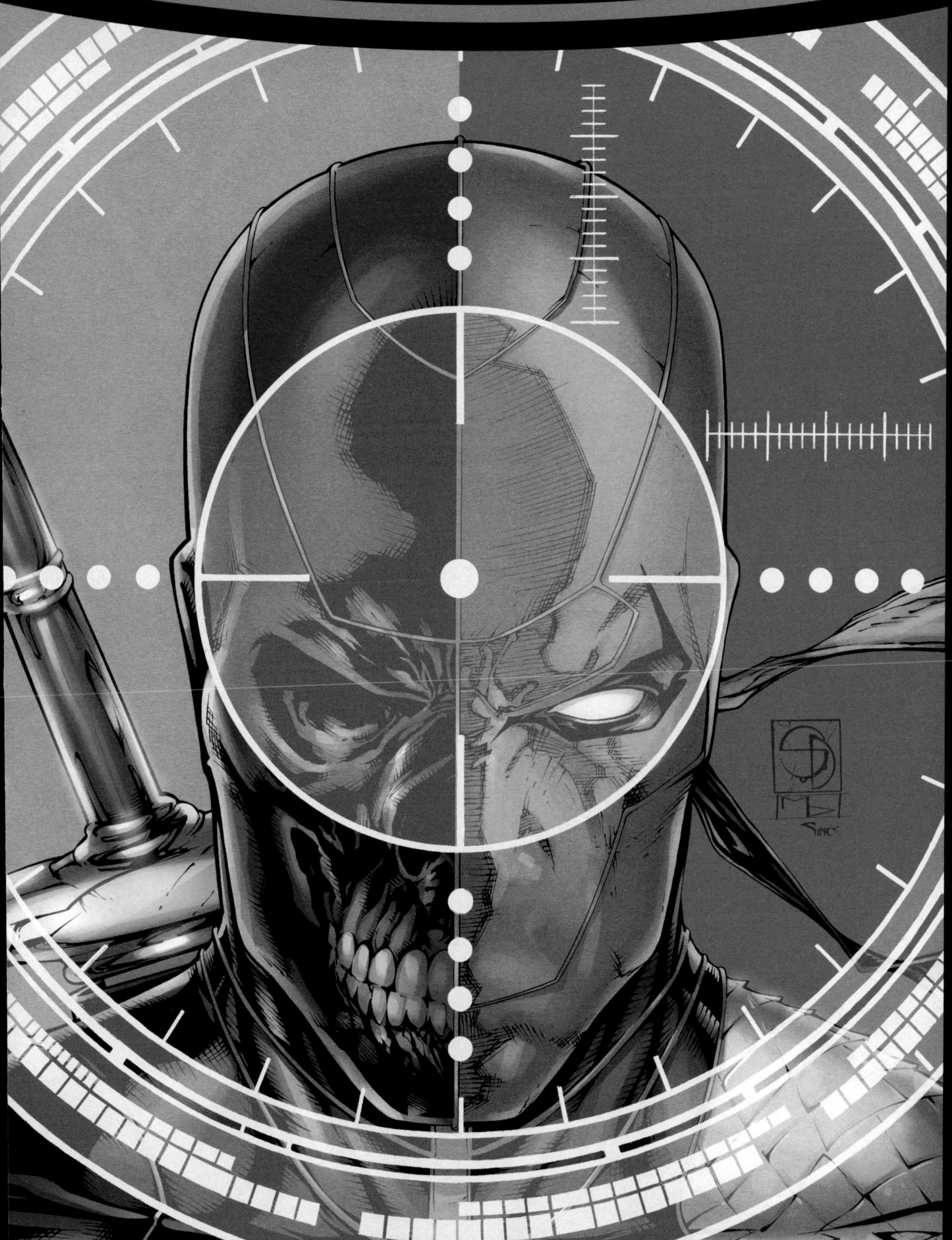

DEATHSTROKE

VOL.1 THE PROFESSIONAL

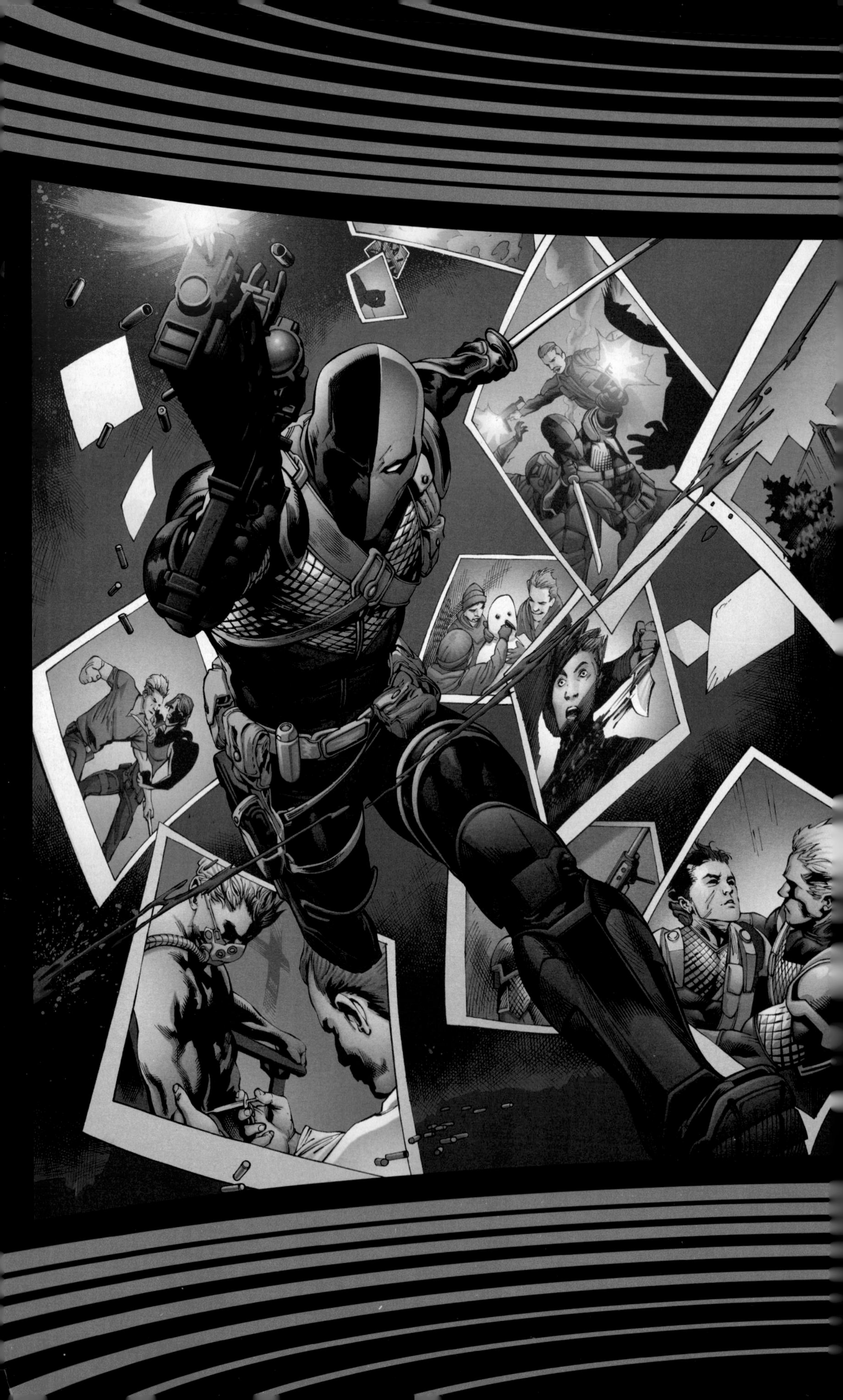

DEATHSTROKE
VOL.1 THE PROFESSIONAL

CHRISTOPHER PRIEST
writer

CARLO PAGULAYAN * **JASON PAZ** * **LARRY HAMA** * **JOE BENNETT**
MARK MORALES * **BELARDINO BRABO**
artists

JEROMY COX
colorist

WILLIE SCHUBERT
letterer

ACO and ROMULO FAJARDO JR.
collection cover artists

ACO and ROMULO FAJARDO JR.
CARLO PAGULAYAN, JASON PAZ and ROMULO FAJARDO JR.
original series covers

DEATHSTROKE created by **MARV WOLFMAN** and **GEORGE PÉREZ**
RAVAGER created by **MARV WOLFMAN** and **GEORGE PÉREZ**
BATMAN created by **BOB KANE** with **BILL FINGER**

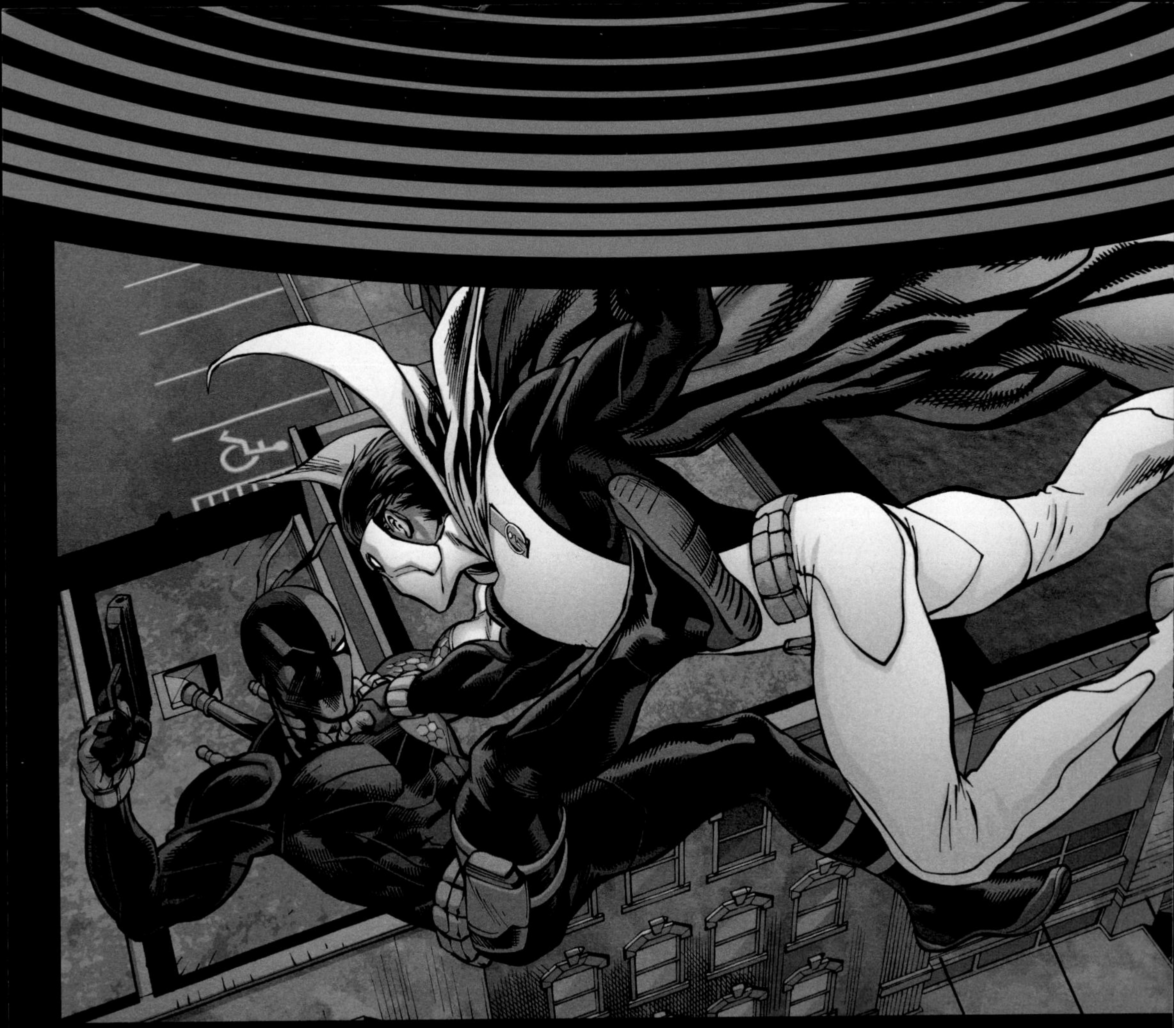

ALEX ANTONE Editor - Original Series * **BRITTANY HOLZHERR** Assistant Editor - Original Series
JEB WOODARD Group Editor - Collected Editions * **SCOTT NYBAKKEN** Editor - Collected Edition
STEVE COOK Design Director - Books * **DAMIAN RYLAND** Publication Design

BOB HARRAS Senior VP - Editor-in-Chief, DC Comics

DIANE NELSON President * **DAN DiDIO** Publisher * **JIM LEE** Publisher * **GEOFF JOHNS** President & Chief Creative Officer
AMIT DESAI Executive VP - Business & Marketing Strategy, Direct to Consumer & Global Franchise Management * **SAM ADES** Senior VP - Direct to Consumer
BOBBIE CHASE VP - Talent Development * **MARK CHIARELLO** Senior VP - Art, Design & Collected Editions
JOHN CUNNINGHAM Senior VP - Sales & Trade Marketing * **ANNE DePIES** Senior VP - Business Strategy, Finance & Administration
DON FALLETTI VP - Manufacturing Operations * **LAWRENCE GANEM** VP - Editorial Administration & Talent Relations
ALISON GILL Senior VP - Manufacturing & Operations * **HANK KANALZ** Senior VP - Editorial Strategy & Administration
JAY KOGAN VP - Legal Affairs * **THOMAS LOFTUS** VP - Business Affairs
JACK MAHAN VP - Business Affairs * **NICK J. NAPOLITANO** VP - Manufacturing Administration
EDDIE SCANNELL VP - Consumer Marketing * **COURTNEY SIMMONS** Senior VP - Publicity & Communications
JIM (SKI) SOKOLOWSKI VP - Comic Book Specialty Sales & Trade Marketing * **NANCY SPEARS** VP - Mass, Book, Digital Sales & Trade Marketing

DEATHSTROKE VOL. 1: THE PROFESSIONAL

DC Comics, 2900 West Alameda Ave., Burbank, CA 91505. Printed by LSC Communications, Salem, VA, USA. 2/3/17.
First Printing. ISBN: 978-1-4012-6823-7

Library of Congress Cataloging-in-Publication Data is available.

PEFC Certified
Printed on paper from sustainably managed forests, controlled sources
PEFC
PEFC/29-31-337
www.pefc.org

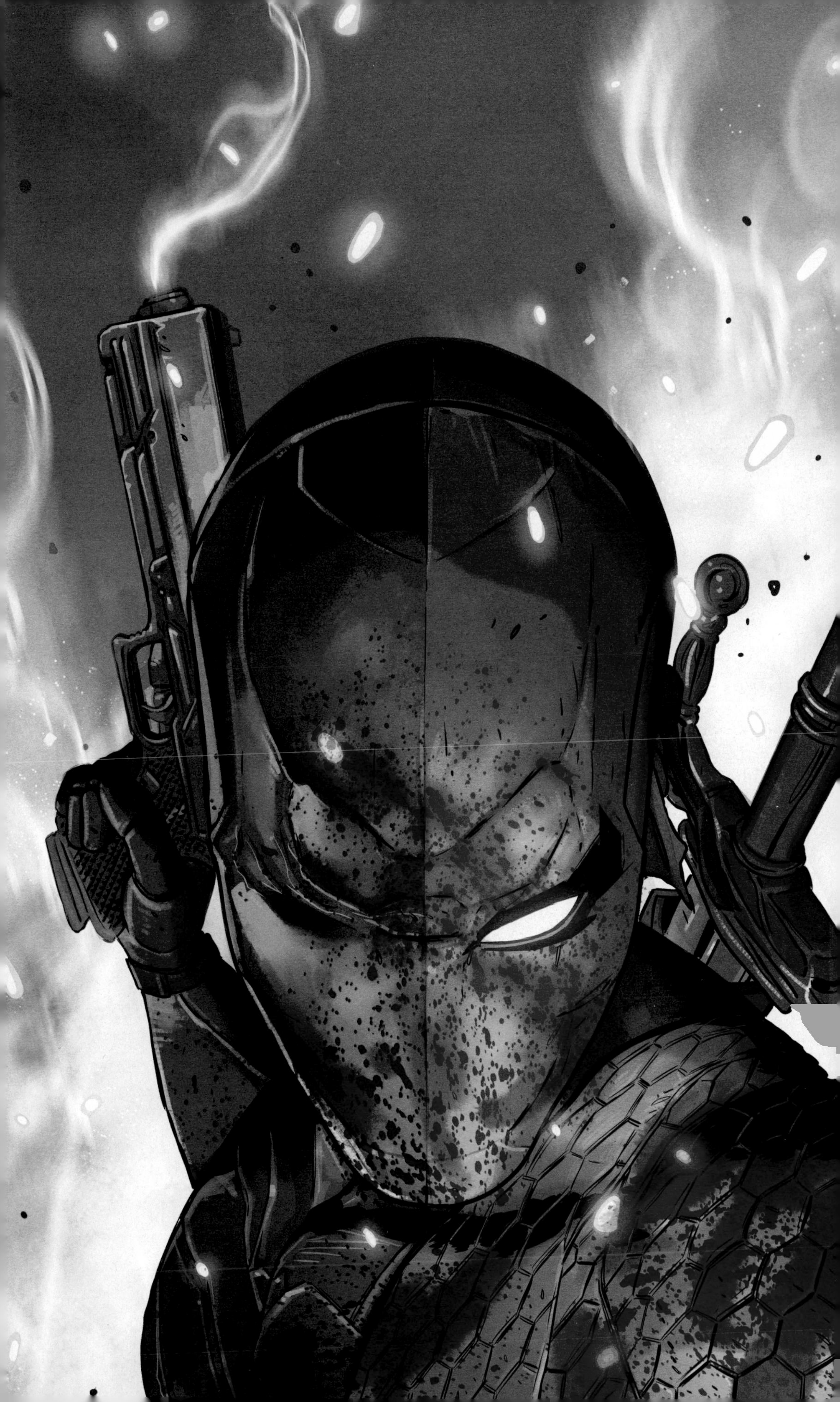

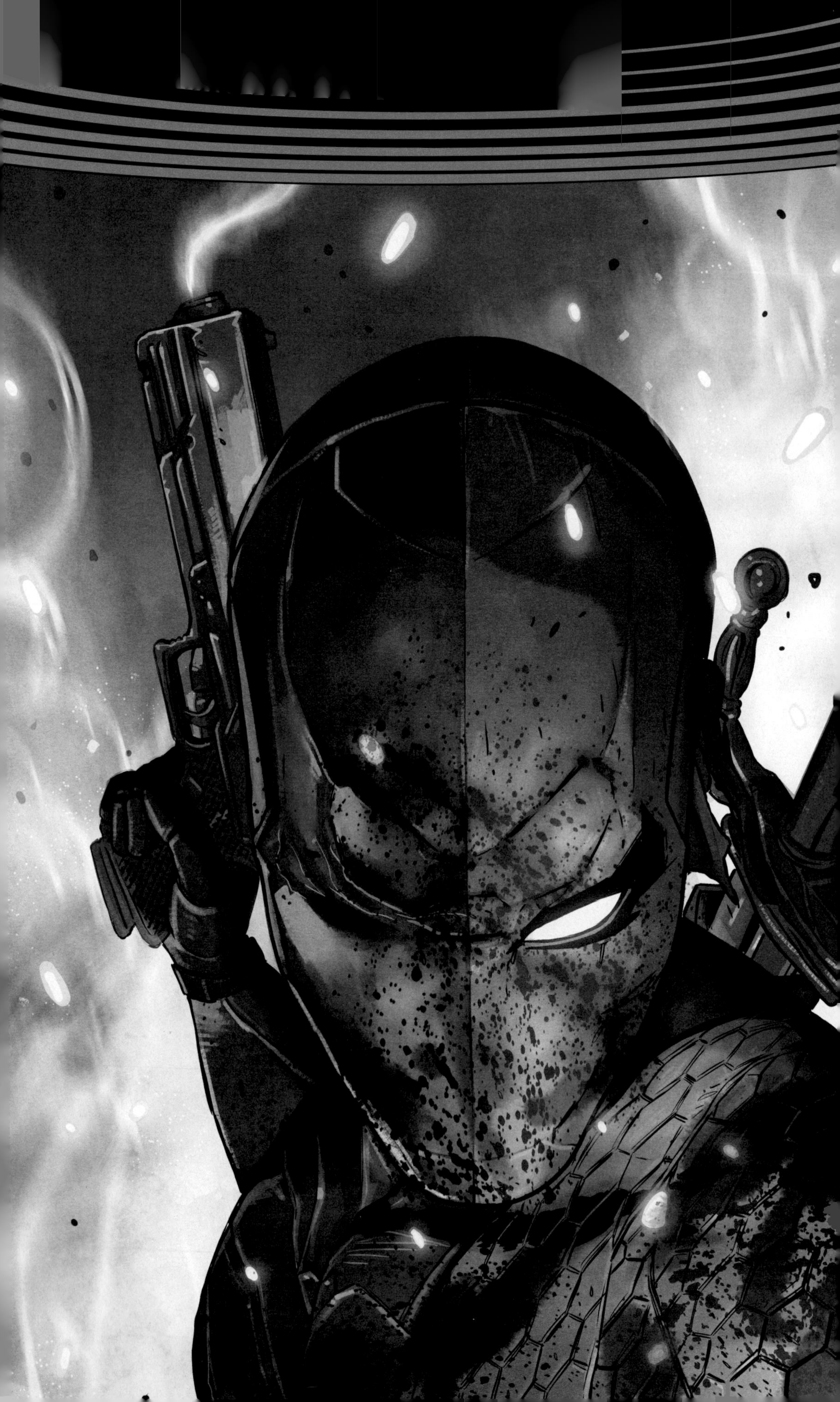

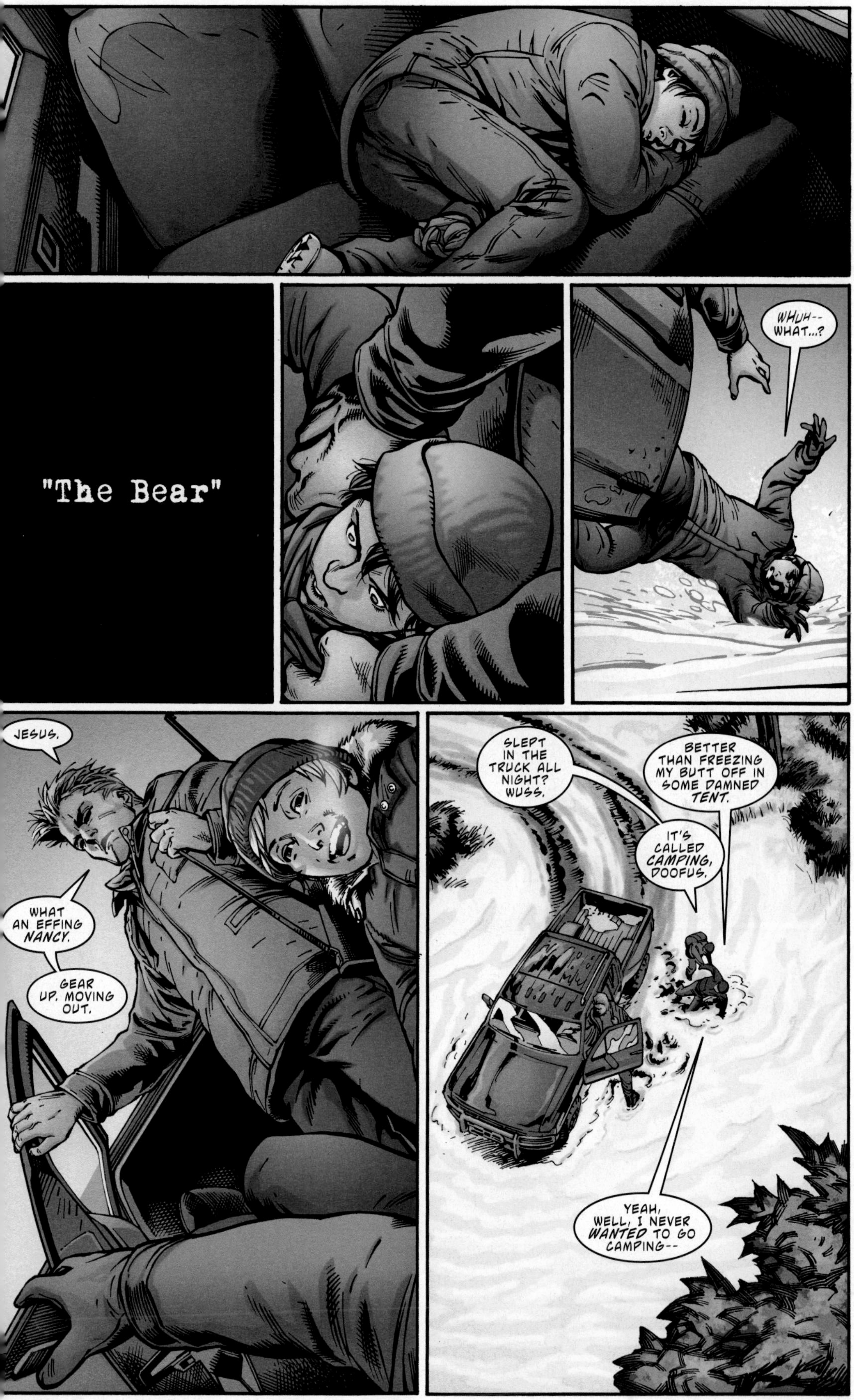
"The Bear"
WHUH--
WHAT...?
JESUS.
WHAT AN EFFING NANCY.
GEAR UP. MOVING OUT.
SLEPT IN THE TRUCK ALL NIGHT? WUSS.
BETTER THAN FREEZING MY BUTT OFF IN SOME DAMNED TENT.
IT'S CALLED CAMPING, DOOFUS.
YEAH, WELL, I NEVER WANTED TO GO CAMPING--

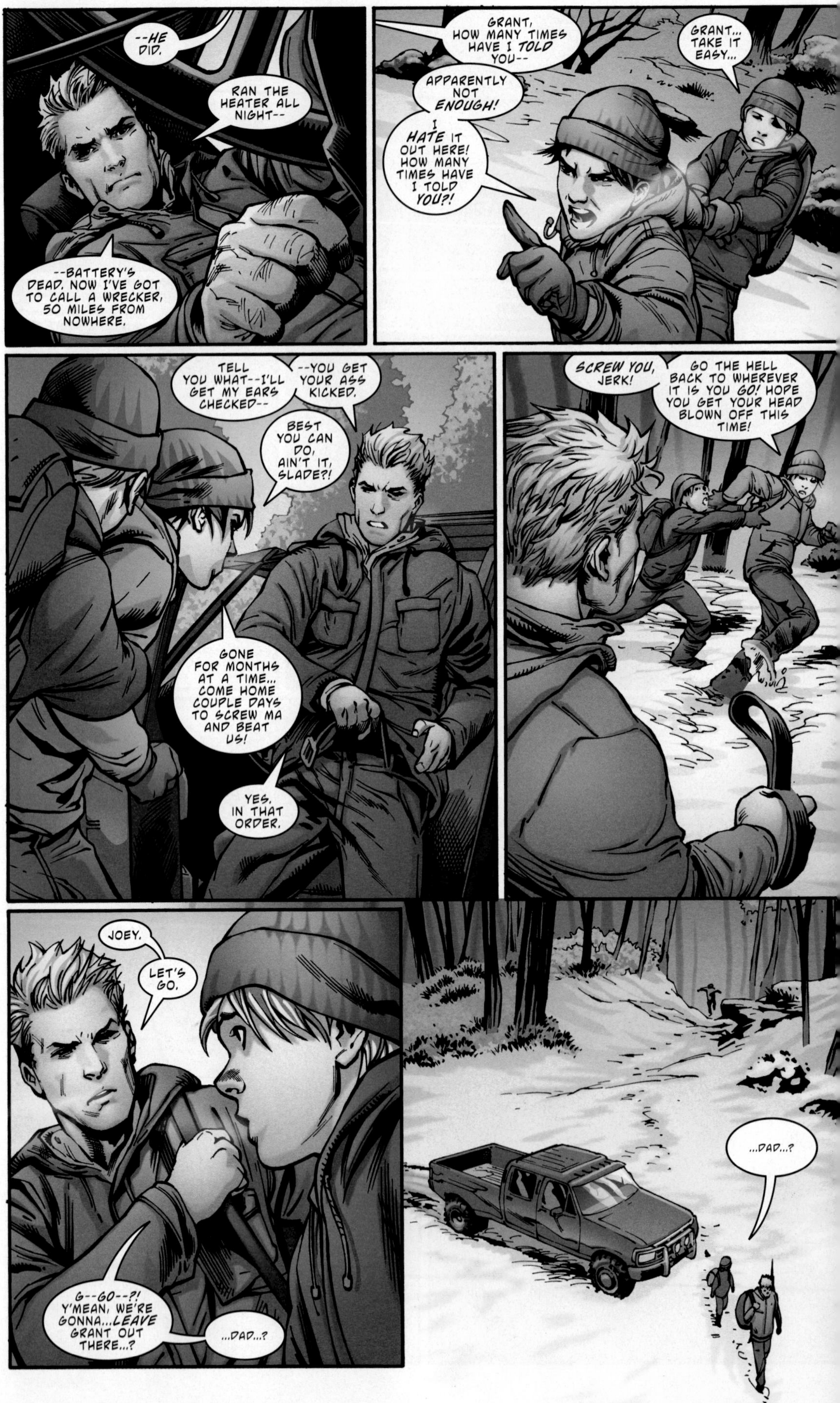
--HE DID.
RAN THE HEATER ALL NIGHT--
--BATTERY'S DEAD. NOW I'VE GOT TO CALL A WRECKER, 50 MILES FROM NOWHERE.
GRANT, HOW MANY TIMES HAVE I TOLD YOU--
APPARENTLY NOT ENOUGH!
I HATE IT OUT HERE! HOW MANY TIMES HAVE I TOLD YOU?!
GRANT... TAKE IT EASY...
TELL YOU WHAT--I'LL GET MY EARS CHECKED--
--YOU GET YOUR ASS KICKED.
BEST YOU CAN DO, AIN'T IT, SLADE?!
GONE FOR MONTHS AT A TIME... COME HOME COUPLE DAYS TO SCREW MA AND BEAT US!
YES, IN THAT ORDER.
SCREW YOU, JERK!
GO THE HELL BACK TO WHEREVER IT IS YOU GO! HOPE YOU GET YOUR HEAD BLOWN OFF THIS TIME!
JOEY.
LET'S GO.
G--GO--?! Y'MEAN, WE'RE GONNA...LEAVE GRANT OUT THERE...?
...DAD...?
...DAD...?

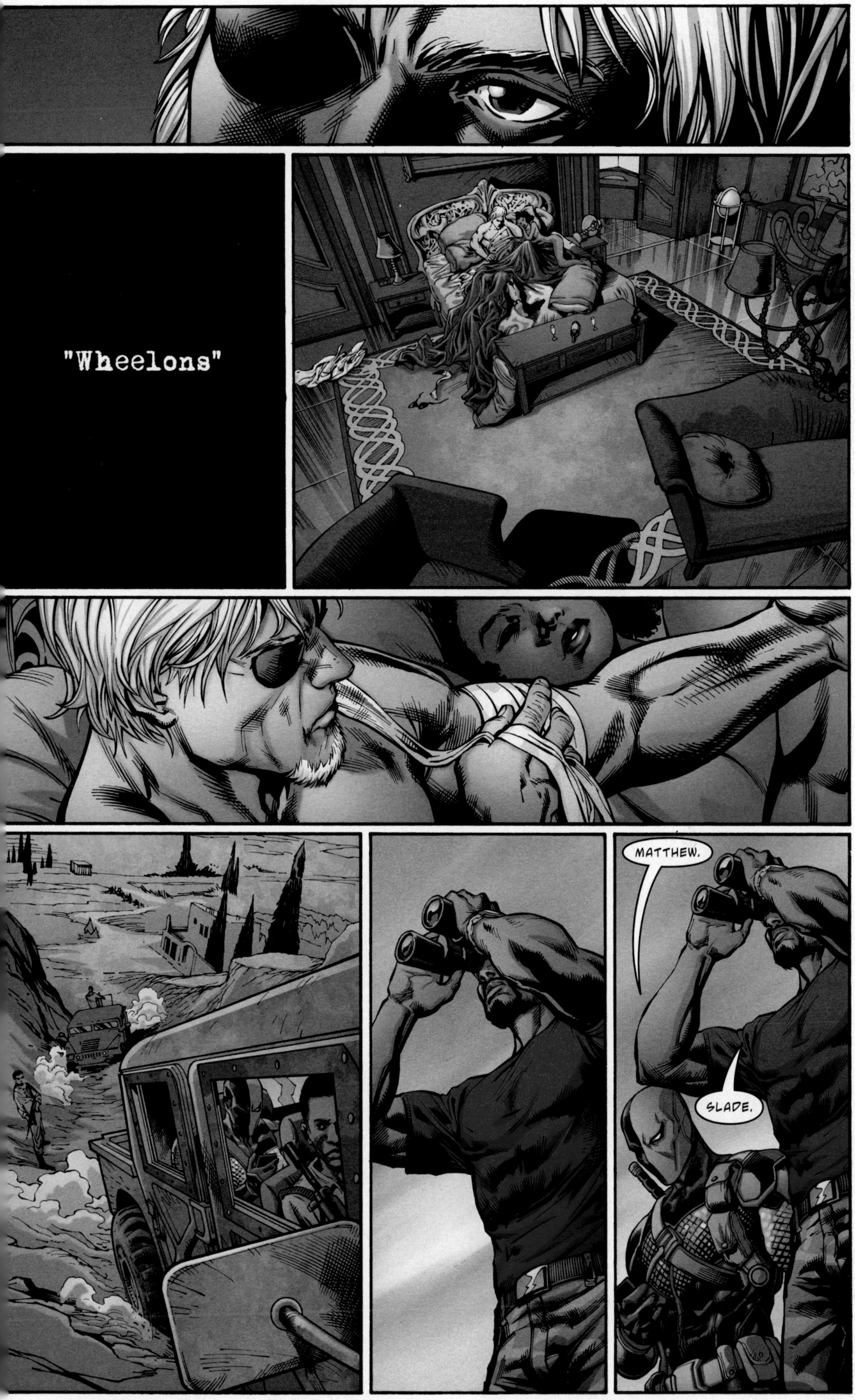
"Wheelons"
MATTHEW.
SLADE.

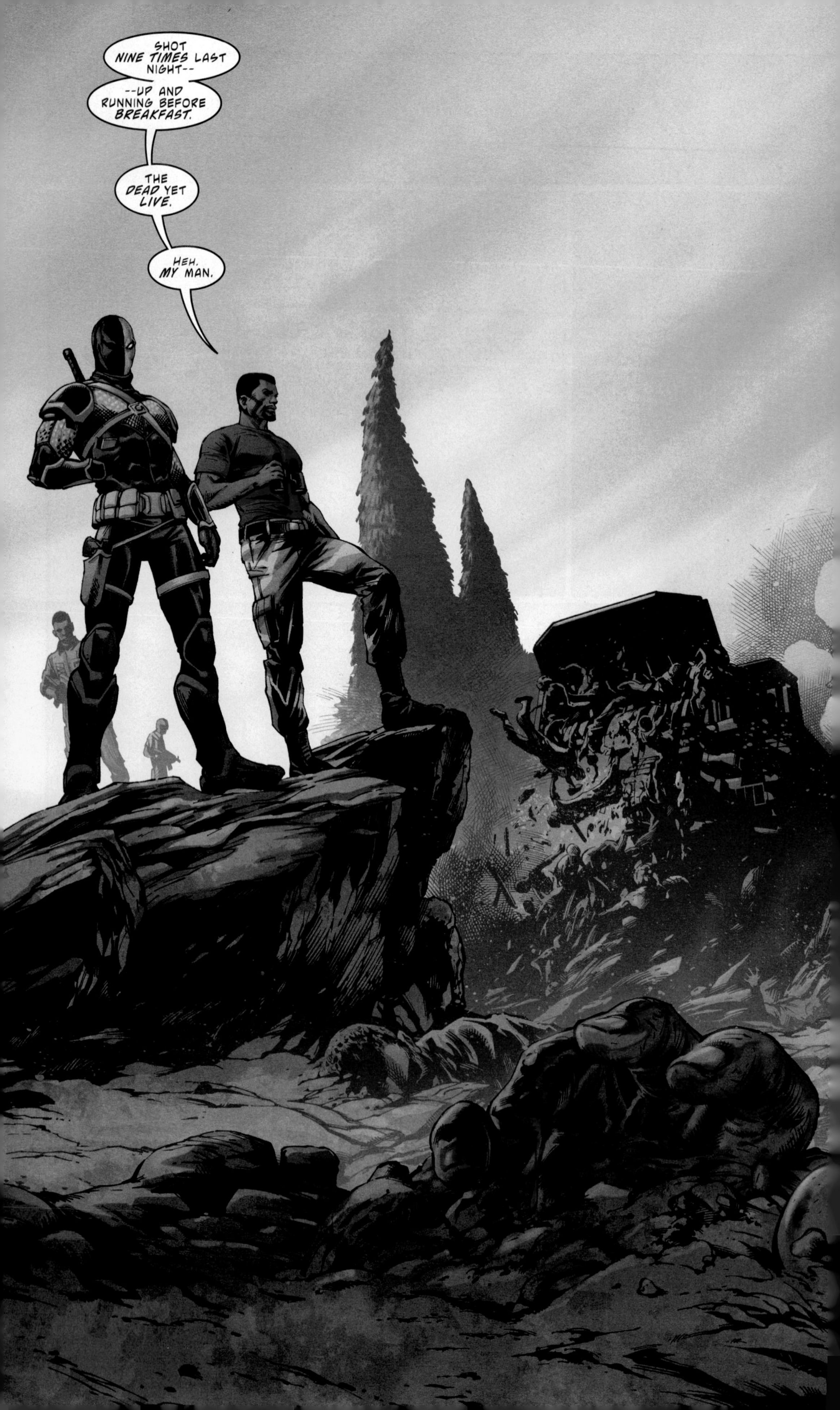
SHOT NINE TIMES LAST NIGHT--
--UP AND RUNNING BEFORE BREAKFAST.
THE DEAD YET LIVE.
HEH. MY MAN.

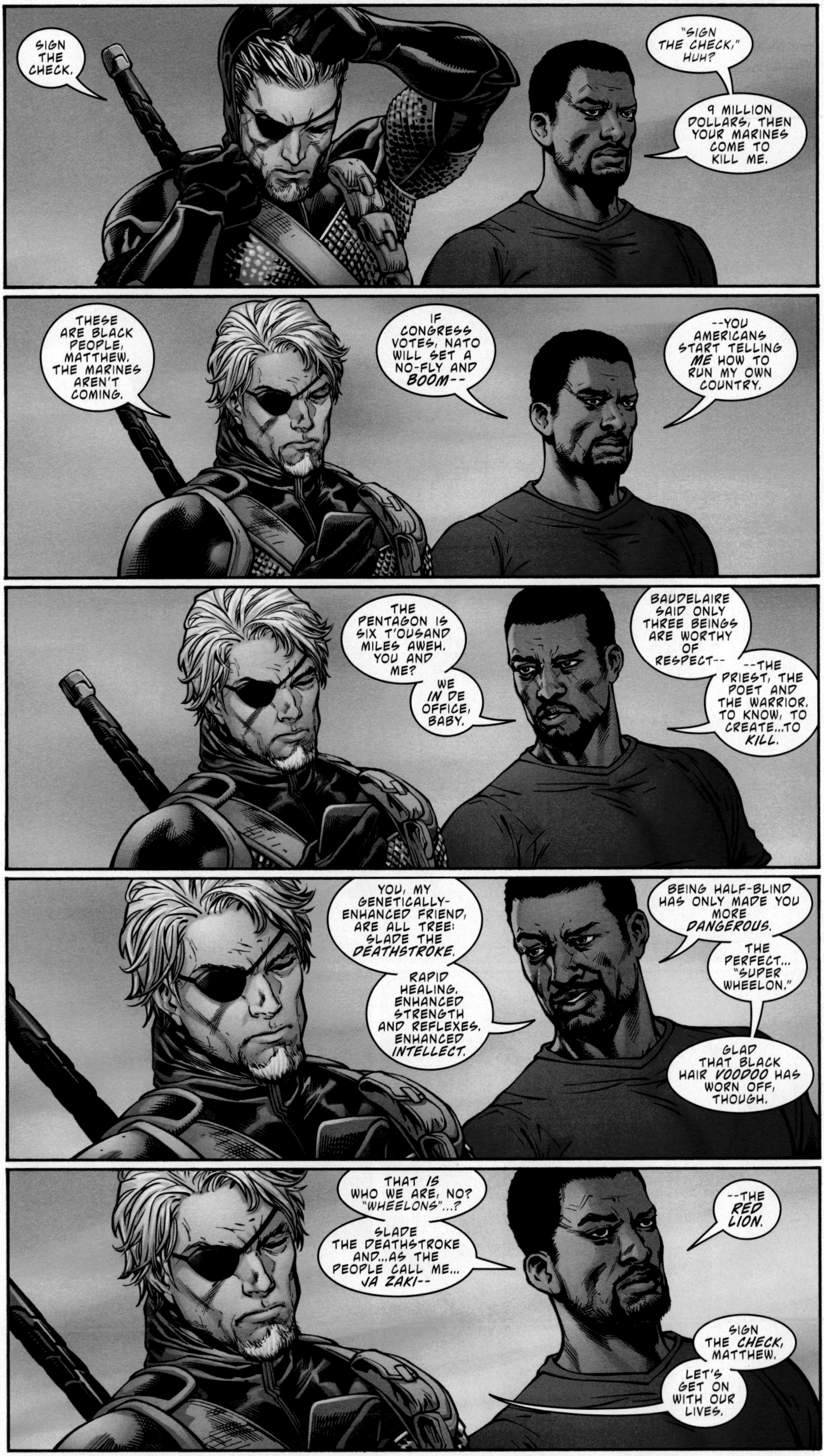
SIGN THE CHECK.
"SIGN THE CHECK," HUH?
9 MILLION DOLLARS, THEN YOUR MARINES COME TO KILL ME.
THESE ARE BLACK PEOPLE, MATTHEW. THE MARINES AREN'T COMING.
IF CONGRESS VOTES, NATO WILL SET A NO-FLY AND *BOOM*--
--YOU AMERICANS START TELLING *ME* HOW TO RUN MY OWN COUNTRY.
THE PENTAGON IS SIX T'OUSAND MILES AWEH. YOU AND ME?
WE *IN* DE OFFICE, BABY.
BAUDELAIRE SAID ONLY THREE BEINGS ARE WORTHY OF RESPECT--
--THE PRIEST, THE POET AND THE WARRIOR. TO KNOW, TO CREATE...TO *KILL*.
YOU, MY GENETICALLY-ENHANCED FRIEND, ARE ALL TREE: SLADE THE *DEATHSTROKE*.
RAPID HEALING. ENHANCED STRENGTH AND REFLEXES. ENHANCED *INTELLECT*.
BEING HALF-BLIND HAS ONLY MADE YOU MORE *DANGEROUS*.
THE PERFECT... "SUPER WHEELON."
GLAD THAT BLACK HAIR *VOODOO* HAS WORN OFF, THOUGH.
THAT *IS* WHO WE ARE, NO? "WHEELONS"...?
SLADE THE DEATHSTROKE AND...AS THE PEOPLE CALL ME... *JA ZAKI*--
--THE *RED LION*.
SIGN THE *CHECK*, MATTHEW.
LET'S GET ON WITH OUR LIVES.

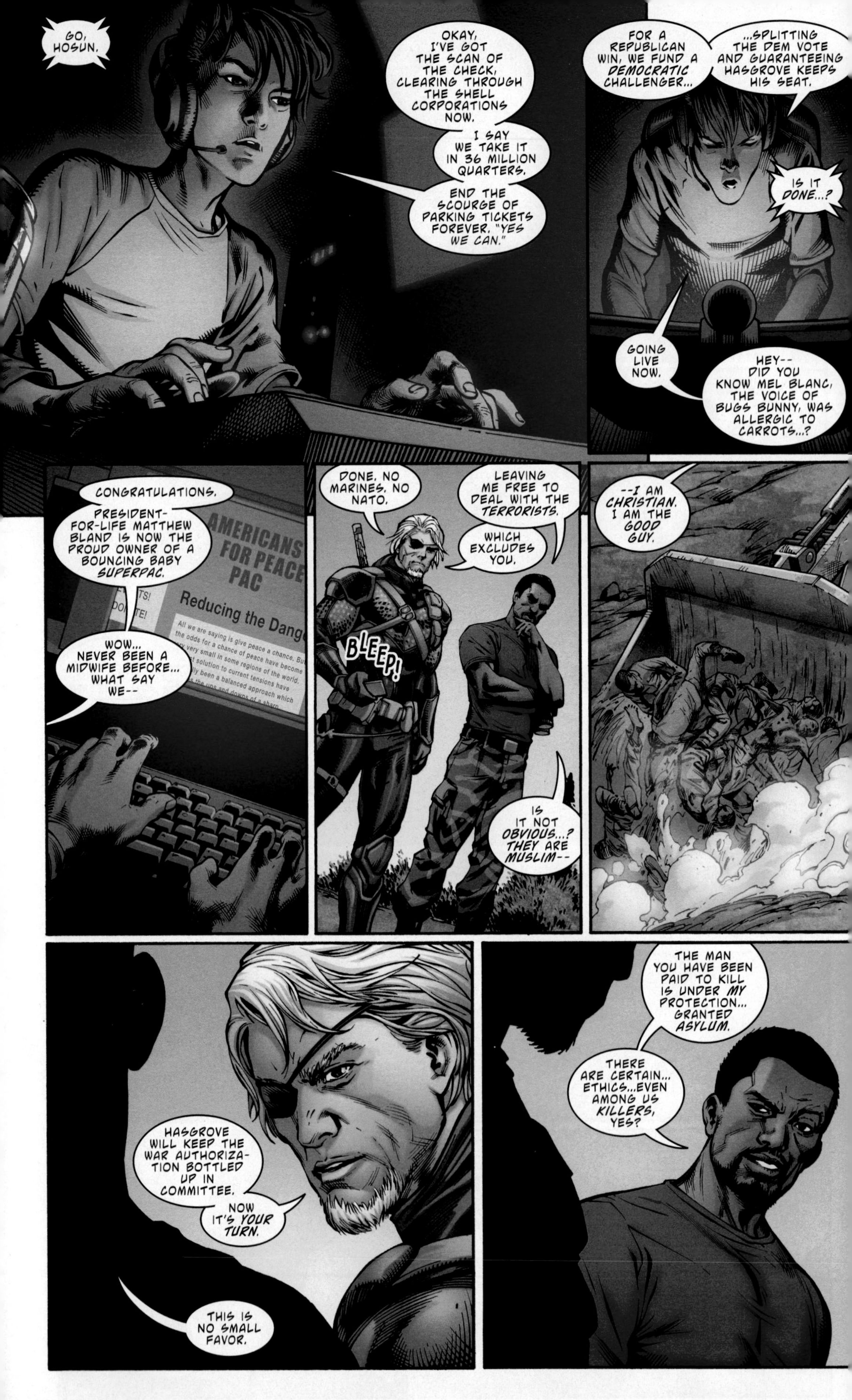
GO, HOSUN.
OKAY, I'VE GOT THE SCAN OF THE CHECK, CLEARING THROUGH THE SHELL CORPORATIONS NOW.
I SAY WE TAKE IT IN 36 MILLION QUARTERS.
END THE SCOURGE OF PARKING TICKETS FOREVER. "YES WE CAN."
FOR A REPUBLICAN WIN, WE FUND A *DEMOCRATIC* CHALLENGER...
...SPLITTING THE DEM VOTE AND GUARANTEEING HASGROVE KEEPS HIS SEAT.
IS IT *DONE*...?
GOING LIVE NOW.
HEY-- DID YOU KNOW MEL BLANC, THE VOICE OF BUGS BUNNY, WAS ALLERGIC TO CARROTS...?
CONGRATULATIONS.
PRESIDENT-FOR-LIFE MATTHEW BLAND IS NOW THE PROUD OWNER OF A BOUNCING BABY *SUPERPAC*.
AMERICANS FOR PEACE PAC
WOW... NEVER BEEN A MIDWIFE BEFORE... WHAT SAY WE--
DONE. NO MARINES. NO NATO.
LEAVING ME FREE TO DEAL WITH THE *TERRORISTS*.
WHICH EXCLUDES YOU.
BLEEP!
IS IT NOT *OBVIOUS*...? *THEY* ARE *MUSLIM*--
--I AM *CHRISTIAN*. I AM THE *GOOD GUY*.
HASGROVE WILL KEEP THE WAR AUTHORIZATION BOTTLED UP IN COMMITTEE.
NOW IT'S *YOUR TURN*.
THIS IS NO SMALL FAVOR.
THE MAN YOU HAVE BEEN PAID TO KILL IS UNDER *MY* PROTECTION... GRANTED *ASYLUM*.
THERE ARE CERTAIN... ETHICS...EVEN AMONG US *KILLERS*, YES?

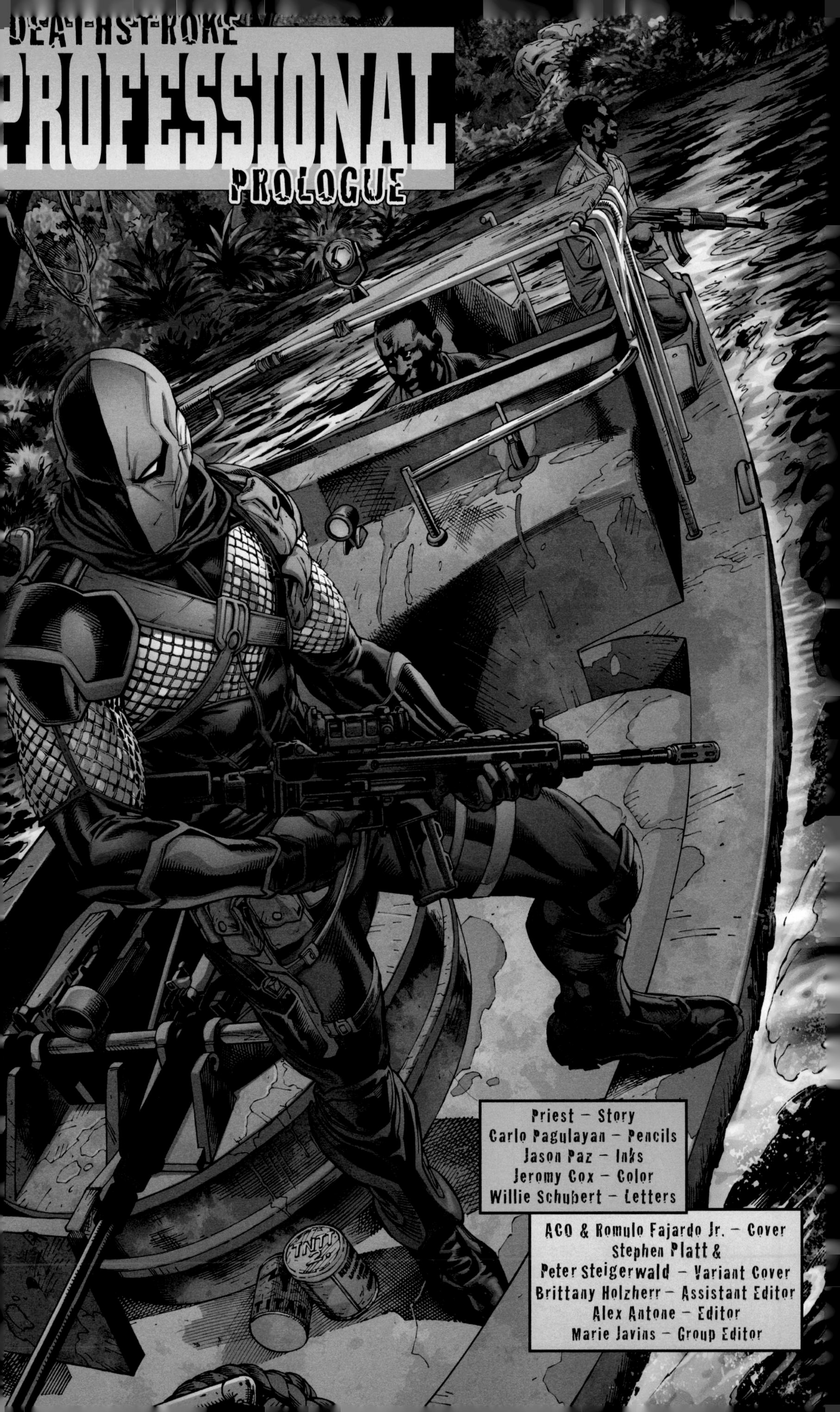
DEATHSTROKE
PROFESSIONAL
PROLOGUE
Priest – Story
Carlo Pagulayan – Pencils
Jason Paz – Inks
Jeromy Cox – Color
Willie Schubert – Letters
ACO & Romulo Fajardo Jr. – Cover
Stephen Platt &
Peter Steigerwald – Variant Cover
Brittany Holzherr – Assistant Editor
Alex Antone – Editor
Marie Javins – Group Editor

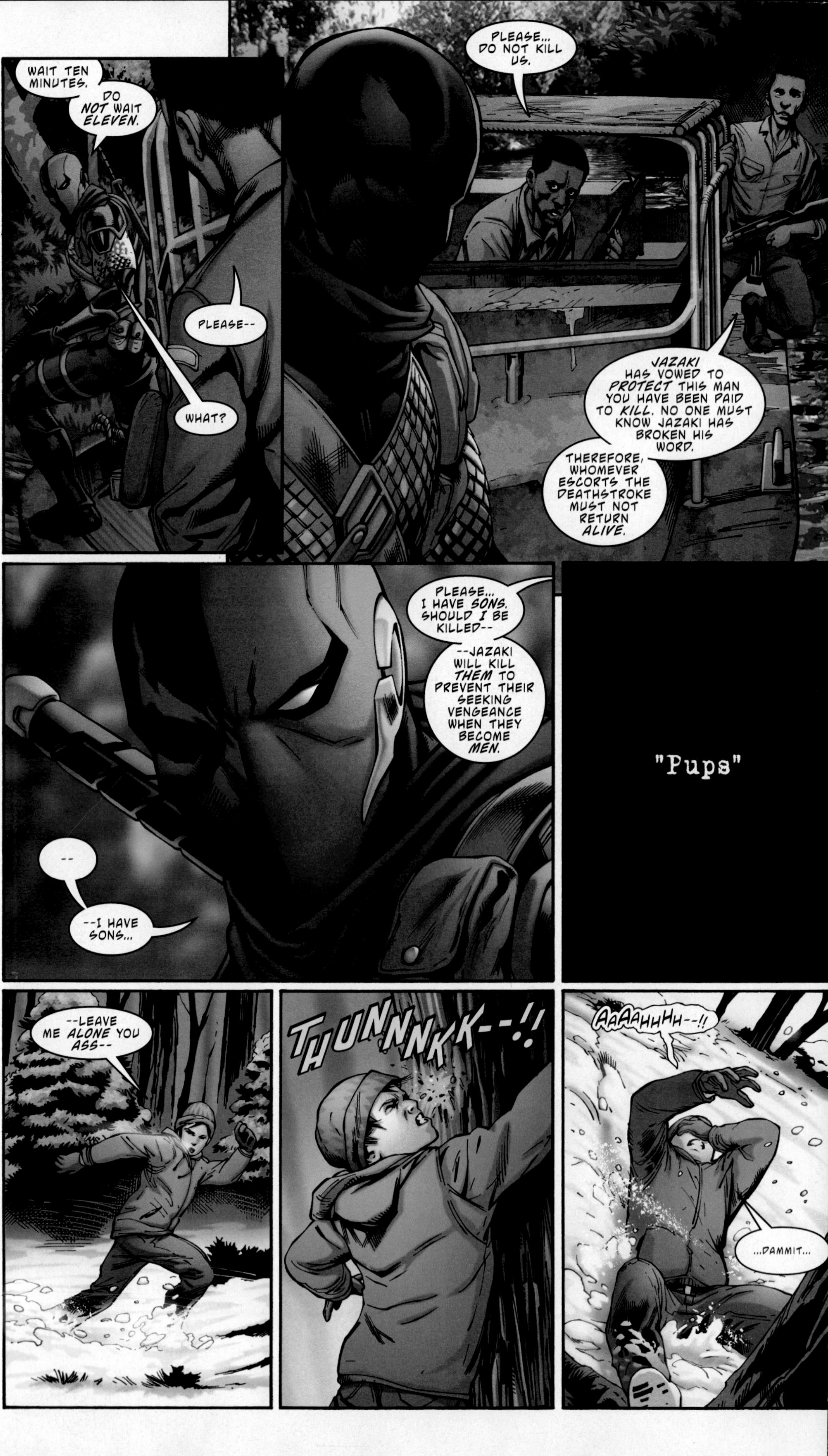
PLEASE... DO NOT KILL US.
WAIT TEN MINUTES.
DO NOT WAIT ELEVEN.
PLEASE--
WHAT?
JAZAKI HAS VOWED TO PROTECT THIS MAN YOU HAVE BEEN PAID TO KILL. NO ONE MUST KNOW JAZAKI HAS BROKEN HIS WORD.
THEREFORE, WHOMEVER ESCORTS THE DEATHSTROKE MUST NOT RETURN ALIVE.
PLEASE... I HAVE SONS. SHOULD I BE KILLED--
--JAZAKI WILL KILL THEM TO PREVENT THEIR SEEKING VENGEANCE WHEN THEY BECOME MEN.
--
--I HAVE SONS...
"Pups"
--LEAVE ME ALONE YOU ASS--
THUNNNKK--!!
AAAAHHHH--!!
...DAMMIT...

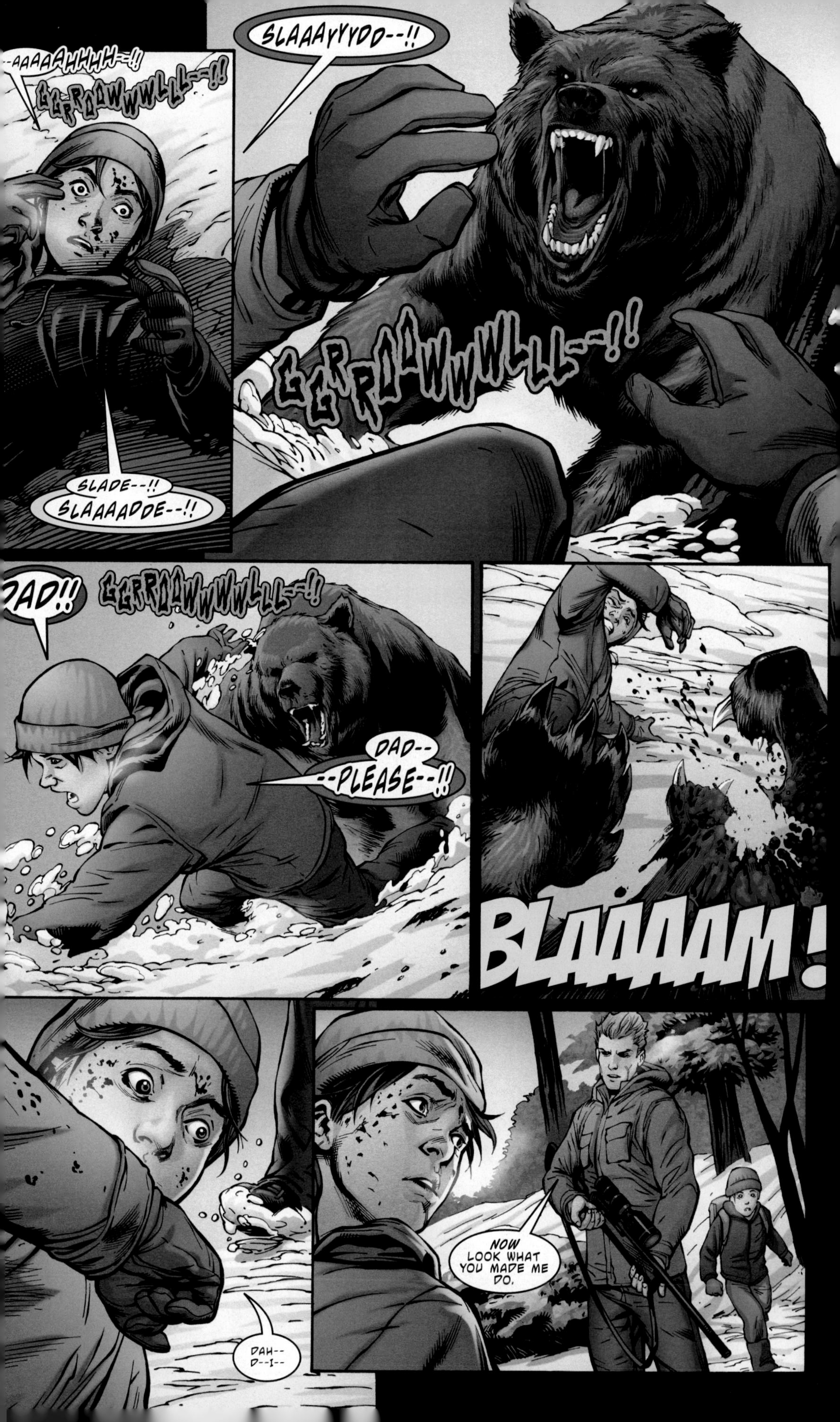

--AAAAAHHHH--!!
GGRROOWWWLLL--!!
SLADE--!!
SLAAAADDE--!!
SLAAAYYYDD--!!
GGRROOWWWLLL--!!
DAD!!
GGRROOWWWLLL--!!
DAD--
--PLEASE--!!
BLAAAAM!
DAH--
D--I--
NOW LOOK WHAT YOU MADE ME DO.

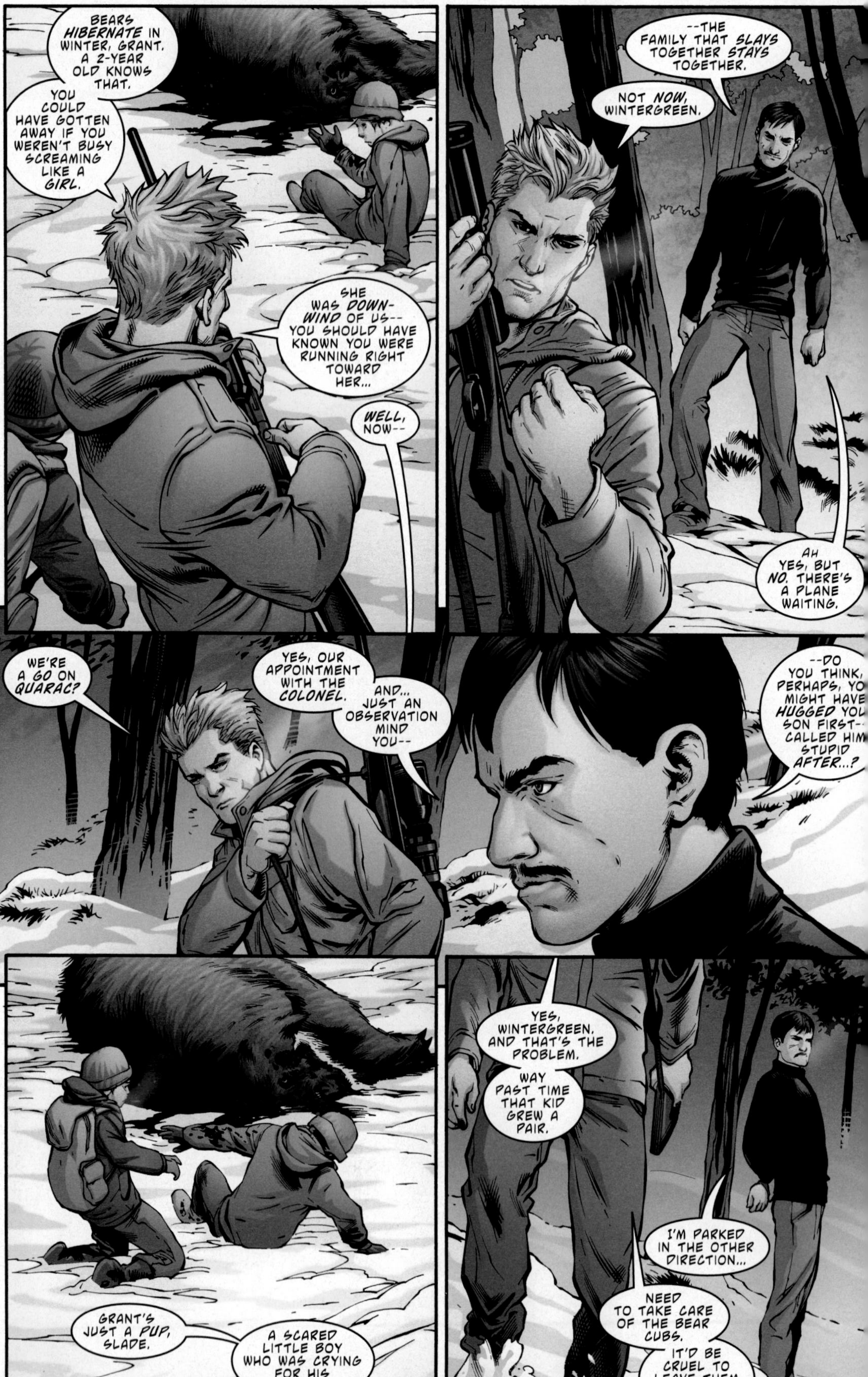
BEARS HIBERNATE IN WINTER, GRANT. A 2-YEAR OLD KNOWS THAT.
YOU COULD HAVE GOTTEN AWAY IF YOU WEREN'T BUSY SCREAMING LIKE A GIRL.
SHE WAS DOWN-WIND OF US--YOU SHOULD HAVE KNOWN YOU WERE RUNNING RIGHT TOWARD HER...
WELL, NOW--
--THE FAMILY THAT SLAYS TOGETHER STAYS TOGETHER.
NOT NOW, WINTERGREEN.
AH YES, BUT NO. THERE'S A PLANE WAITING.
WE'RE A GO ON QUARAC?
YES, OUR APPOINTMENT WITH THE COLONEL.
AND... JUST AN OBSERVATION MIND YOU--
--DO YOU THINK, PERHAPS, YO MIGHT HAVE HUGGED YOU SON FIRST-- CALLED HIM STUPID AFTER...?
GRANT'S JUST A PUP, SLADE.
A SCARED LITTLE BOY WHO WAS CRYING FOR HIS FATHER.
YES, WINTERGREEN. AND THAT'S THE PROBLEM.
WAY PAST TIME THAT KID GREW A PAIR.
I'M PARKED IN THE OTHER DIRECTION...
NEED TO TAKE CARE OF THE BEAR CUBS.
IT'D BE CRUEL TO LEAVE THEM WITHOUT A MOTHER.

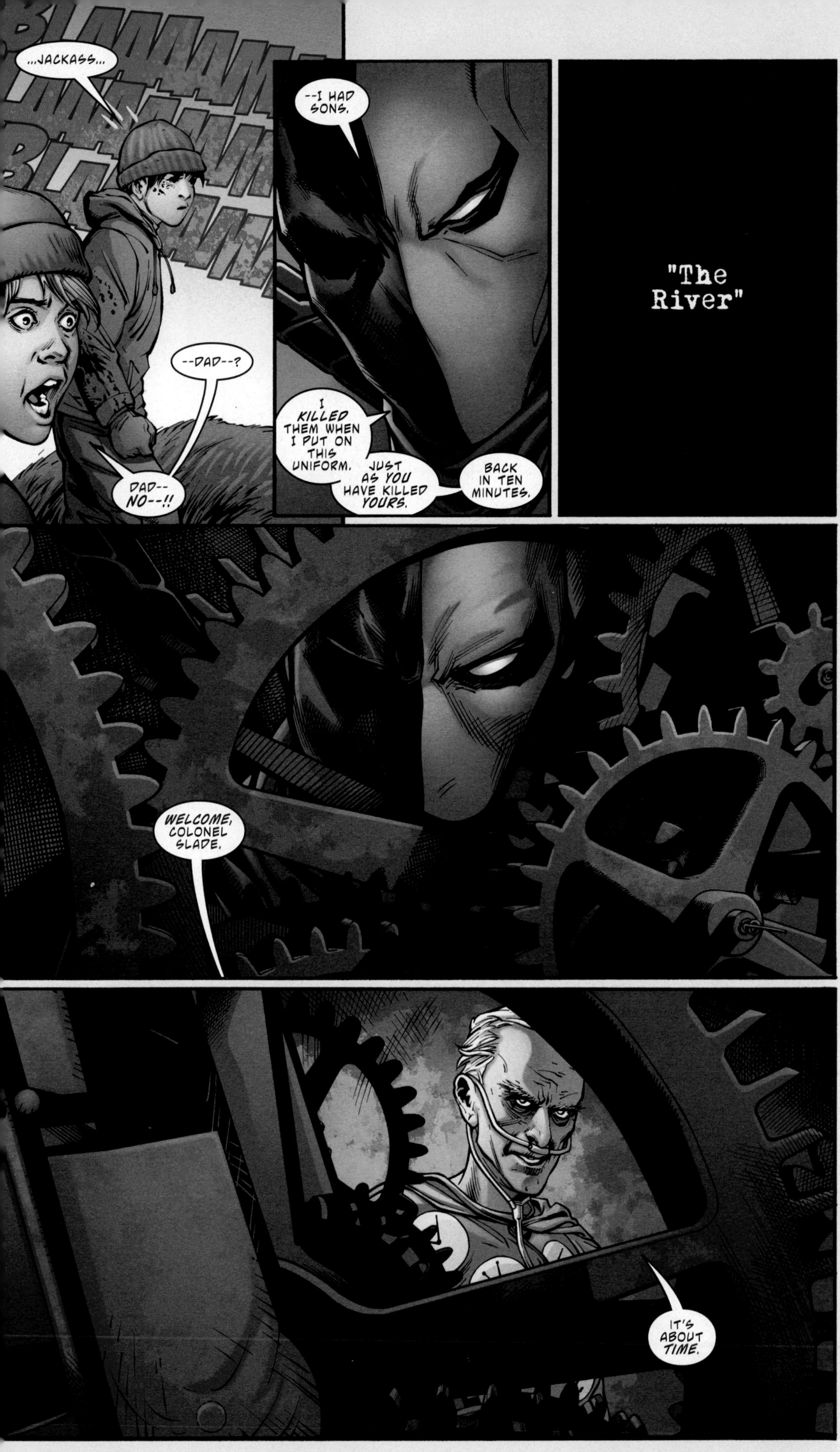
...JACKASS...
--DAD--?
DAD-- NO--!!
--I HAD SONS.
I KILLED THEM WHEN I PUT ON THIS UNIFORM.
JUST AS YOU HAVE KILLED YOURS.
BACK IN TEN MINUTES.
"The River"
WELCOME, COLONEL SLADE.
IT'S ABOUT TIME.

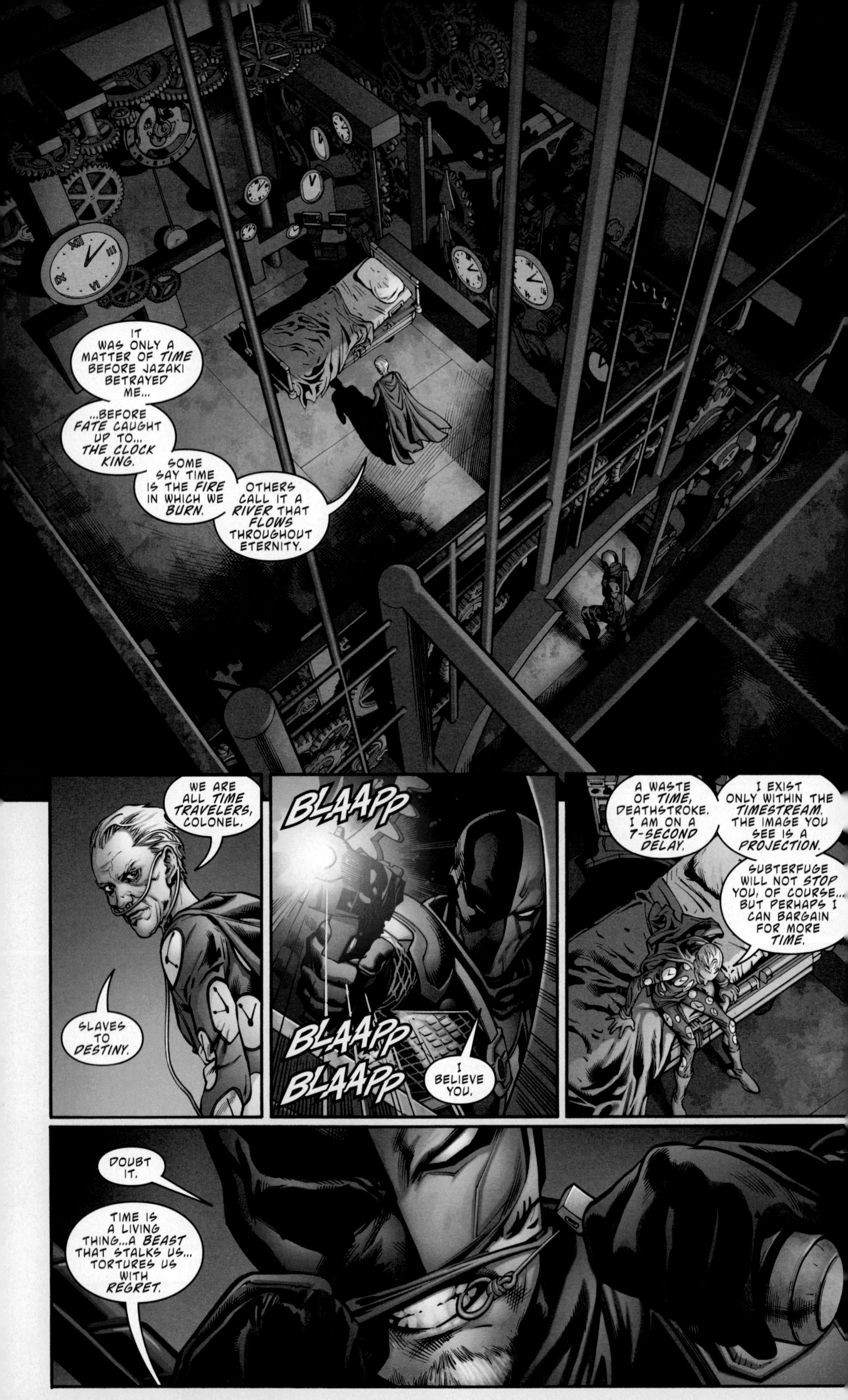
IT WAS ONLY A MATTER OF TIME BEFORE JAZAKI BETRAYED ME...
...BEFORE FATE CAUGHT UP TO... THE CLOCK KING.
SOME SAY TIME IS THE FIRE IN WHICH WE BURN.
OTHERS CALL IT A RIVER THAT FLOWS THROUGHOUT ETERNITY.
WE ARE ALL TIME TRAVELERS, COLONEL.
SLAVES TO DESTINY.
BLAAPP
BLAAPP
BLAAPP
I BELIEVE YOU.
A WASTE OF TIME, DEATHSTROKE. I AM ON A 7-SECOND DELAY.
I EXIST ONLY WITHIN THE TIMESTREAM. THE IMAGE YOU SEE IS A PROJECTION.
SUBTERFUGE WILL NOT STOP YOU, OF COURSE... BUT PERHAPS I CAN BARGAIN FOR MORE TIME.
DOUBT IT.
TIME IS A LIVING THING...A BEAST THAT STALKS US... TORTURES US WITH REGRET.

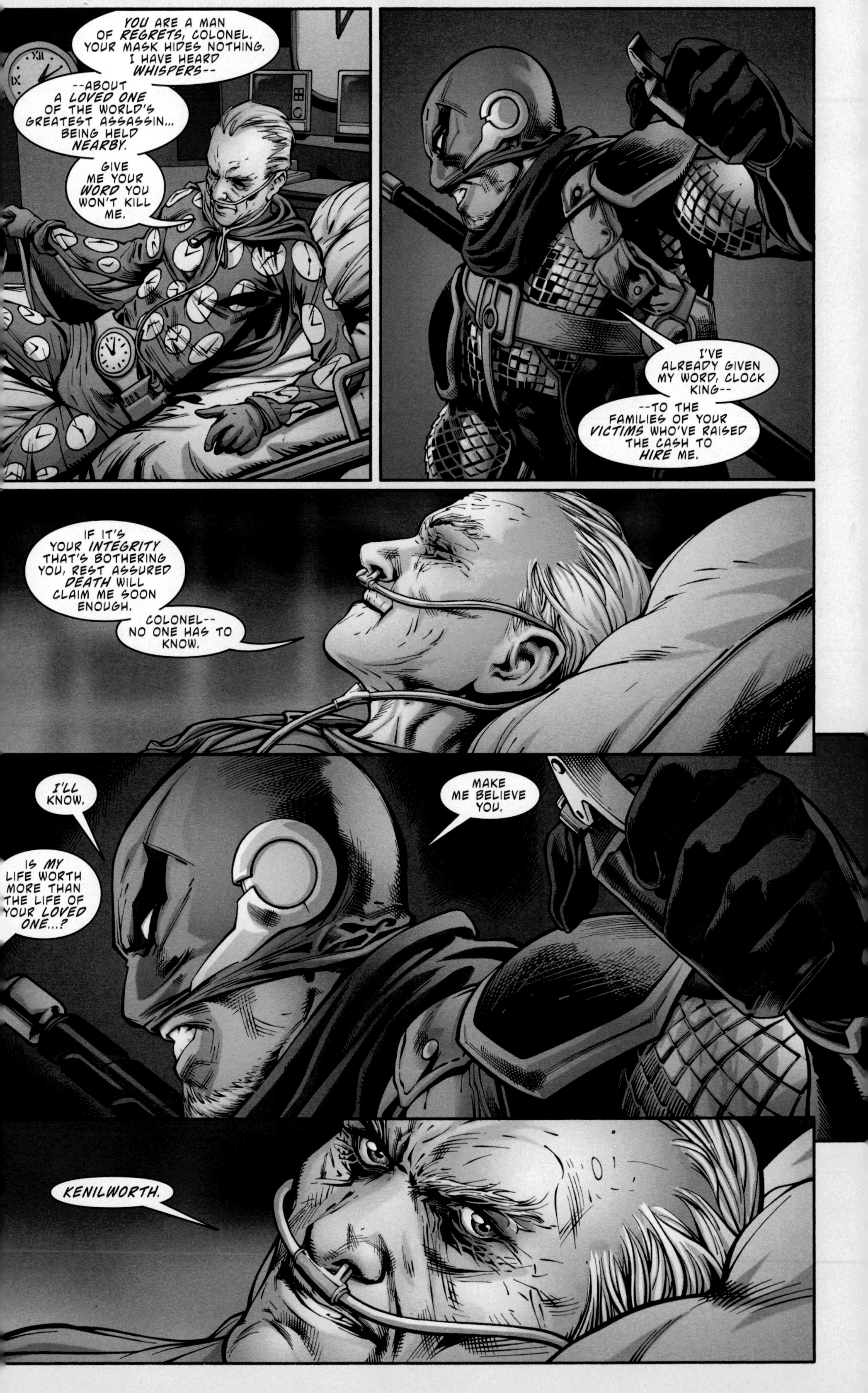
YOU ARE A MAN OF REGRETS, COLONEL. YOUR MASK HIDES NOTHING. I HAVE HEARD WHISPERS--
--ABOUT A LOVED ONE OF THE WORLD'S GREATEST ASSASSIN... BEING HELD NEARBY.
GIVE ME YOUR WORD YOU WON'T KILL ME.
I'VE ALREADY GIVEN MY WORD, CLOCK KING--
--TO THE FAMILIES OF YOUR VICTIMS WHO'VE RAISED THE CASH TO HIRE ME.
IF IT'S YOUR INTEGRITY THAT'S BOTHERING YOU, REST ASSURED DEATH WILL CLAIM ME SOON ENOUGH.
COLONEL-- NO ONE HAS TO KNOW.
I'LL KNOW.
MAKE ME BELIEVE YOU.
IS MY LIFE WORTH MORE THAN THE LIFE OF YOUR LOVED ONE...?
KENILWORTH.

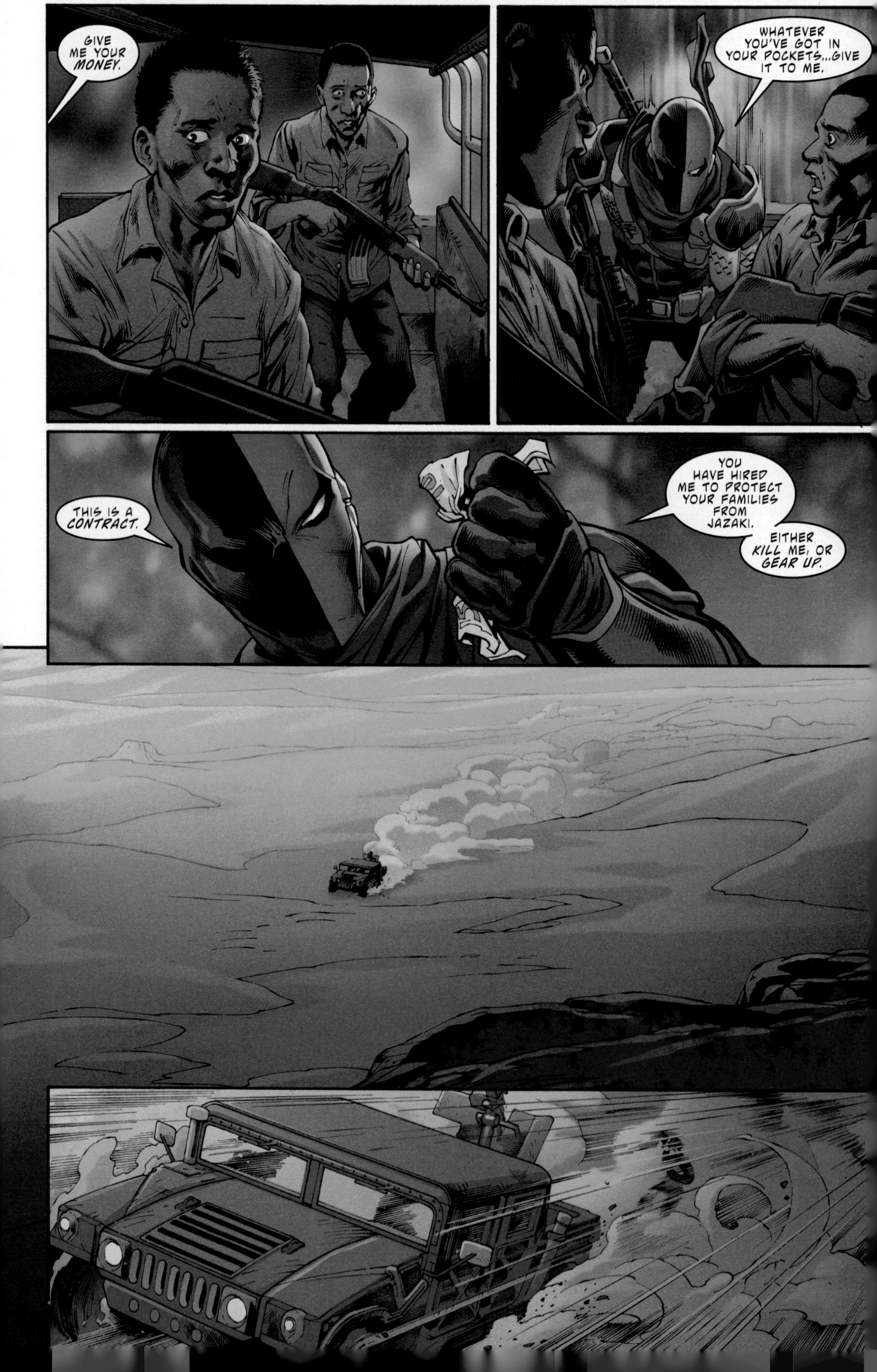
GIVE ME YOUR MONEY.
WHATEVER YOU'VE GOT IN YOUR POCKETS...GIVE IT TO ME.
THIS IS A CONTRACT.
YOU HAVE HIRED ME TO PROTECT YOUR FAMILIES FROM JAZAKI.
EITHER KILL ME, OR GEAR UP.

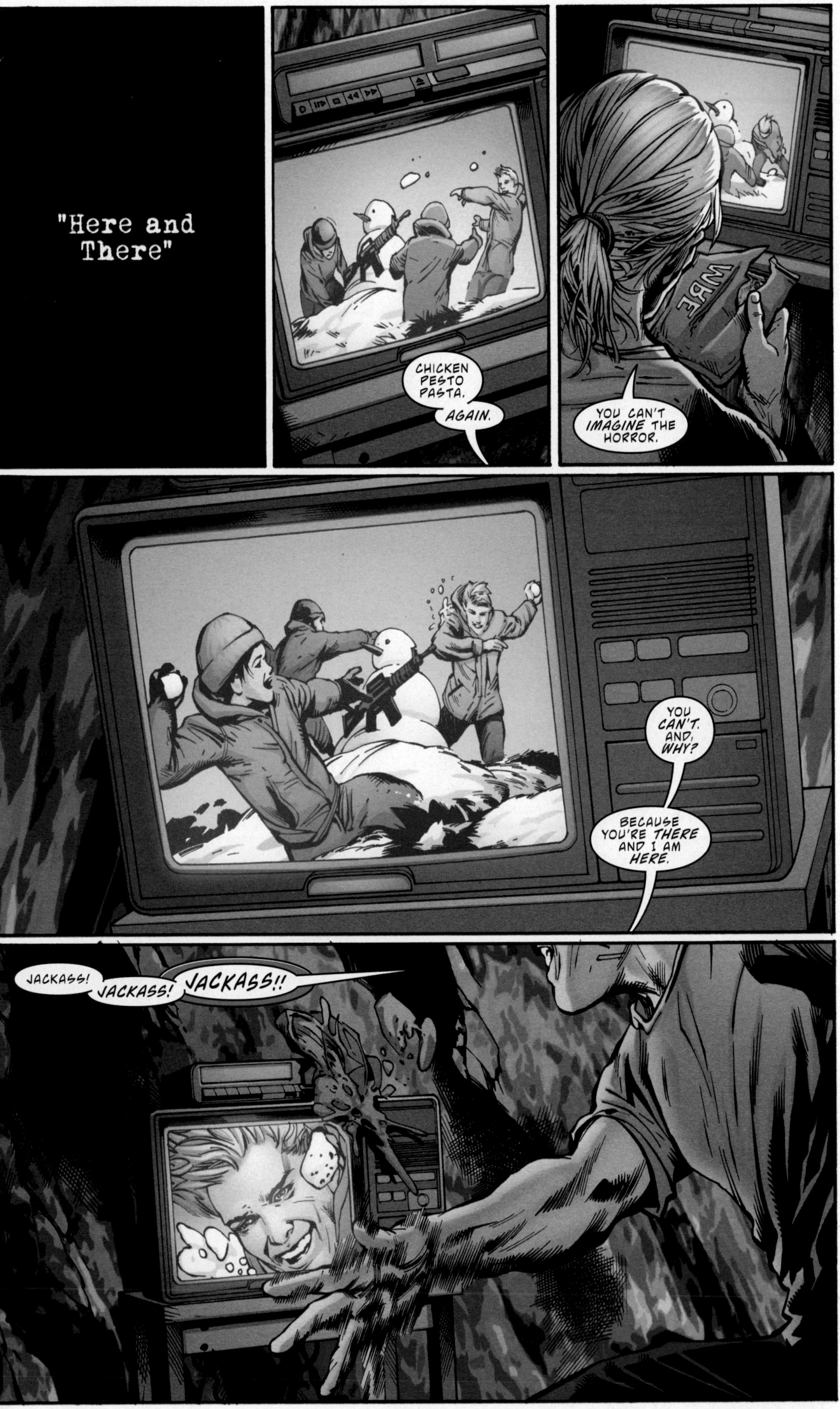

"Here and There"
CHICKEN PESTO PASTA.
AGAIN.
YOU CAN'T IMAGINE THE HORROR.
MRE
YOU CAN'T. AND, WHY?
BECAUSE YOU'RE THERE AND I AM HERE.
JACKASS!
JACKASS!
JACKASS!!

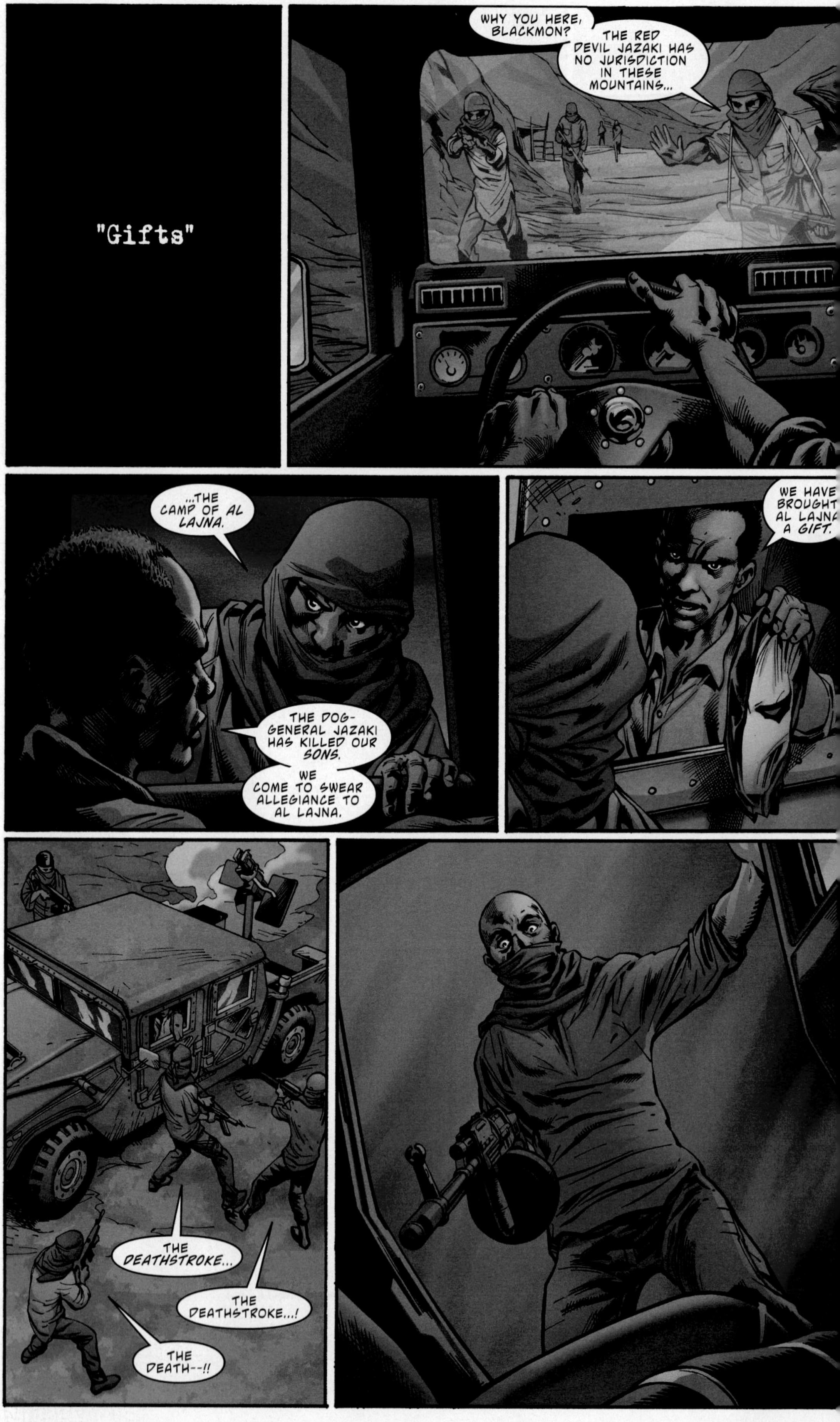
"Gifts"
WHY YOU HERE, BLACKMON?
THE RED DEVIL JAZAKI HAS NO JURISDICTION IN THESE MOUNTAINS...
...THE CAMP OF AL LAJNA.
THE DOG-GENERAL JAZAKI HAS KILLED OUR SONS.
WE COME TO SWEAR ALLEGIANCE TO AL LAJNA.
WE HAVE BROUGHT AL LAJNA A GIFT.
THE DEATHSTROKE...
THE DEATHSTROKE...!
THE DEATH--!!

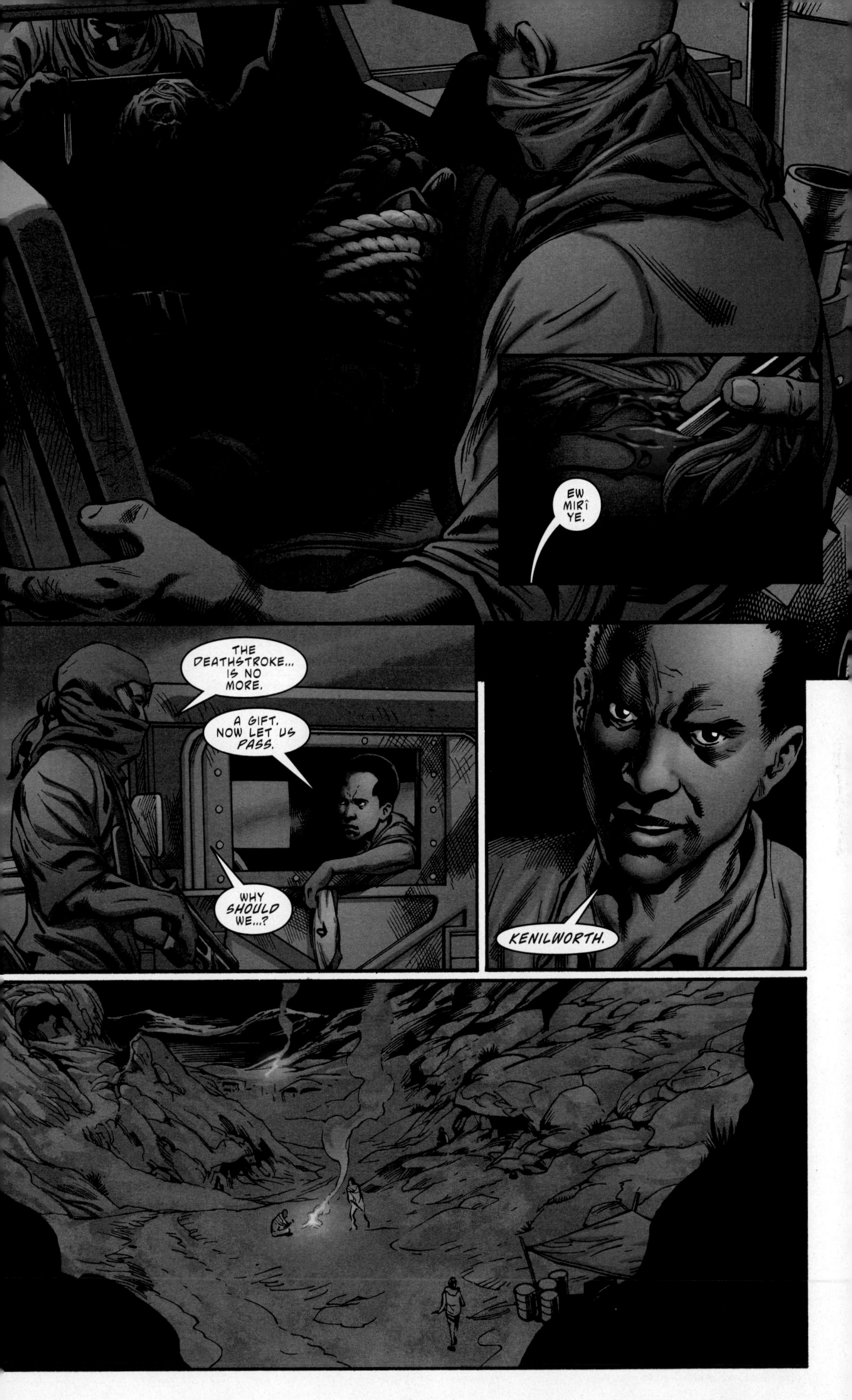
EW MIRÎ YE.
THE DEATHSTROKE... IS NO MORE.
A GIFT. NOW LET US PASS.
WHY SHOULD WE...?
KENILWORTH.

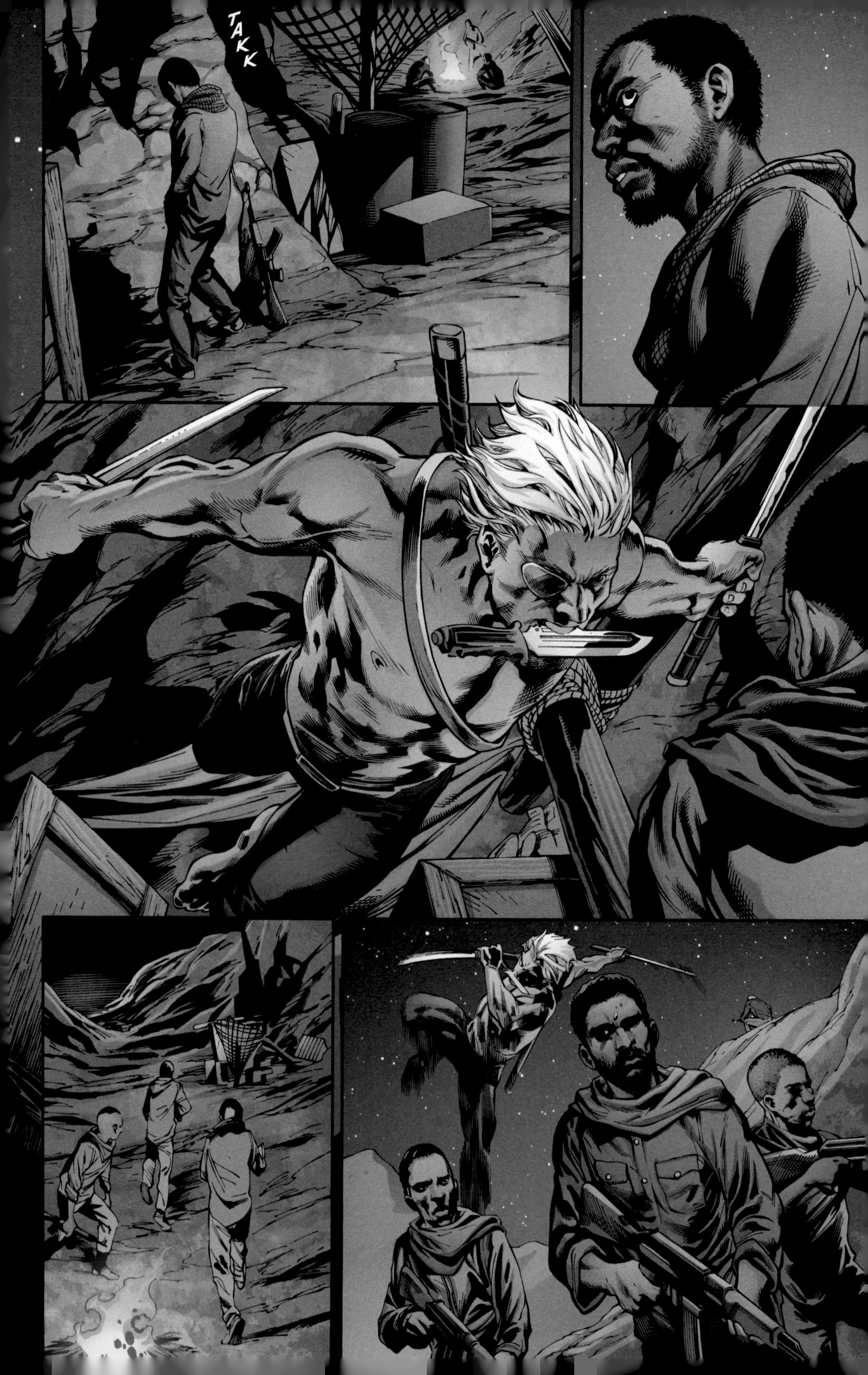
TAKK

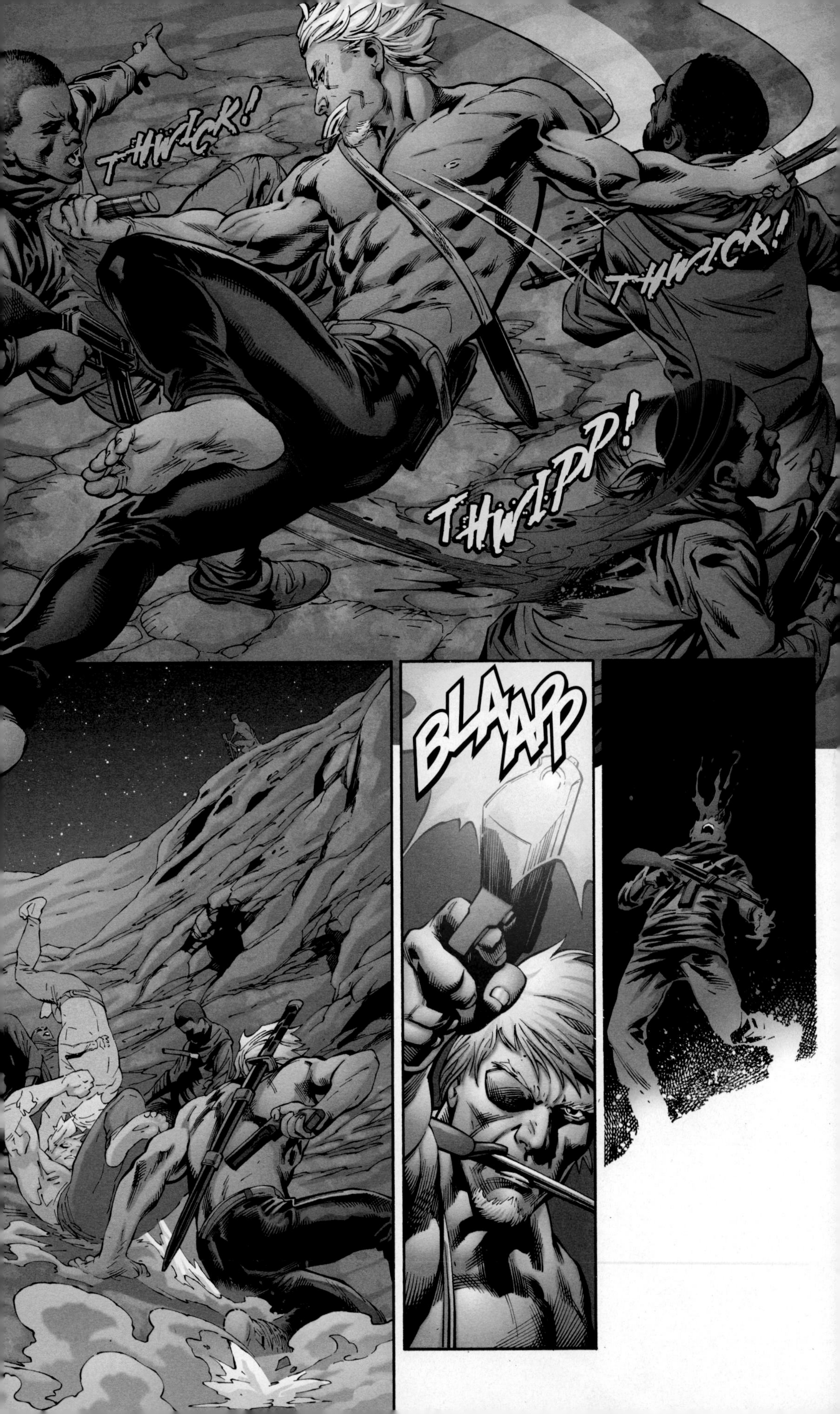
THWICK!
THWICK!
THWIPP!
BLAAPP

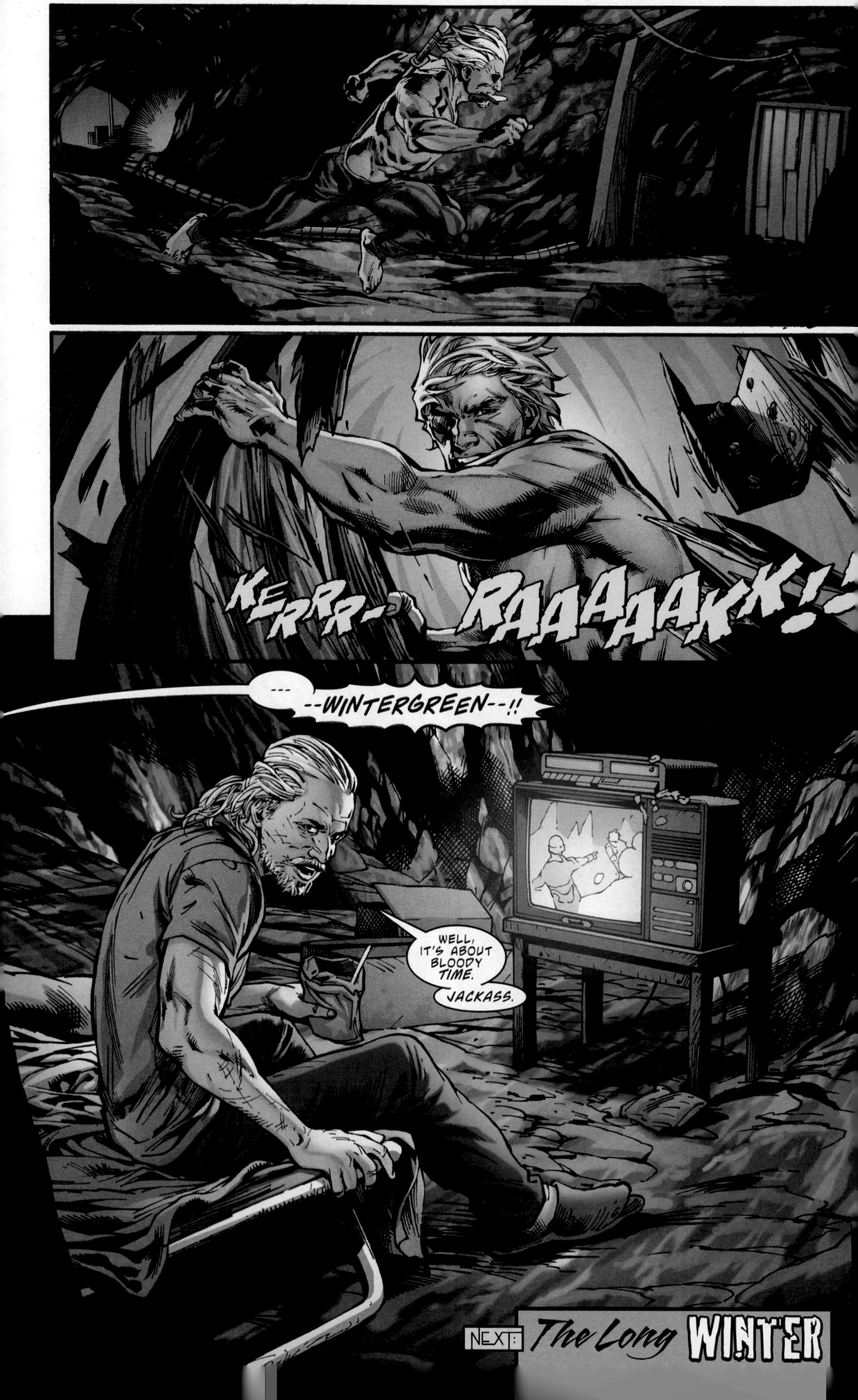
KERRRR--RAAAAAAKK!!

--WINTERGREEN--!!
WELL, IT'S ABOUT BLOODY TIME.
JACKASS.
NEXT: The Long WINTER

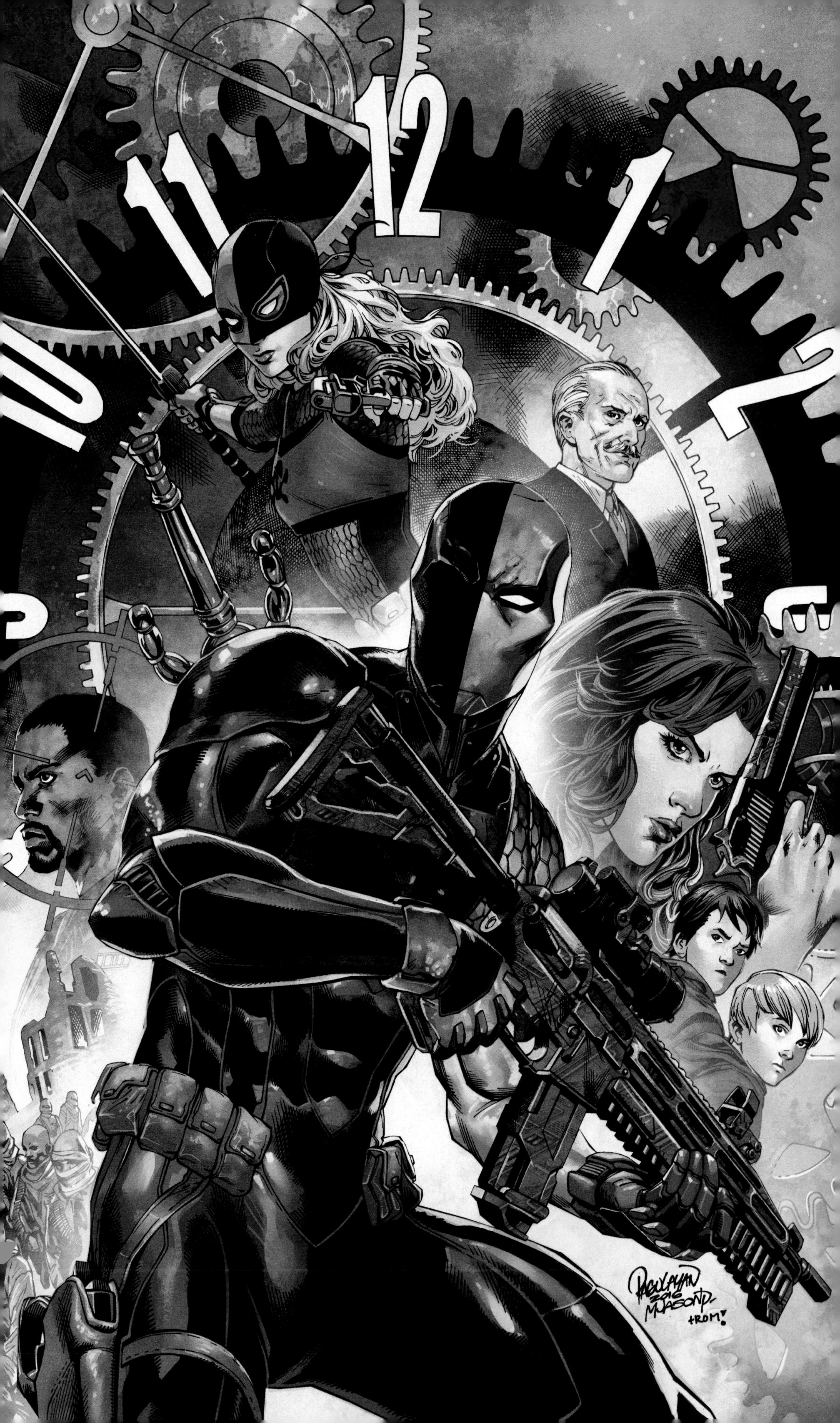
11
12
1

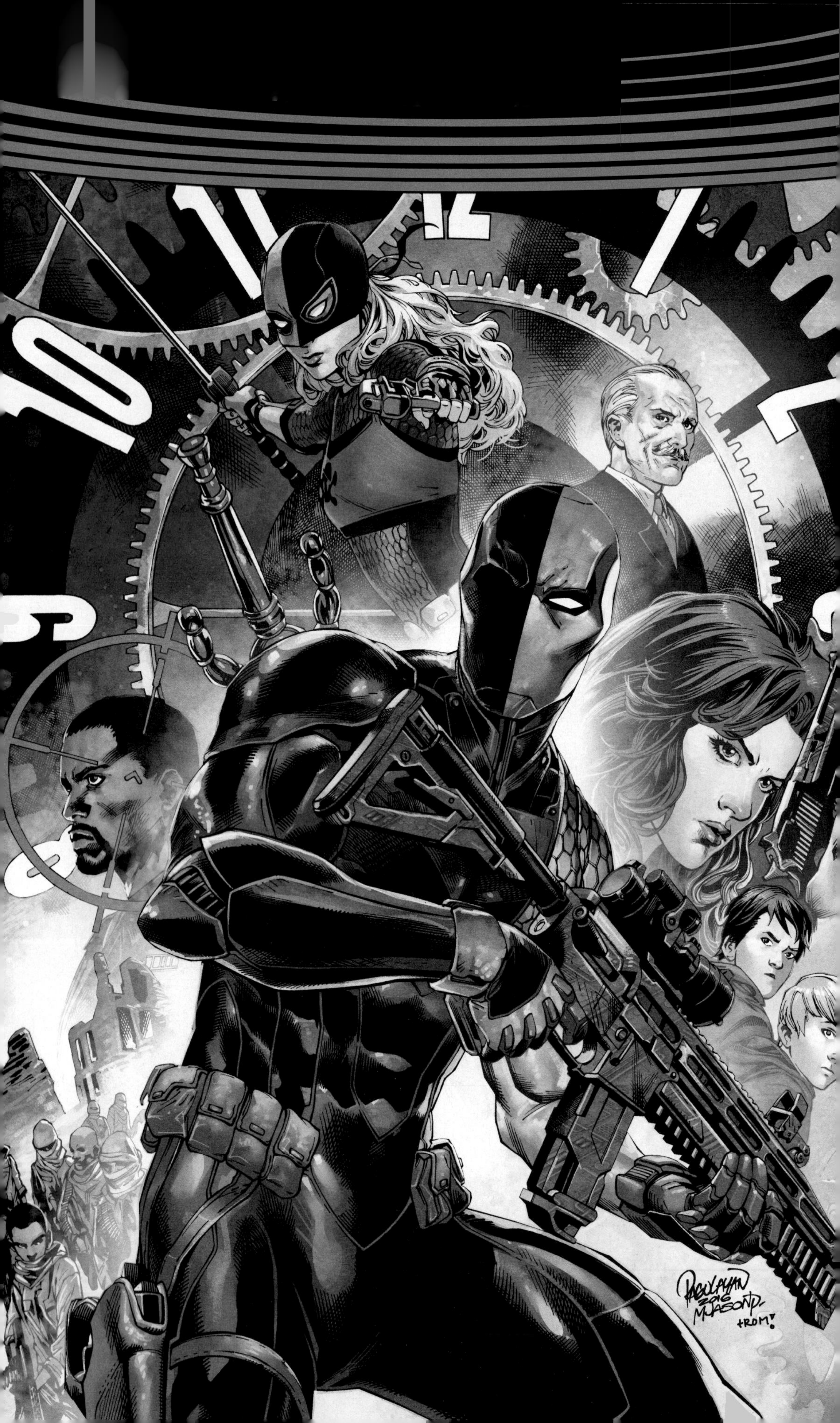

SIGN HERE, CONGRESSMAN HASGROVE.

HOSUN

IN AN AMAZING TURN OF EVENTS, AMERICANS FOR PEACE, A NEW SUPER PAC...

"Whom Nobody Can Deny"

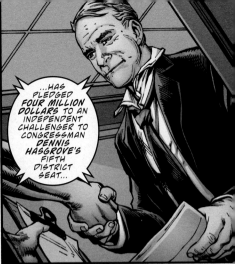

...HAS PLEDGED FOUR MILLION DOLLARS TO AN INDEPENDENT CHALLENGER TO CONGRESSMAN DENNIS HASGROVE'S FIFTH DISTRICT SEAT...

...WHICH WILL SPLIT THE DEMOCRATIC VOTE, VIRTUALLY GUARANTEEING REPUBLICAN HASGROVE'S RE-ELECTION.

"THE SUPER PAC HAS MIRACULOUSLY REVIVED HASGROVE'S CAMPAIGN...

...WHICH HAD PREVIOUSLY BEEN ON THE ROPES, DUE, IN PART, TO HASGROVE'S BLOCKING CONGRESSIONAL AUTHORIZATION...

"...FOR U.S. MILITARY INTERVENTION IN AFRICAN DESPOT MATTHEW BLAND'S ETHNIC GENOCIDE.

"NEEDLESS TO SAY, IT SHOULD NOW BE SMOOTH SAILING FOR HASGROVE...

"...WHILE THE ONE-SIDED SLAUGHTER CONTINUES OVERSEAS..."

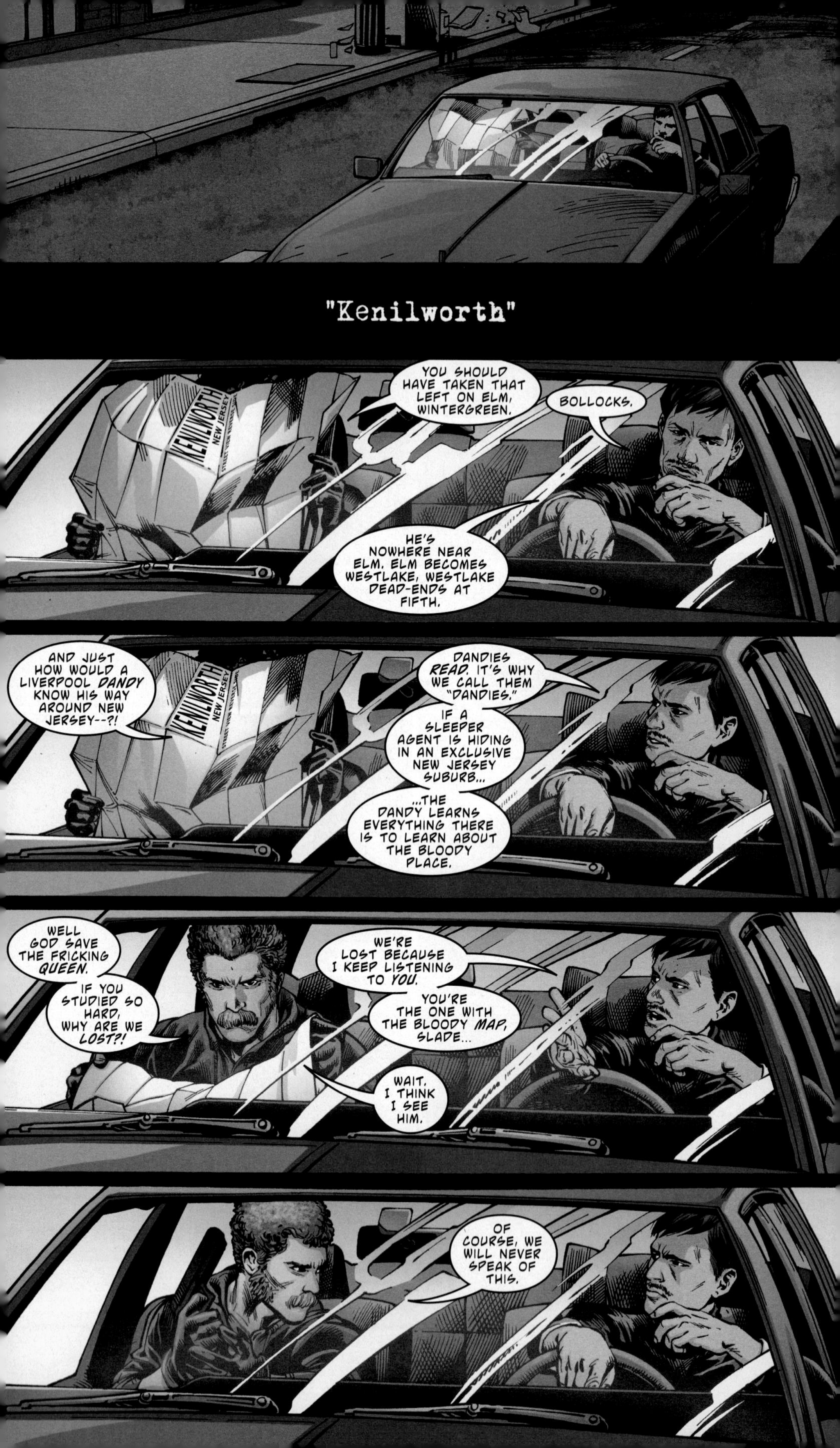
"Kenilworth"
KENILWORTH NEW JERSEY
YOU SHOULD HAVE TAKEN THAT LEFT ON ELM, WINTERGREEN.
BOLLOCKS.
HE'S NOWHERE NEAR ELM. ELM BECOMES WESTLAKE, WESTLAKE DEAD-ENDS AT FIFTH.
AND JUST HOW WOULD A LIVERPOOL *DANDY* KNOW HIS WAY AROUND NEW JERSEY--?!
DANDIES *READ*. IT'S WHY WE CALL THEM "DANDIES."
IF A SLEEPER AGENT IS HIDING IN AN EXCLUSIVE NEW JERSEY SUBURB...
...THE DANDY LEARNS EVERYTHING THERE IS TO LEARN ABOUT THE BLOODY PLACE.
WELL GOD SAVE THE FRICKING *QUEEN*.
IF YOU STUDIED SO HARD, WHY ARE WE *LOST*?!
WE'RE LOST BECAUSE I KEEP LISTENING TO *YOU*.
YOU'RE THE ONE WITH THE BLOODY *MAP*, SLADE...
WAIT, I THINK I SEE HIM.
OF COURSE, WE WILL NEVER SPEAK OF THIS.

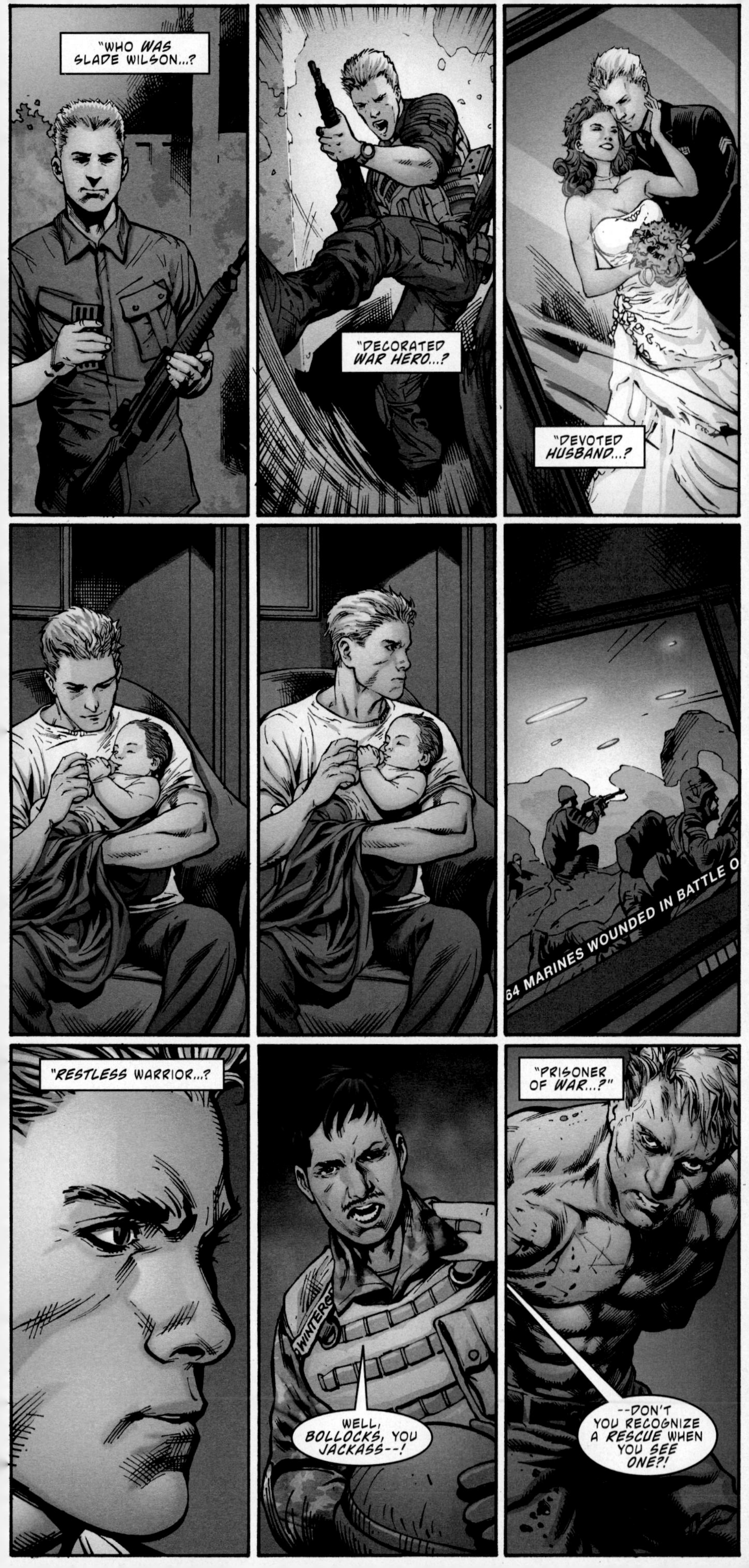
"WHO WAS SLADE WILSON...?
"DECORATED WAR HERO...?
"DEVOTED HUSBAND...?
64 MARINES WOUNDED IN BATTLE O
"RESTLESS WARRIOR...?
WINTERG
WELL, BOLLOCKS, YOU JACKASS--!
"PRISONER OF WAR...?"
--DON'T YOU RECOGNIZE A RESCUE WHEN YOU SEE ONE?!

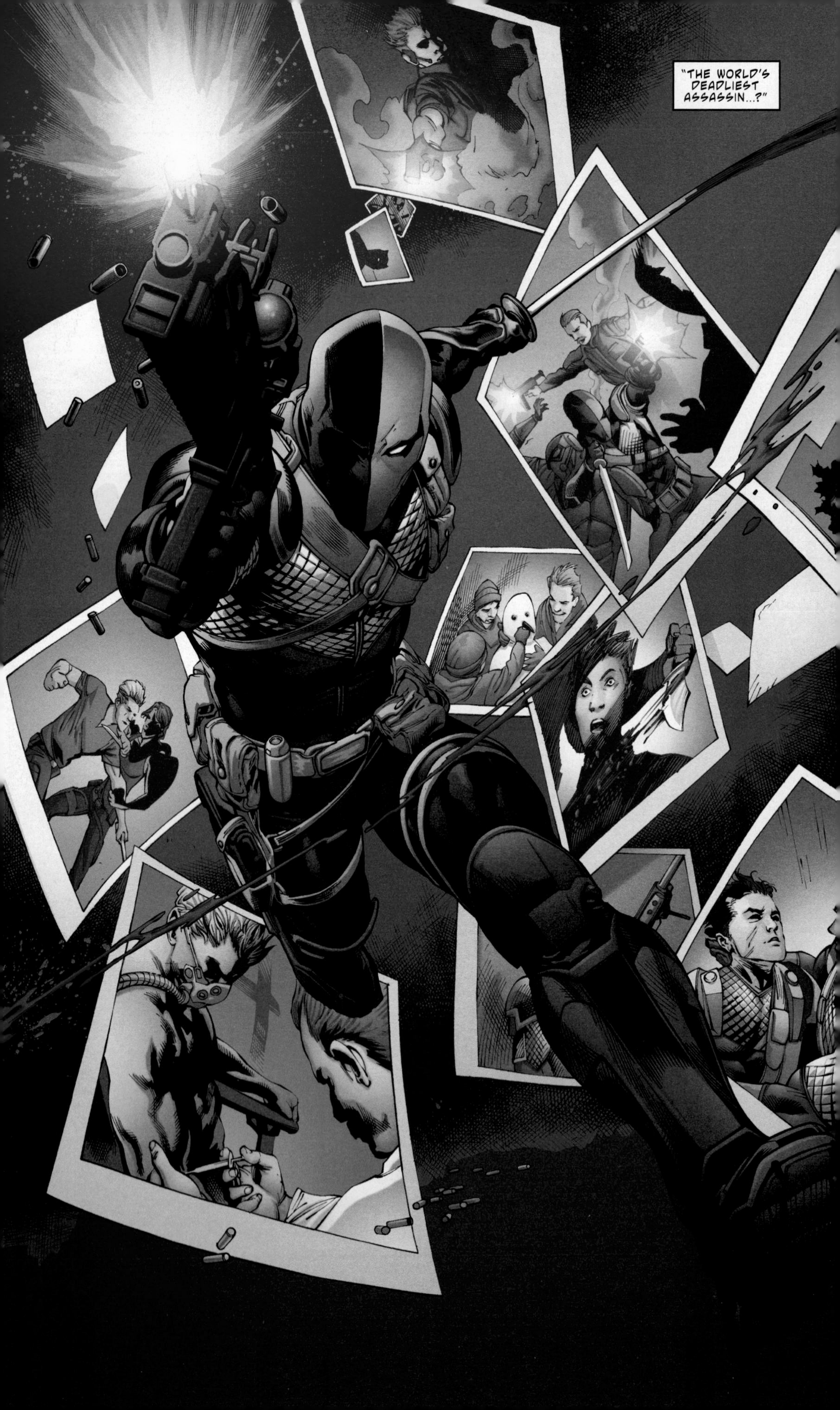
"THE WORLD'S DEADLIEST ASSASSIN...?"

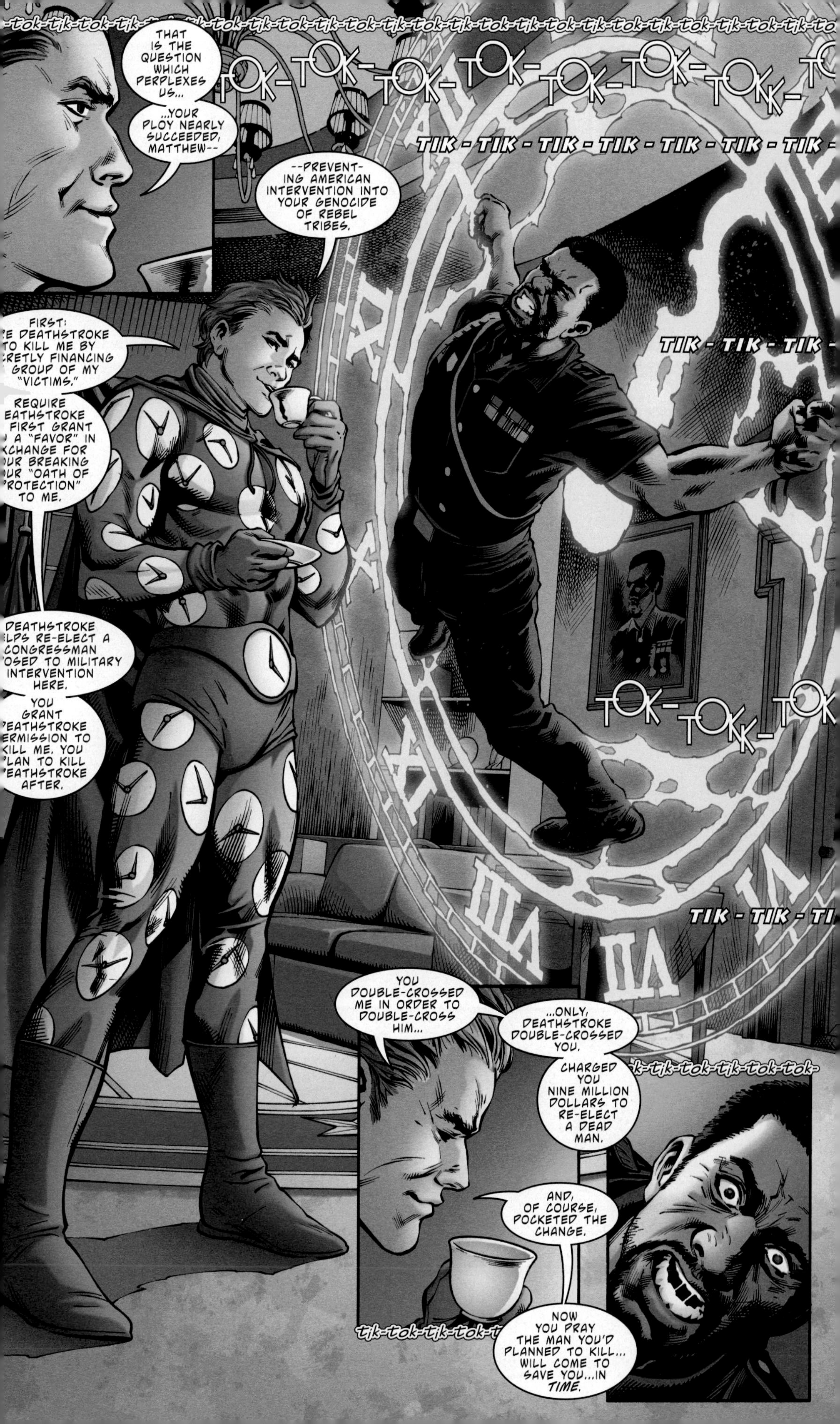
-tok-tik-tok-tik-tik-tok-tik-tok-tik-tok-tik-tok-tik-tok-tik-tok-tik-tok-tik-to
THAT IS THE QUESTION WHICH PERPLEXES US...
...YOUR PLOY NEARLY SUCCEEDED, MATTHEW--
TOK-TOK-TOK-TOK-TOK-TOK-TOK-TOK-TO
TIK - TIK - TIK - TIK - TIK - TIK - TIK -
--PREVENTING AMERICAN INTERVENTION INTO YOUR GENOCIDE OF REBEL TRIBES.
FIRST: E DEATHSTROKE TO KILL ME BY CRETLY FINANCING GROUP OF MY "VICTIMS."
REQUIRE EATHSTROKE FIRST GRANT A "FAVOR" IN XCHANGE FOR UR BREAKING UR "OATH OF ROTECTION" TO ME.
TIK - TIK - TIK -
DEATHSTROKE ELPS RE-ELECT A CONGRESSMAN OSED TO MILITARY INTERVENTION HERE.
YOU GRANT EATHSTROKE ERMISSION TO ILL ME. YOU LAN TO KILL EATHSTROKE AFTER.
TOK-TOK-TOK
TIK - TIK - TI
YOU DOUBLE-CROSSED ME IN ORDER TO DOUBLE-CROSS HIM...
...ONLY, DEATHSTROKE DOUBLE-CROSSED YOU.
CHARGED YOU NINE MILLION DOLLARS TO RE-ELECT A DEAD MAN.
ok-tik-tok-tik-tok-tok-
AND, OF COURSE, POCKETED THE CHANGE.
tik-tok-tik-tok-t
NOW YOU PRAY THE MAN YOU'D PLANNED TO KILL... WILL COME TO SAVE YOU...IN *TIME*.

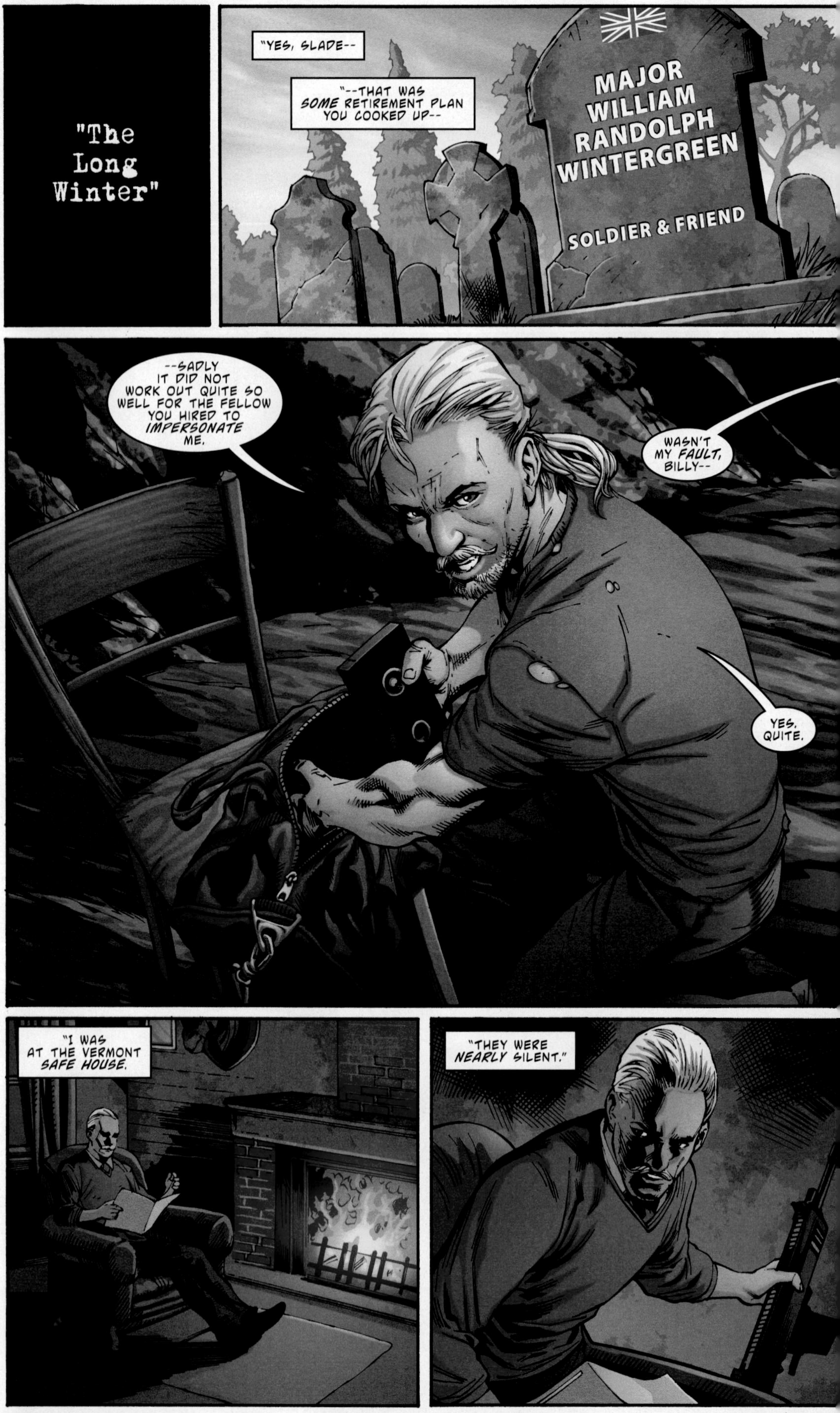
"The Long Winter"
"YES, SLADE--
"--THAT WAS SOME RETIREMENT PLAN YOU COOKED UP--
MAJOR WILLIAM RANDOLPH WINTERGREEN
SOLDIER & FRIEND
--SADLY IT DID NOT WORK OUT QUITE SO WELL FOR THE FELLOW YOU HIRED TO IMPERSONATE ME.
WASN'T MY FAULT, BILLY--
YES. QUITE.
"I WAS AT THE VERMONT SAFE HOUSE.
"THEY WERE NEARLY SILENT."

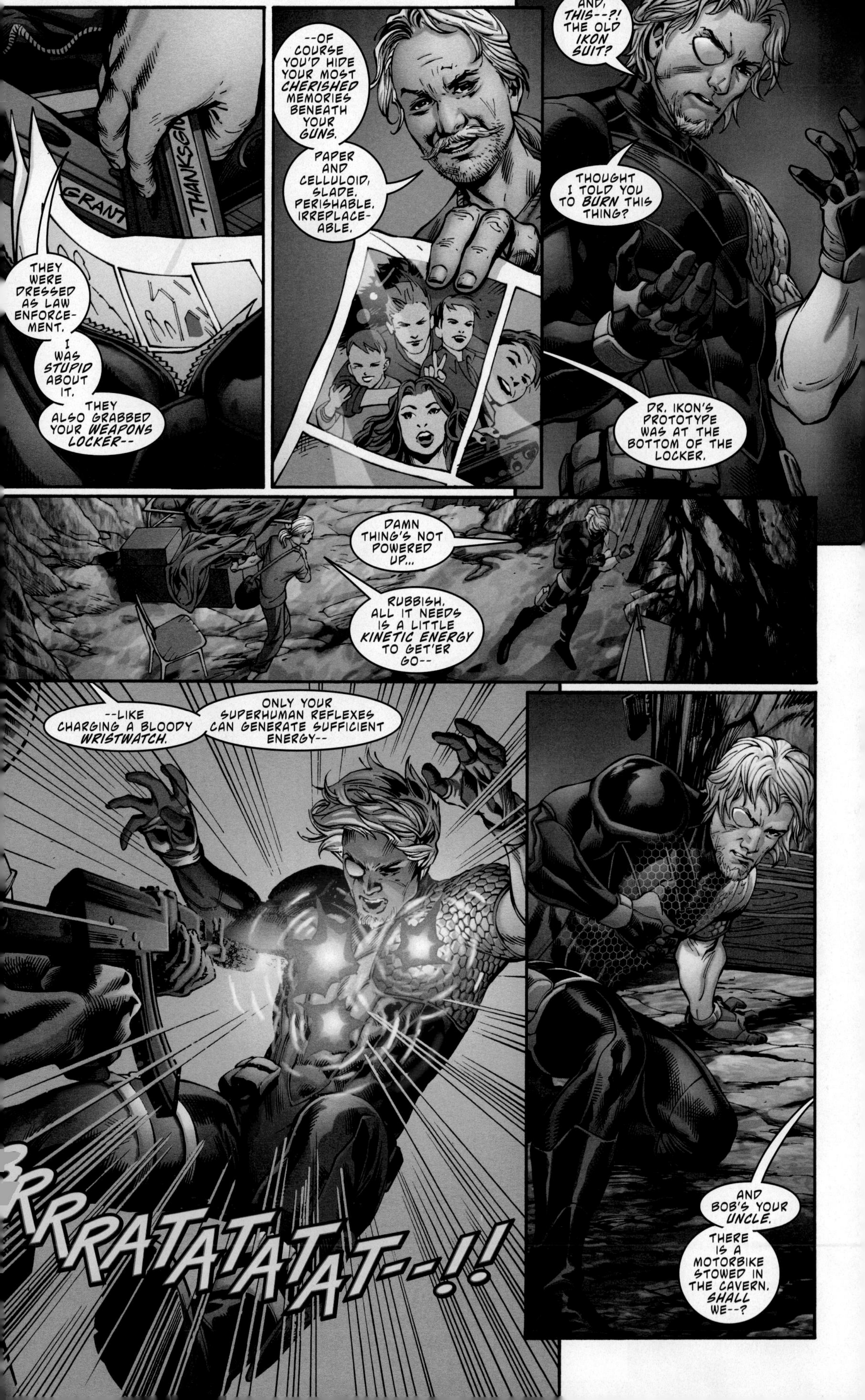
THEY WERE DRESSED AS LAW ENFORCEMENT.
I WAS STUPID ABOUT IT.
THEY ALSO GRABBED YOUR WEAPONS LOCKER--
--OF COURSE YOU'D HIDE YOUR MOST CHERISHED MEMORIES BENEATH YOUR GUNS.
PAPER AND CELLULOID, SLADE. PERISHABLE. IRREPLACEABLE.
GRANT
THANKSGIV
AND, THIS--?! THE OLD IKON SUIT?
THOUGHT I TOLD YOU TO BURN THIS THING?
DR. IKON'S PROTOTYPE WAS AT THE BOTTOM OF THE LOCKER.
DAMN THING'S NOT POWERED UP...
RUBBISH. ALL IT NEEDS IS A LITTLE KINETIC ENERGY TO GET'ER GO--
ONLY YOUR SUPERHUMAN REFLEXES CAN GENERATE SUFFICIENT ENERGY--
--LIKE CHARGING A BLOODY WRISTWATCH.
BRRRATATATAT--!!
AND BOB'S YOUR UNCLE.
THERE IS A MOTORBIKE STOWED IN THE CAVERN. SHALL WE--?

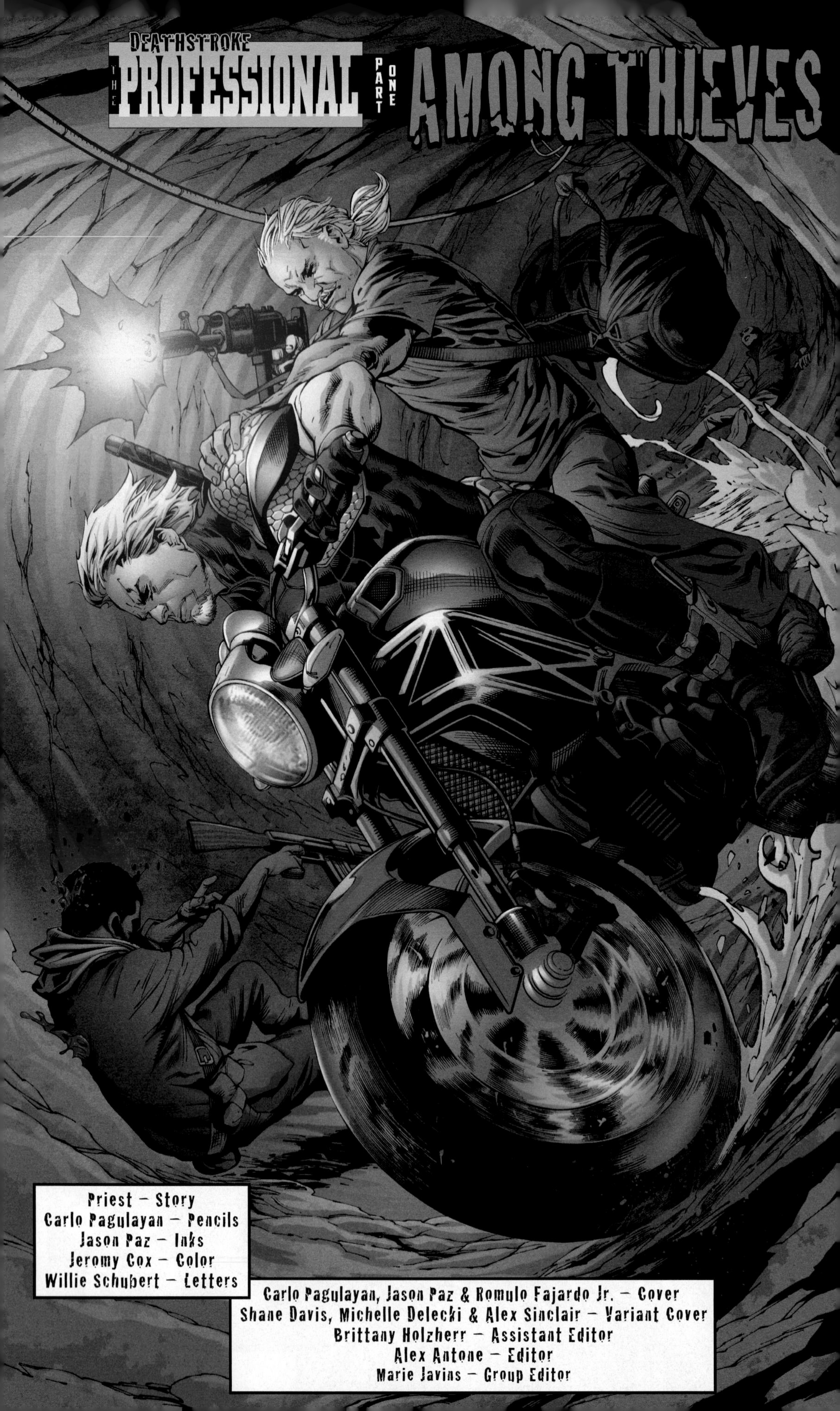
DEATHSTROKE
THE PROFESSIONAL PART ONE
AMONG THIEVES
Priest – Story
Carlo Pagulayan – Pencils
Jason Paz – Inks
Jeromy Cox – Color
Willie Schubert – Letters
Carlo Pagulayan, Jason Paz & Romulo Fajardo Jr. – Cover
Shane Davis, Michelle Delecki & Alex Sinclair – Variant Cover
Brittany Holzherr – Assistant Editor
Alex Antone – Editor
Marie Javins – Group Editor

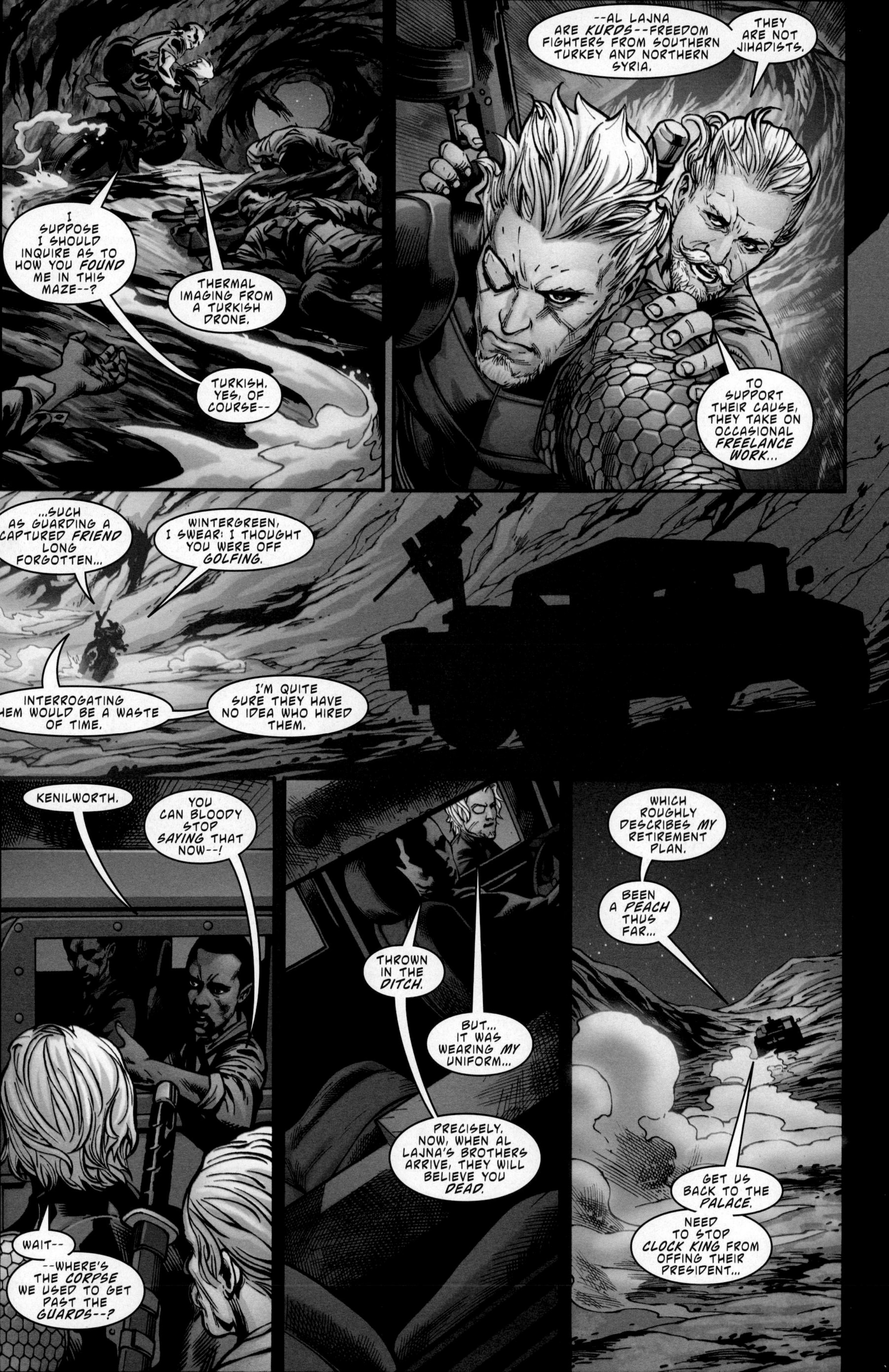

I SUPPOSE I SHOULD INQUIRE AS TO HOW YOU FOUND ME IN THIS MAZE--?
THERMAL IMAGING FROM A TURKISH DRONE.
TURKISH. YES, OF COURSE--
--AL LAJNA ARE KURDS--FREEDOM FIGHTERS FROM SOUTHERN TURKEY AND NORTHERN SYRIA.
THEY ARE NOT JIHADISTS.
TO SUPPORT THEIR CAUSE, THEY TAKE ON OCCASIONAL FREELANCE WORK...
...SUCH AS GUARDING A CAPTURED FRIEND LONG FORGOTTEN...
WINTERGREEN, I SWEAR: I THOUGHT YOU WERE OFF GOLFING.
INTERROGATING THEM WOULD BE A WASTE OF TIME.
I'M QUITE SURE THEY HAVE NO IDEA WHO HIRED THEM.
KENILWORTH.
YOU CAN BLOODY STOP SAYING THAT NOW--!
WAIT--
--WHERE'S THE CORPSE WE USED TO GET PAST THE GUARDS--?
THROWN IN THE DITCH.
BUT... IT WAS WEARING MY UNIFORM...
PRECISELY. NOW, WHEN AL LAJNA'S BROTHERS ARRIVE, THEY WILL BELIEVE YOU DEAD.
WHICH ROUGHLY DESCRIBES MY RETIREMENT PLAN.
BEEN A PEACH THUS FAR...
GET US BACK TO THE PALACE.
NEED TO STOP CLOCK KING FROM OFFING THEIR PRESIDENT...

"Countdown"

TOK-TOK-TOK-TOK

TIK-TIK-TIK-TIK-TIK-

WHERE ARE YOU, JAZAKI...? WHERE IN TIME?

LOST IN THE BEAUTIFUL MUSIC...HOW I DO LOVE IT...

PARDON...

WILLIAM RANDOLPH WINTERGREEN.

A SQUADRON 22 OF HER MAJESTY'S SPECIAL AIR SERVICE.

RETIRED, OF COURSE.

TIK-TIK-TIK

tok-tik-tok-tik-t

TOK-TOK-TOK-TOK

tik-tok-t

YOU'RE WELCOME. FOR THE RESCUE.

YES... COLONEL SLADE HAS MADE A CONTRACT WITH THESE YOUNG MEN--

TIK-TIK-

ok-tik-tok-tik-to

--TO PROTECT THEIR LOVED ONES.

HE CANNOT ALLOW PRESIDENT BLAND'S DEMISE, AS THAT WOULD DESTABILIZE THE COUNTRY.

tok-tik-tok-tik-tok-tik-tok-

WE SHALL RETIRE WITH YOUR PROMISE TO NOT KILL THE PRESIDENT.

I SEE. WELL, PERMIT ME TO PRESENT A COUNTER-OFFER--

TIK-TIK-TIK-TI

TOK-TOK-

SZACKK--!

--A JOURNEY THROUGH THE RAVAGES OF TIME--!!

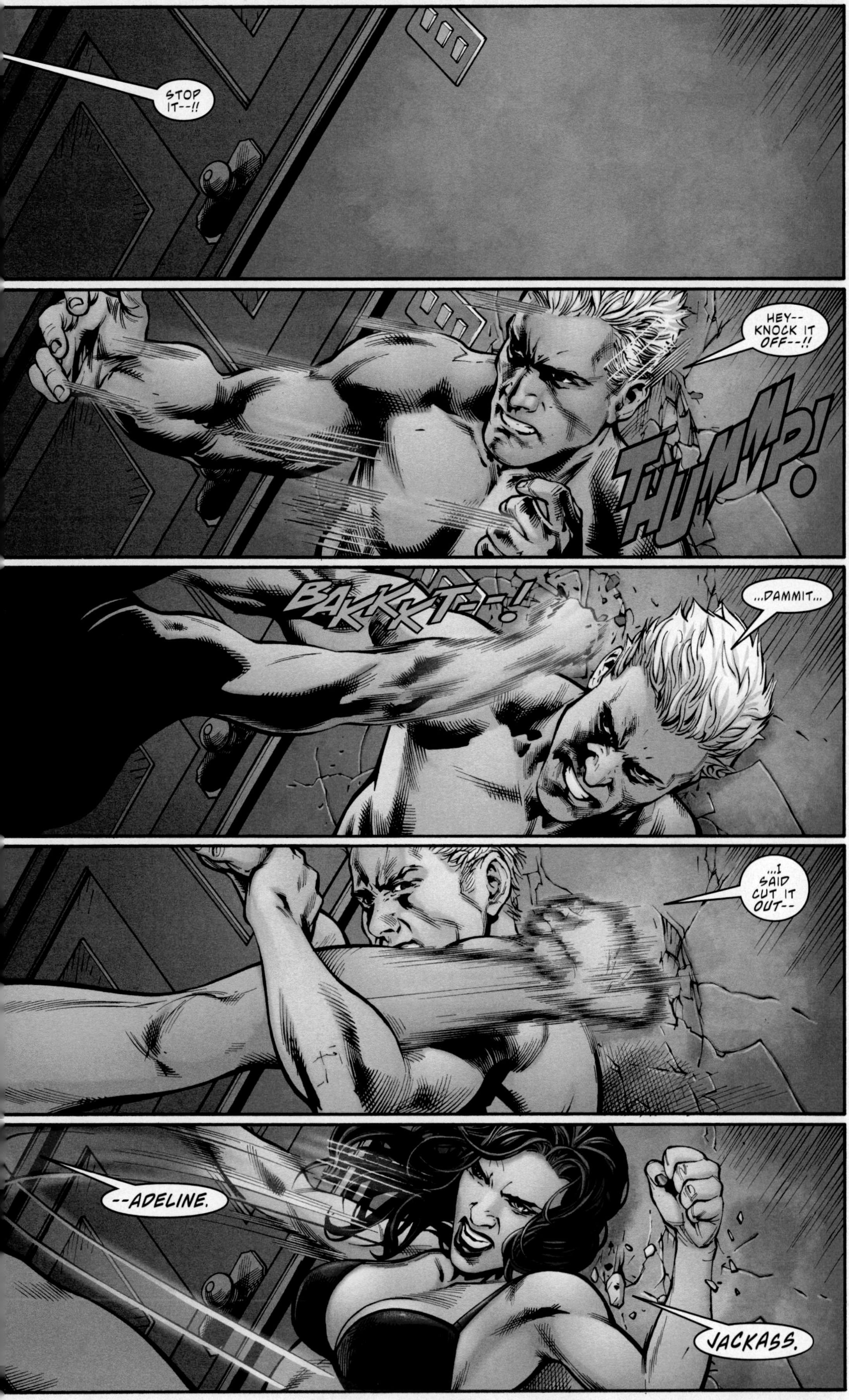
STOP IT--!!
HEY-- KNOCK IT OFF--!!
THUMMP!
BAKKKT--!
...DAMMIT...
...I SAID CUT IT OUT--
--ADELINE.
JACKASS.

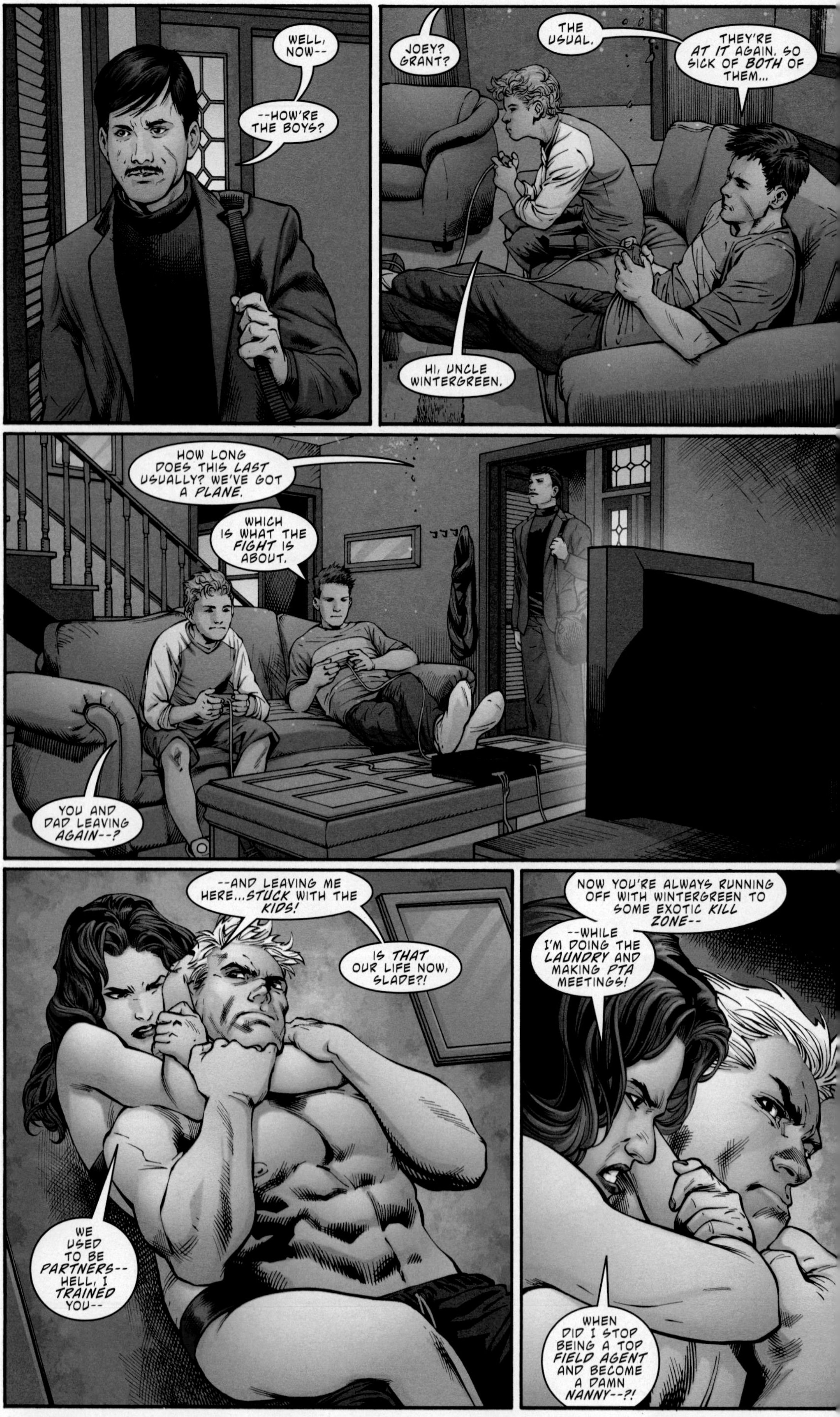
WELL, NOW--
--HOW'RE THE BOYS?
JOEY? GRANT?
THE USUAL.
THEY'RE AT IT AGAIN. SO SICK OF BOTH OF THEM...
HI, UNCLE WINTERGREEN.
HOW LONG DOES THIS LAST USUALLY? WE'VE GOT A PLANE.
WHICH IS WHAT THE FIGHT IS ABOUT.
YOU AND DAD LEAVING AGAIN--?
--AND LEAVING ME HERE...STUCK WITH THE KIDS!
IS THAT OUR LIFE NOW, SLADE?!
WE USED TO BE PARTNERS-- HELL, I TRAINED YOU--
NOW YOU'RE ALWAYS RUNNING OFF WITH WINTERGREEN TO SOME EXOTIC KILL ZONE--
--WHILE I'M DOING THE LAUNDRY AND MAKING PTA MEETINGS!
WHEN DID I STOP BEING A TOP FIELD AGENT AND BECOME A DAMN NANNY--?!

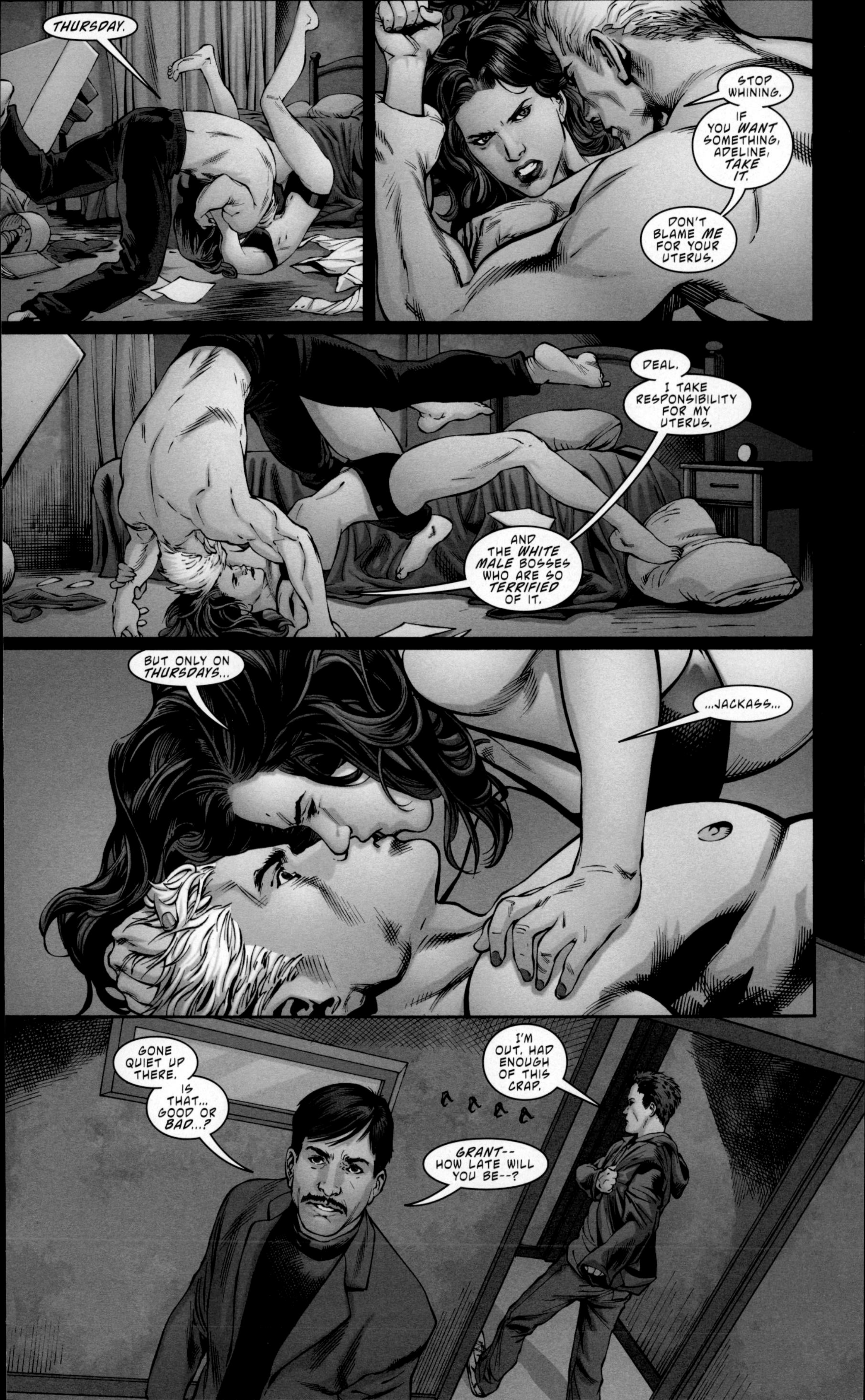
THURSDAY.
STOP WHINING.
IF YOU WANT SOMETHING, ADELINE, TAKE IT.
DON'T BLAME ME FOR YOUR UTERUS.
DEAL.
I TAKE RESPONSIBILITY FOR MY UTERUS.
AND THE WHITE MALE BOSSES WHO ARE SO TERRIFIED OF IT.
BUT ONLY ON THURSDAYS...
...JACKASS...
GONE QUIET UP THERE.
IS THAT... GOOD OR BAD...?
I'M OUT. HAD ENOUGH OF THIS CRAP.
GRANT-- HOW LATE WILL YOU BE--?

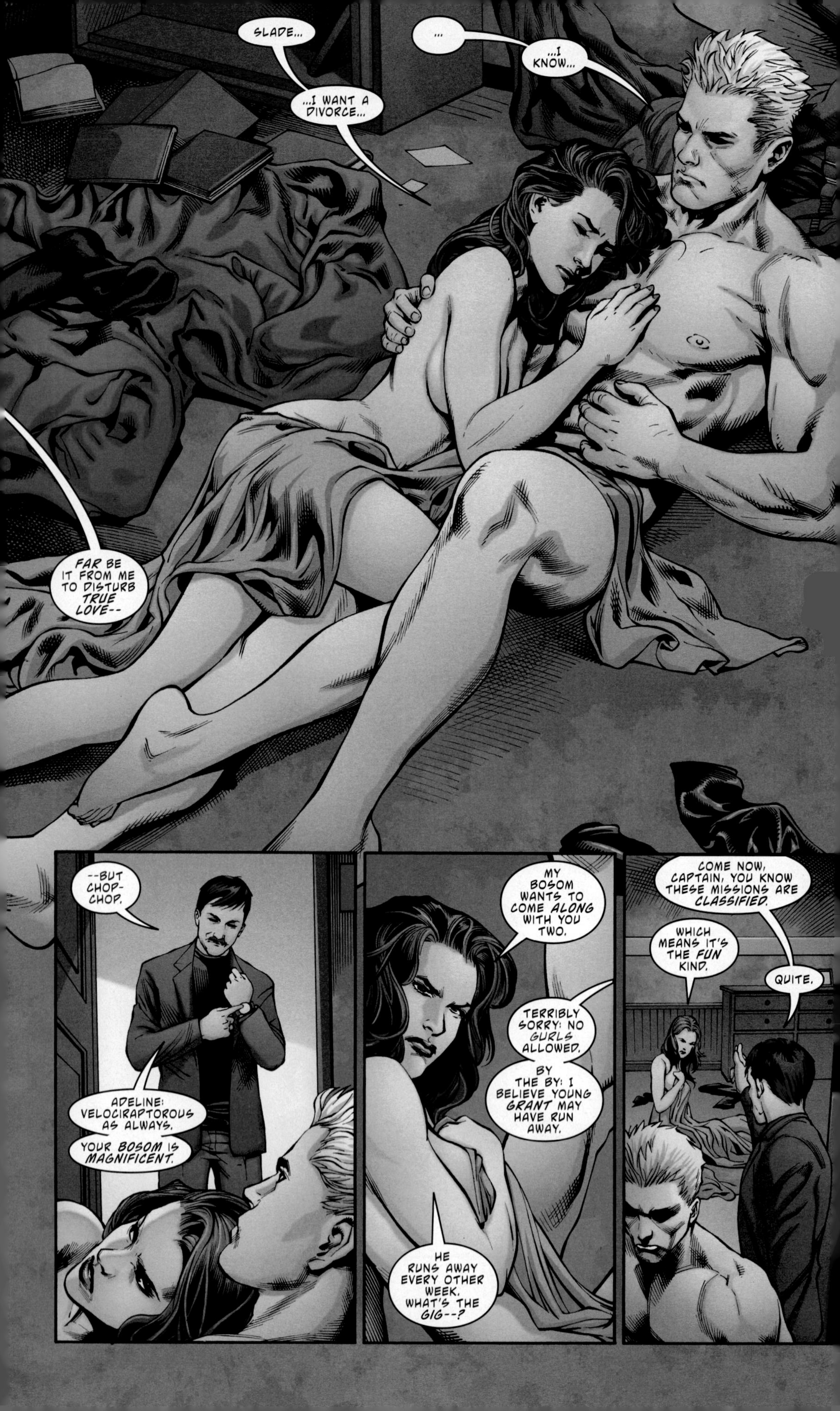

SLADE...
...I WANT A DIVORCE...
...
...I KNOW...
FAR BE IT FROM ME TO DISTURB *TRUE LOVE*--
--BUT CHOP-CHOP.
ADELINE: VELOCIRAPTOROUS AS ALWAYS.
YOUR *BOSOM* IS *MAGNIFICENT*.
MY BOSOM WANTS TO COME *ALONG* WITH YOU TWO.
TERRIBLY SORRY: NO *GURLS* ALLOWED.
BY THE BY: I BELIEVE YOUNG *GRANT* MAY HAVE RUN AWAY.
HE RUNS AWAY EVERY OTHER WEEK. WHAT'S THE *GIG*--?
COME NOW, CAPTAIN, YOU KNOW THESE MISSIONS ARE *CLASSIFIED*.
WHICH MEANS IT'S THE *FUN* KIND.
QUITE.

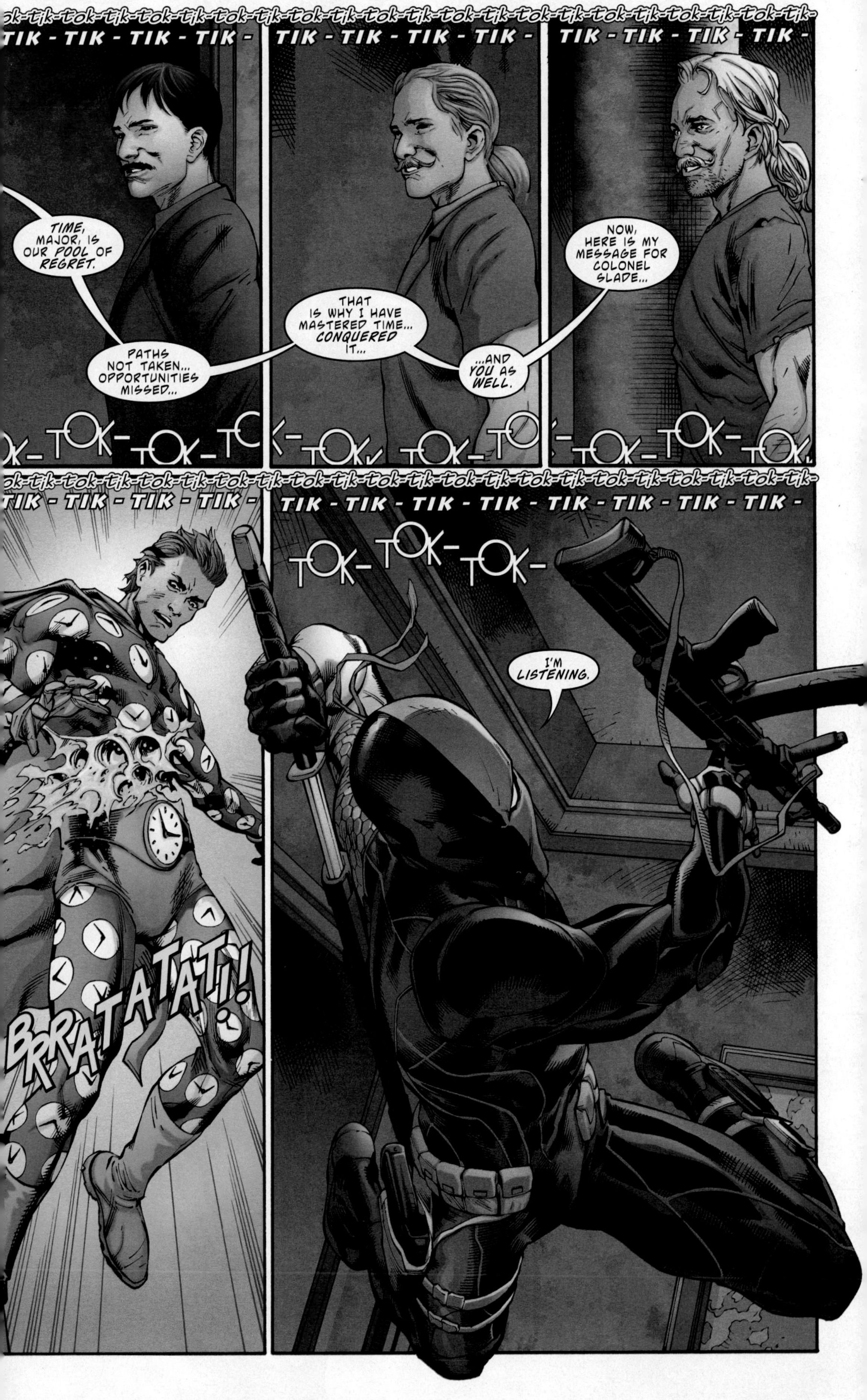
tok-tik-tok-tik-tok-tik-tok-tik-tok-tik-tok-tik-tok-tik-tok-tik-tok-tik-tok-tik-tok-tik-
TIK - TIK - TIK - TIK - TIK - TIK - TIK - TIK - TIK - TIK - TIK - TIK -
TIME, MAJOR, IS OUR POOL OF REGRET.
PATHS NOT TAKEN... OPPORTUNITIES MISSED...
THAT IS WHY I HAVE MASTERED TIME... CONQUERED IT...
...AND YOU AS WELL.
NOW, HERE IS MY MESSAGE FOR COLONEL SLADE...
TOK-TOK-TOK-TOK-TOK-TOK-TOK-TOK-TOK-TOK-TOK-
tok-tik-tok-tik-tok-tik-tok-tik-tok-tik-tok-tik-tok-tik-tok-tik-tok-tik-tok-tik-tok-tik-
TIK - TIK - TIK - TIK - TIK - TIK - TIK - TIK - TIK - TIK - TIK - TIK -
TOK-TOK-TOK-
BRRATATATT!
I'M LISTENING.

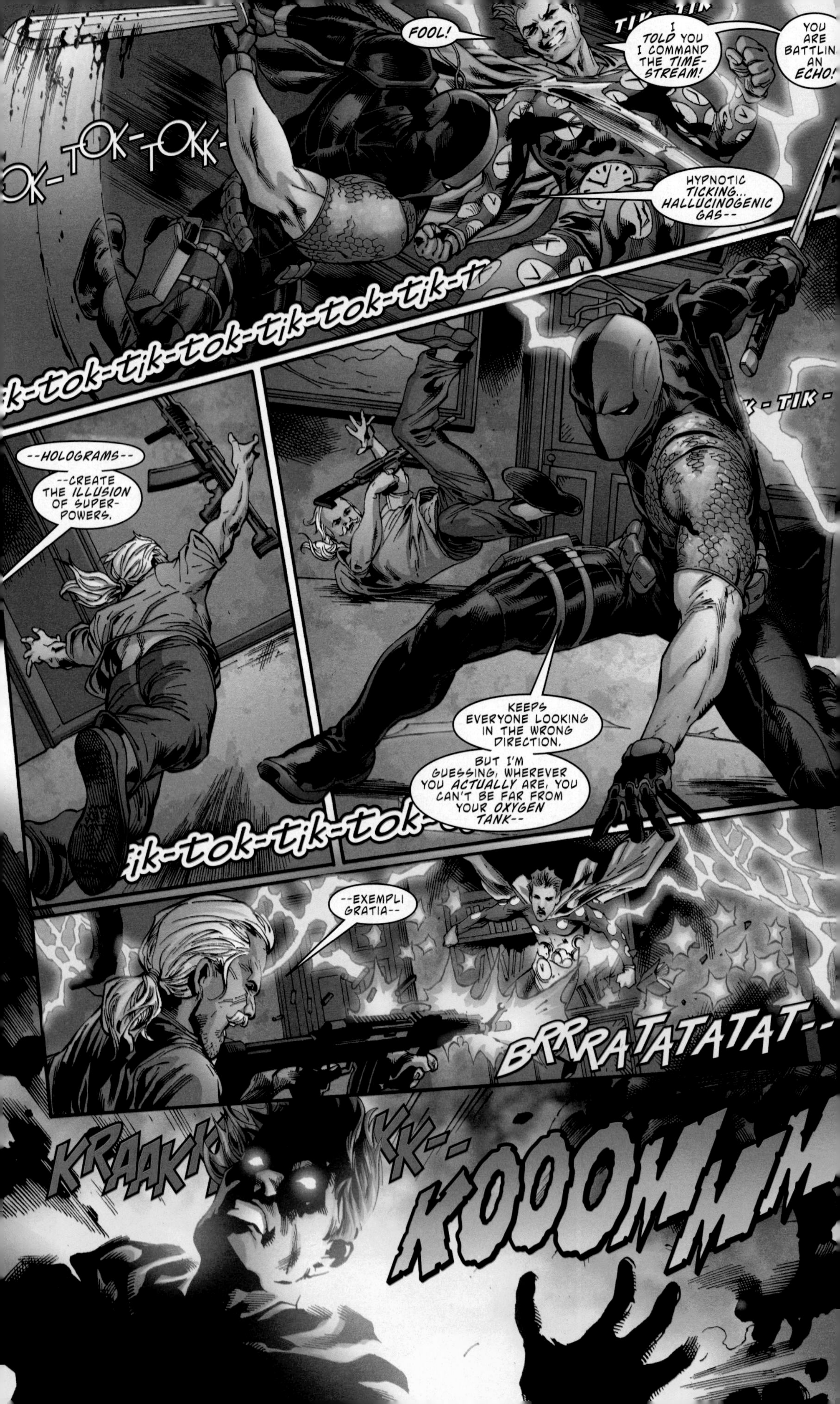
FOOL!
TIK-TIK
I TOLD YOU I COMMAND THE TIME-STREAM!
YOU ARE BATTLIN AN ECHO!
OK-TOK-TOKK-
HYPNOTIC TICKING... HALLUCINOGENIC GAS--
k-tok-tik-tok-tik-tok-tik-t
K-TIK-
--HOLOGRAMS--
--CREATE THE ILLUSION OF SUPER-POWERS.
KEEPS EVERYONE LOOKING IN THE WRONG DIRECTION.
BUT I'M GUESSING, WHEREVER YOU ACTUALLY ARE, YOU CAN'T BE FAR FROM YOUR OXYGEN TANK--
ik-tok-tik-tok-
--EXEMPLI GRATIA--
BRRRATATATAT--
KRAAKK
KK--
KOOOMM

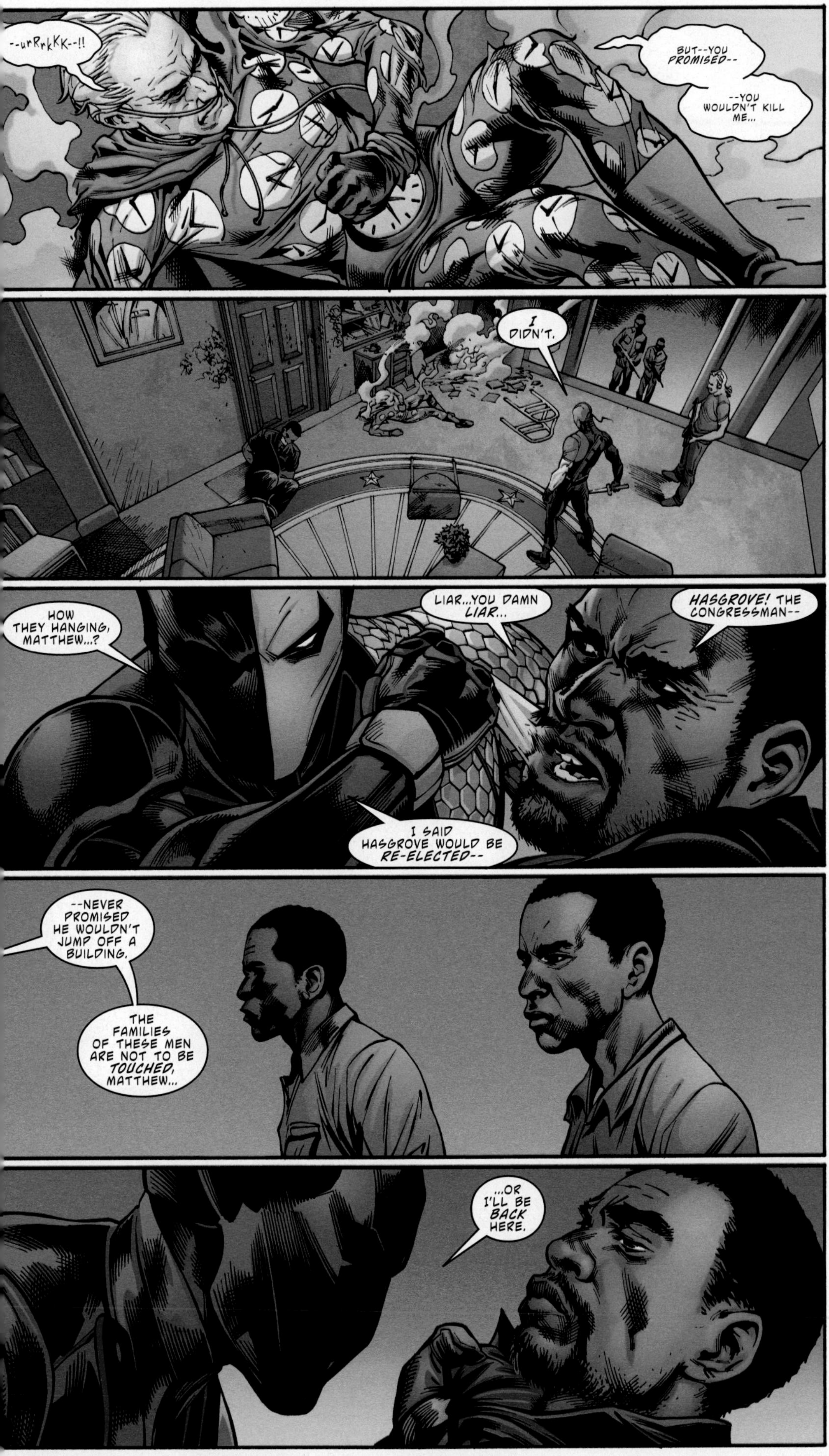
--urRrkKK--!!
BUT--YOU PROMISED--
--YOU WOULDN'T KILL ME...
I DIDN'T.
HOW THEY HANGING, MATTHEW...?
LIAR...YOU DAMN LIAR...
HASGROVE! THE CONGRESSMAN--
I SAID HASGROVE WOULD BE RE-ELECTED--
--NEVER PROMISED HE WOULDN'T JUMP OFF A BUILDING.
THE FAMILIES OF THESE MEN ARE NOT TO BE TOUCHED, MATTHEW...
...OR I'LL BE BACK HERE.

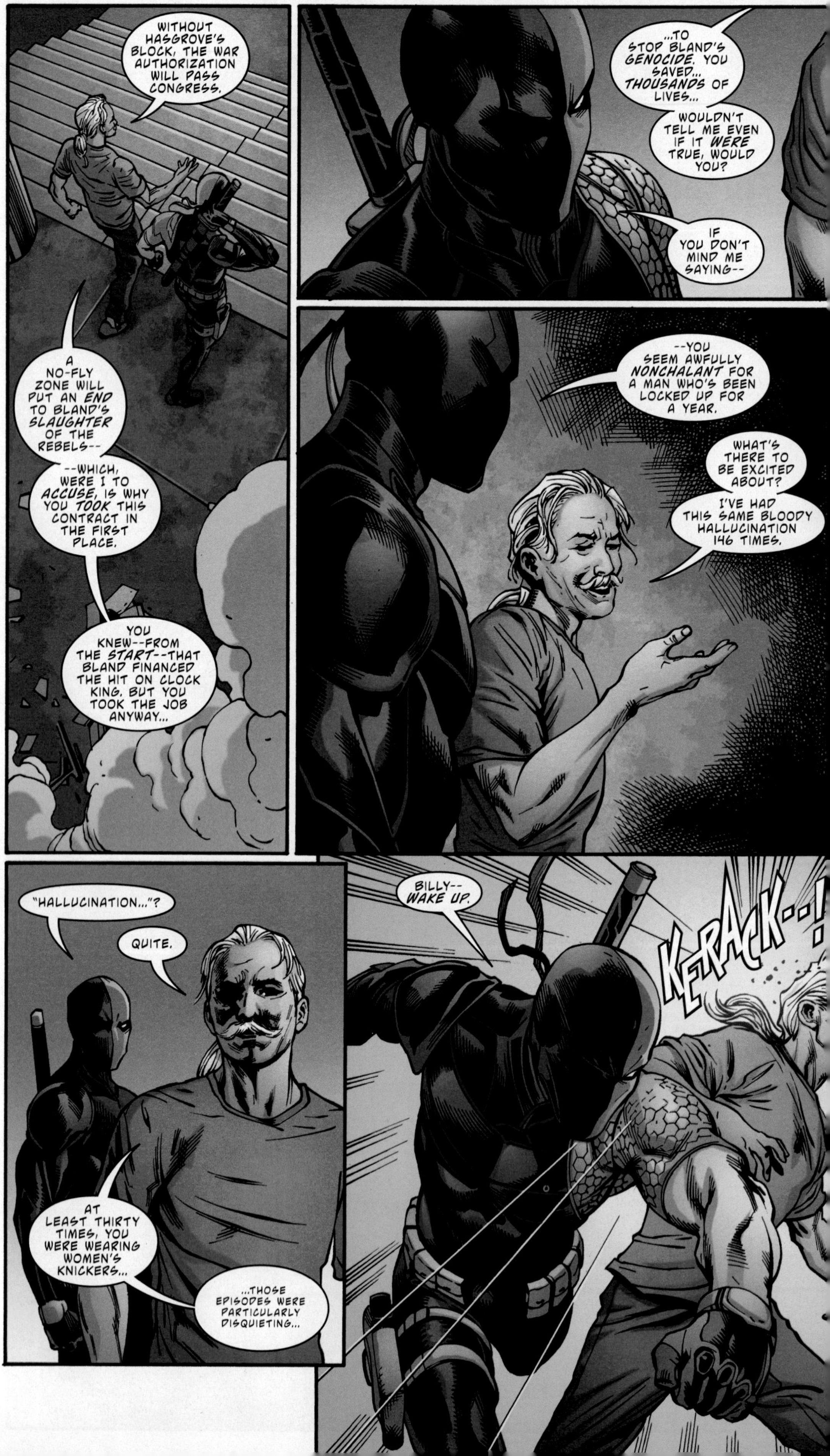
WITHOUT HASGROVE'S BLOCK, THE WAR AUTHORIZATION WILL PASS CONGRESS.
A NO-FLY ZONE WILL PUT AN END TO BLAND'S SLAUGHTER OF THE REBELS--
--WHICH, WERE I TO ACCUSE, IS WHY YOU TOOK THIS CONTRACT IN THE FIRST PLACE.
YOU KNEW--FROM THE START--THAT BLAND FINANCED THE HIT ON CLOCK KING. BUT YOU TOOK THE JOB ANYWAY...
...TO STOP BLAND'S GENOCIDE. YOU SAVED... THOUSANDS OF LIVES...
WOULDN'T TELL ME EVEN IF IT WERE TRUE, WOULD YOU?
IF YOU DON'T MIND ME SAYING--
--YOU SEEM AWFULLY NONCHALANT FOR A MAN WHO'S BEEN LOCKED UP FOR A YEAR.
WHAT'S THERE TO BE EXCITED ABOUT?
I'VE HAD THIS SAME BLOODY HALLUCINATION 146 TIMES.
"HALLUCINATION..."?
QUITE.
AT LEAST THIRTY TIMES, YOU WERE WEARING WOMEN'S KNICKERS...
...THOSE EPISODES WERE PARTICULARLY DISQUIETING...
BILLY-- WAKE UP.
KERACK--!

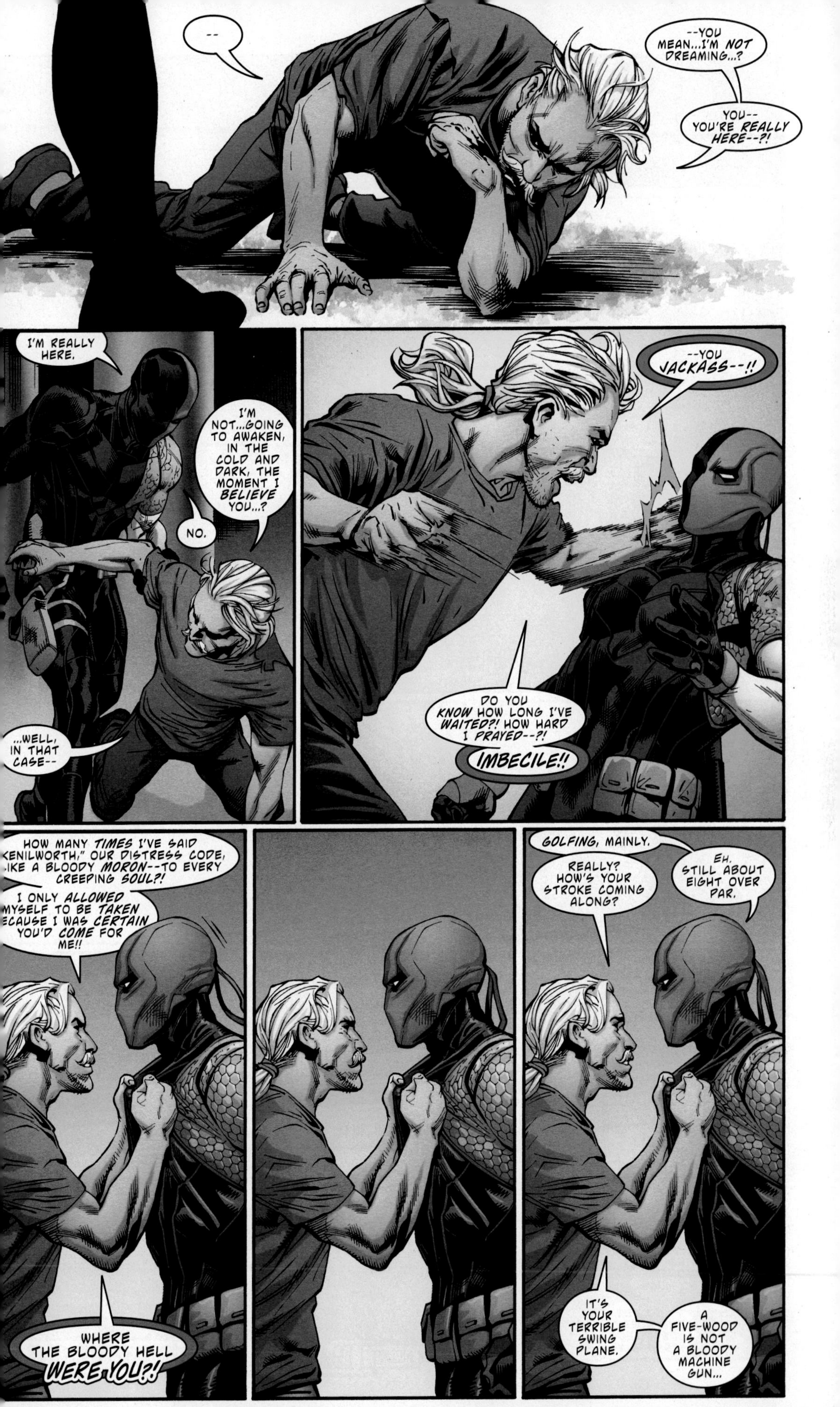
--
--YOU MEAN...I'M NOT DREAMING...?
YOU-- YOU'RE REALLY HERE--?!
I'M REALLY HERE.
I'M NOT...GOING TO AWAKEN, IN THE COLD AND DARK, THE MOMENT I BELIEVE YOU...?
NO.
...WELL, IN THAT CASE--
--YOU JACKASS--!!
DO YOU KNOW HOW LONG I'VE WAITED?! HOW HARD I PRAYED--?!
IMBECILE!!
HOW MANY TIMES I'VE SAID "KENILWORTH," OUR DISTRESS CODE, LIKE A BLOODY MORON--TO EVERY CREEPING SOUL?!
I ONLY ALLOWED MYSELF TO BE TAKEN BECAUSE I WAS CERTAIN YOU'D COME FOR ME!!
WHERE THE BLOODY HELL WERE YOU?!
GOLFING, MAINLY.
REALLY? HOW'S YOUR STROKE COMING ALONG?
EH. STILL ABOUT EIGHT OVER PAR.
IT'S YOUR TERRIBLE SWING PLANE.
A FIVE-WOOD IS NOT A BLOODY MACHINE GUN...

"Laundry"

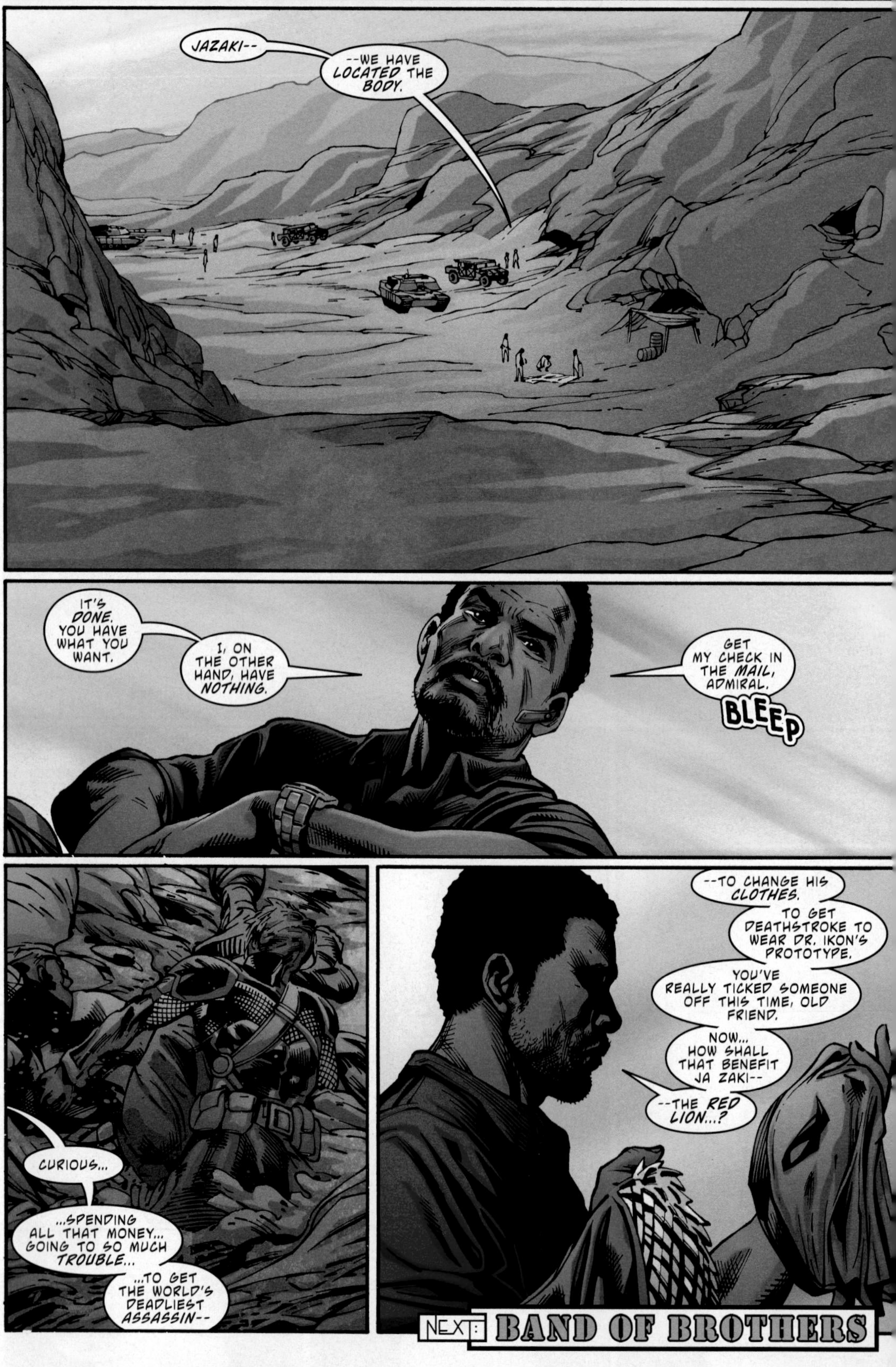
JAZAKI--
--WE HAVE LOCATED THE BODY.
IT'S DONE. YOU HAVE WHAT YOU WANT.
I, ON THE OTHER HAND, HAVE NOTHING.
GET MY CHECK IN THE MAIL, ADMIRAL.
BLEEP
CURIOUS...
...SPENDING ALL THAT MONEY... GOING TO SO MUCH TROUBLE...
...TO GET THE WORLD'S DEADLIEST ASSASSIN--
--TO CHANGE HIS CLOTHES.
TO GET DEATHSTROKE TO WEAR DR. IKON'S PROTOTYPE.
YOU'VE REALLY TICKED SOMEONE OFF THIS TIME, OLD FRIEND.
NOW... HOW SHALL THAT BENEFIT JA ZAKI--
--THE RED LION...?
NEXT: BAND OF BROTHERS

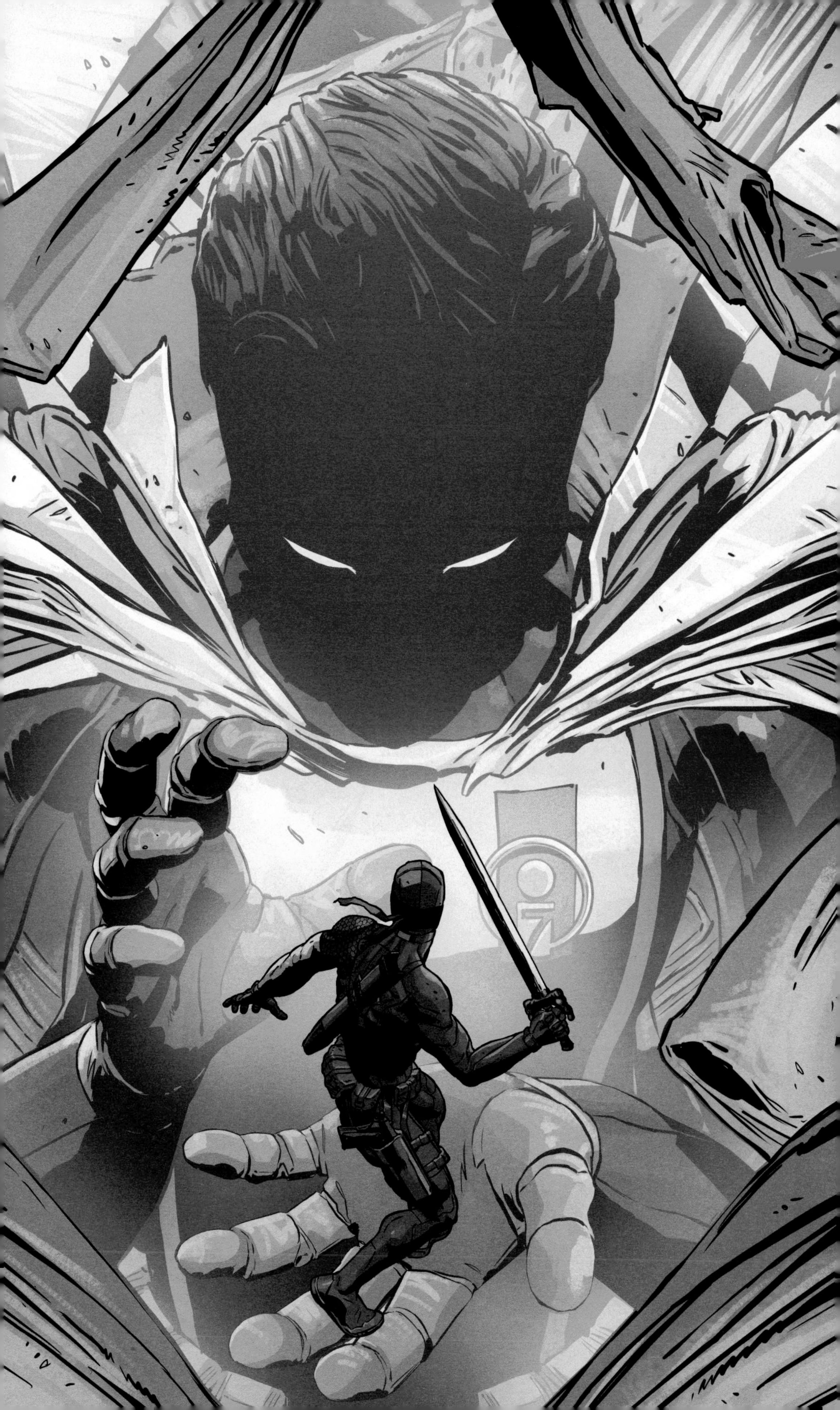

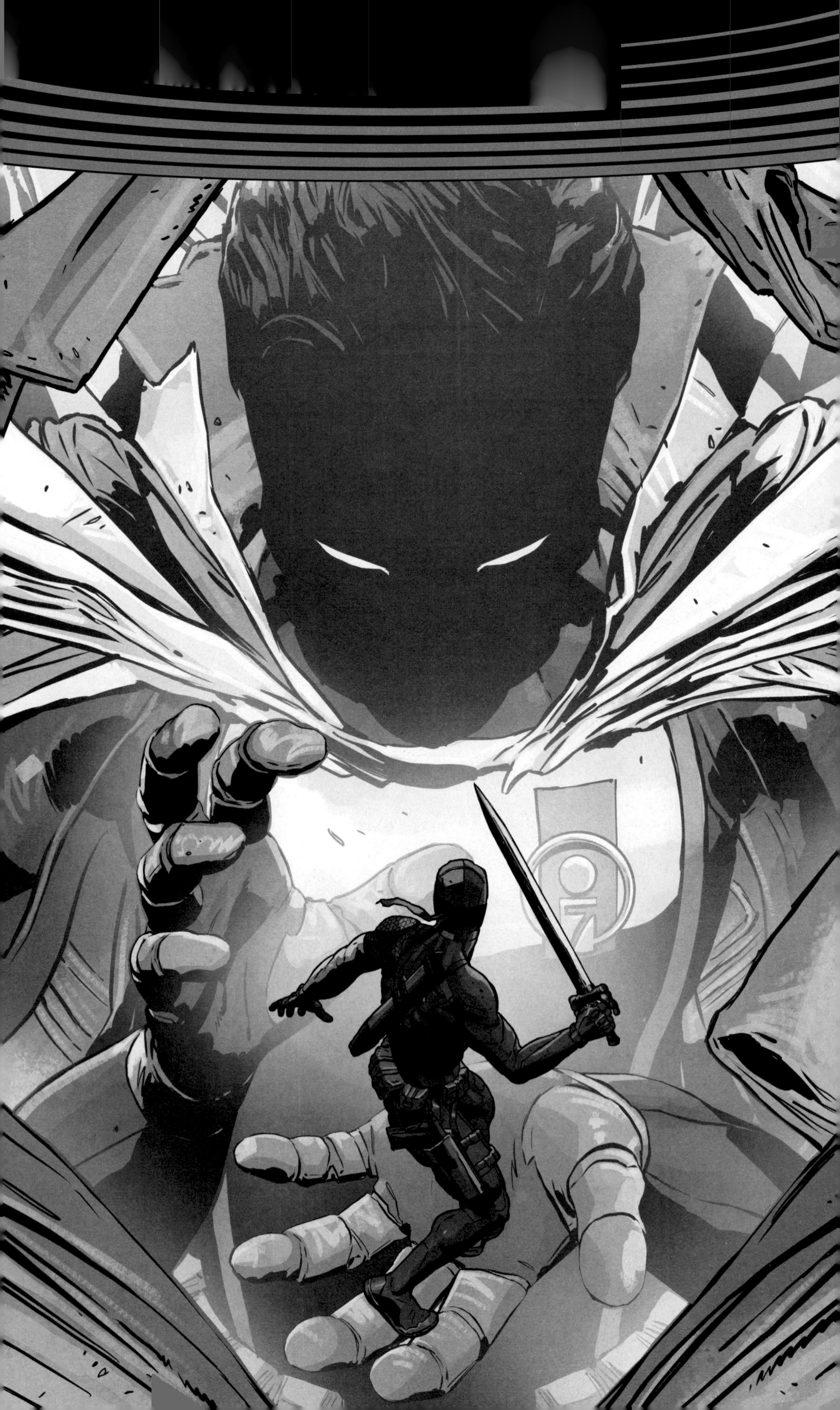

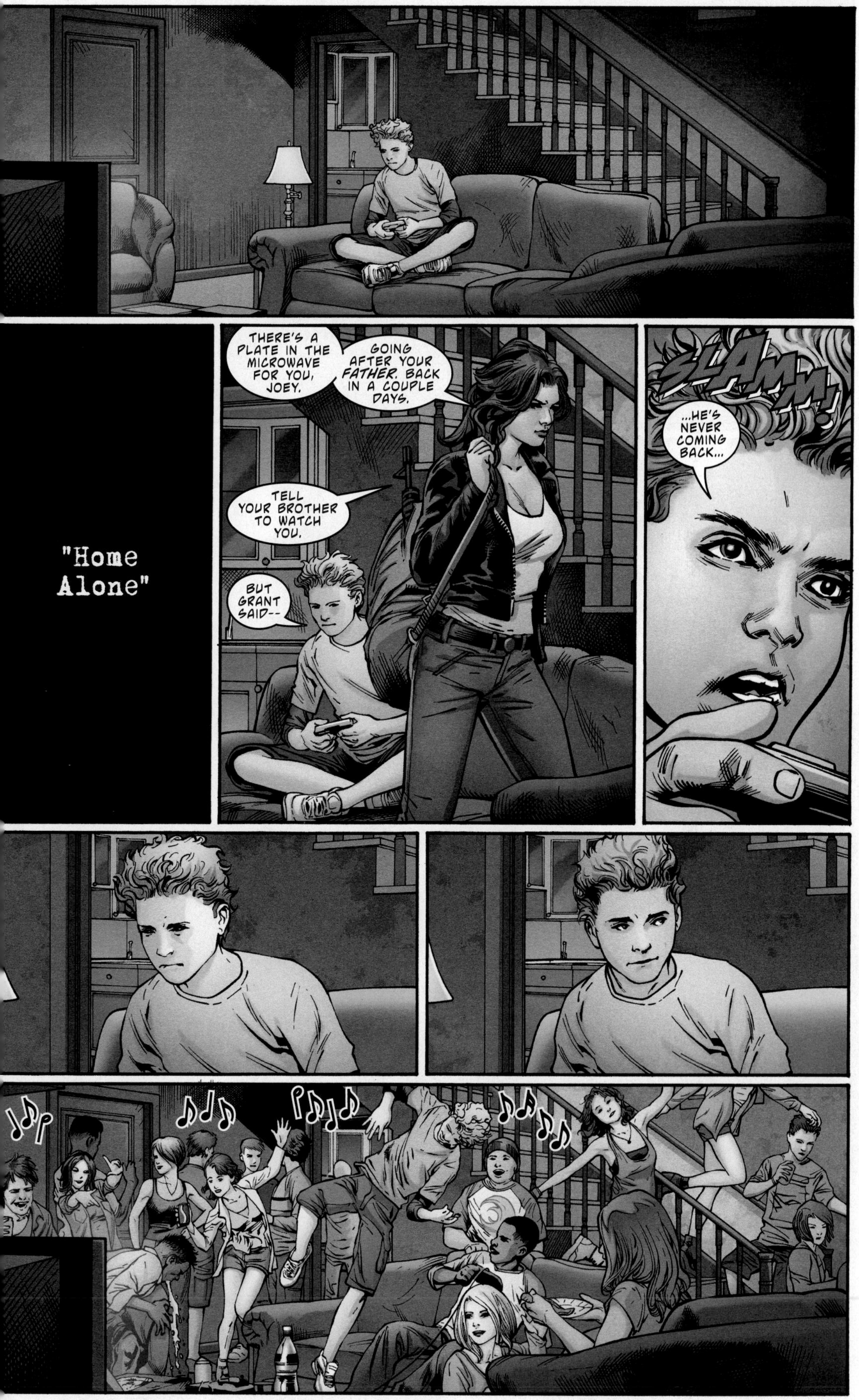
"Home Alone"
THERE'S A PLATE IN THE MICROWAVE FOR YOU, JOEY.
GOING AFTER YOUR FATHER. BACK IN A COUPLE DAYS.
TELL YOUR BROTHER TO WATCH YOU.
BUT GRANT SAID--
SLAMM!
...HE'S NEVER COMING BACK...

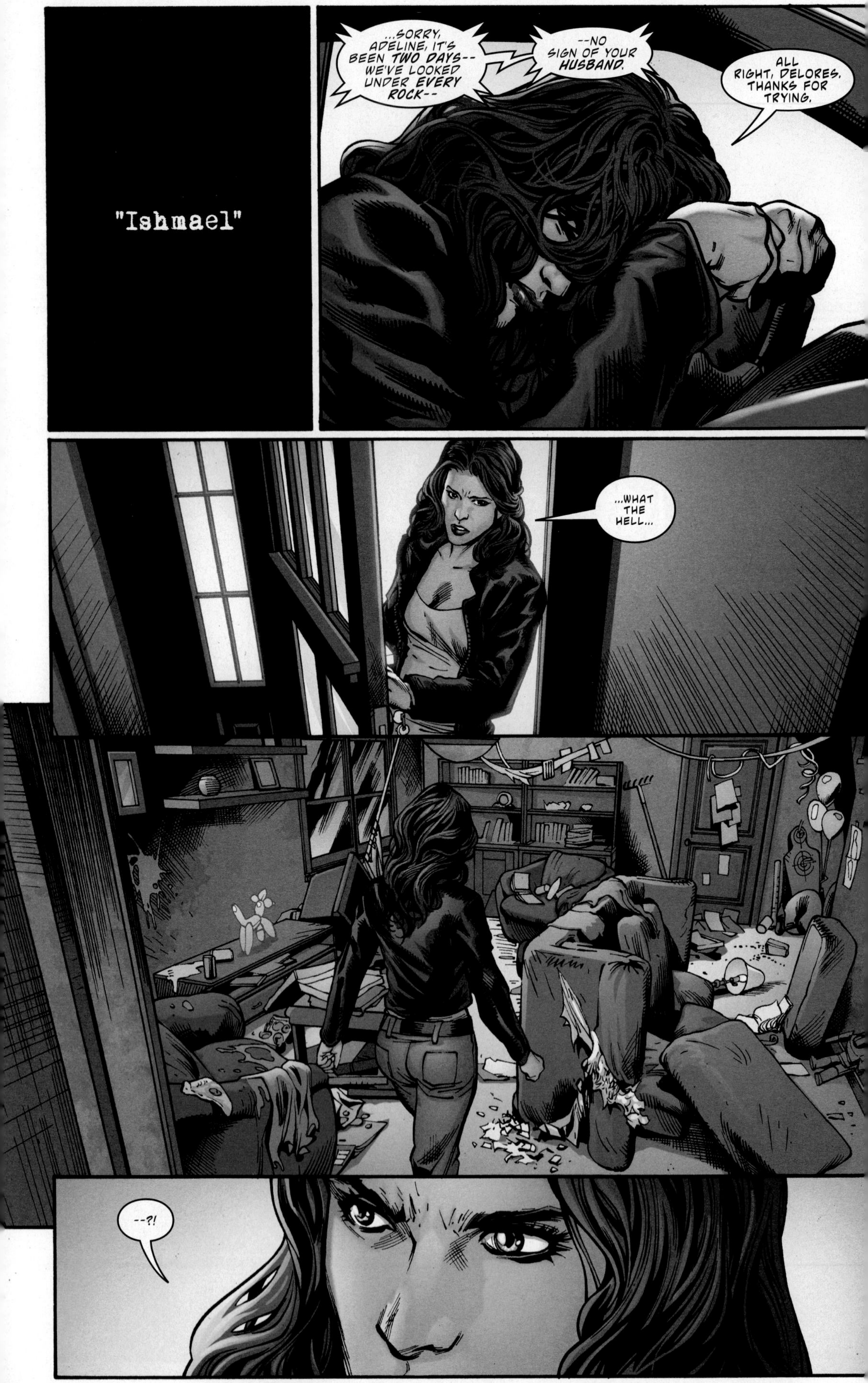
"Ishmael"
...SORRY, ADELINE, IT'S BEEN TWO DAYS-- WE'VE LOOKED UNDER EVERY ROCK--
--NO SIGN OF YOUR HUSBAND.
ALL RIGHT, DELORES. THANKS FOR TRYING.
...WHAT THE HELL...
--?!

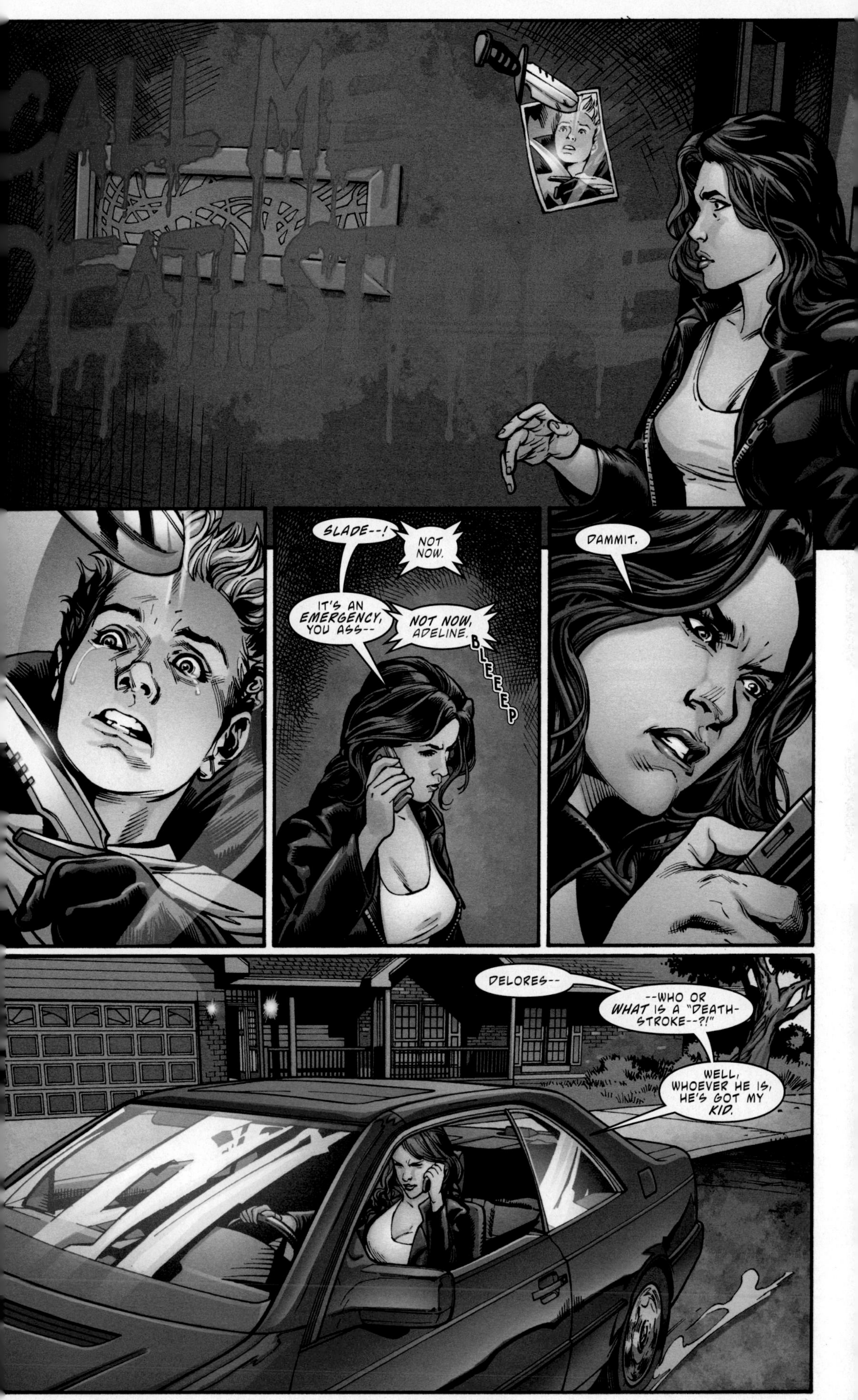
SLADE--!
NOT NOW.
IT'S AN EMERGENCY, YOU ASS--
NOT NOW, ADELINE.
BLEEEP
DAMMIT.
DELORES--
--WHO OR WHAT IS A "DEATH-STROKE--?!"
WELL, WHOEVER HE IS, HE'S GOT MY KID.

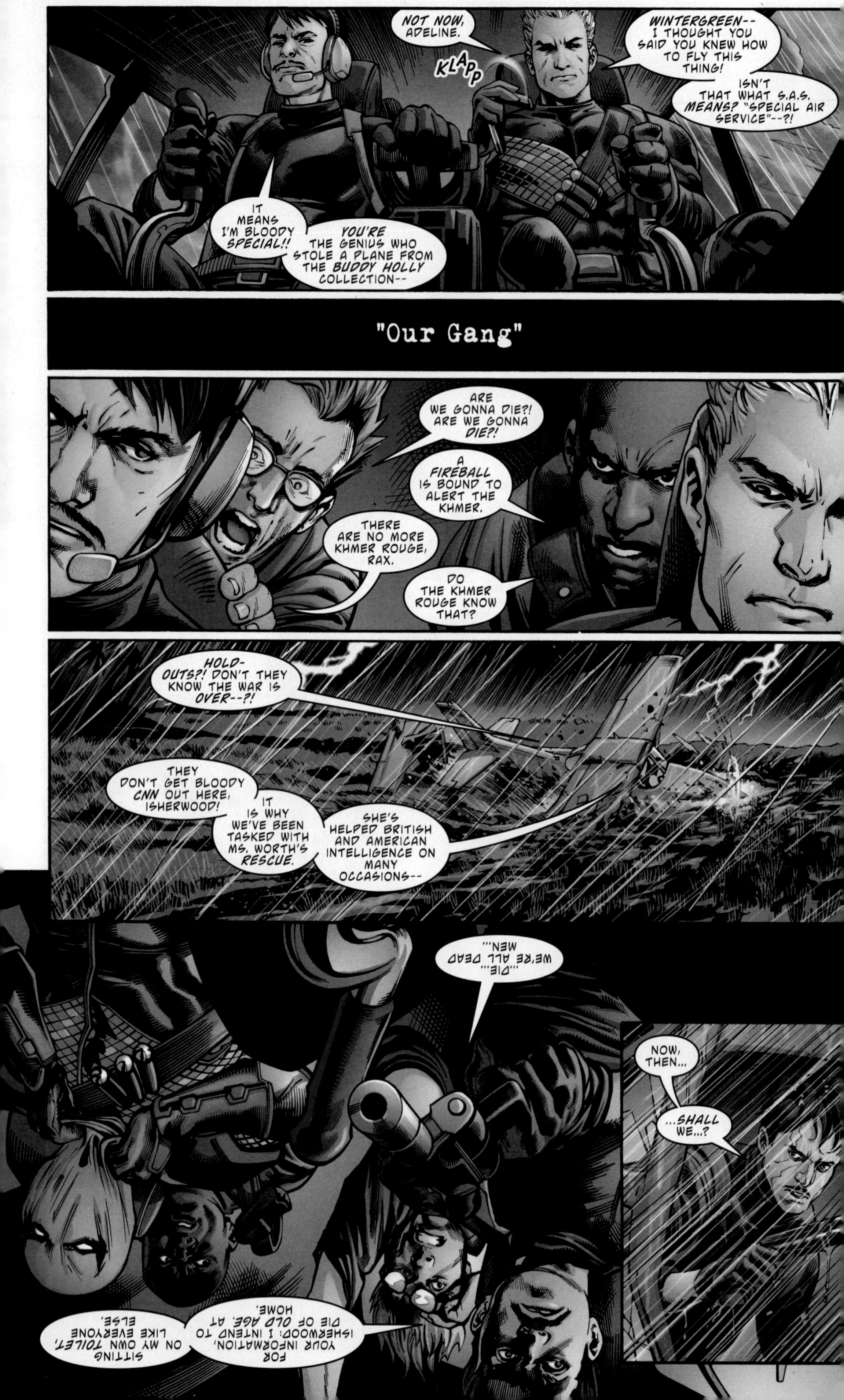

NOT NOW, ADELINE.
KLAPP
WINTERGREEN-- I THOUGHT YOU SAID YOU KNEW HOW TO FLY THIS THING!
ISN'T THAT WHAT S.A.S. MEANS? "SPECIAL AIR SERVICE"--?!
IT MEANS I'M BLOODY SPECIAL!!
YOU'RE THE GENIUS WHO STOLE A PLANE FROM THE BUDDY HOLLY COLLECTION--
"Our Gang"
ARE WE GONNA DIE?! ARE WE GONNA DIE?!
A FIREBALL IS BOUND TO ALERT THE KHMER.
THERE ARE NO MORE KHMER ROUGE, RAX.
DO THE KHMER ROUGE KNOW THAT?
HOLD-OUTS?! DON'T THEY KNOW THE WAR IS OVER--?!
THEY DON'T GET BLOODY CNN OUT HERE, ISHERWOOD!
IT IS WHY WE'VE BEEN TASKED WITH MS. WORTH'S RESCUE.
SHE'S HELPED BRITISH AND AMERICAN INTELLIGENCE ON MANY OCCASIONS--
...DIE... WE'RE ALL DEAD MEN.
FOR YOUR INFORMATION, ISHERWOOD: I INTEND TO DIE OF OLD AGE, AT HOME,
SITTING ON MY OWN TOILET, LIKE EVERYONE ELSE.
NOW, THEN...
...SHALL WE...?

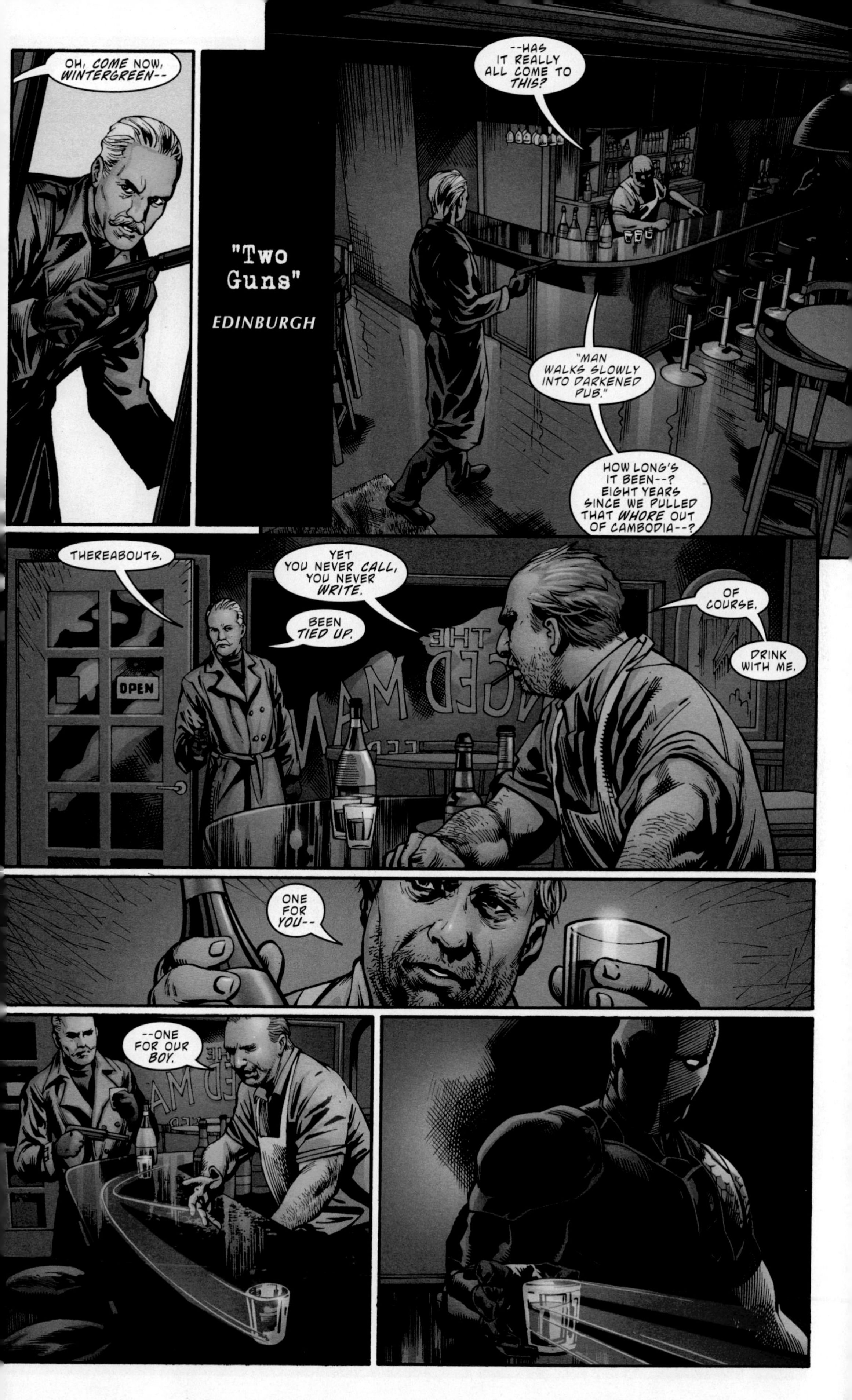

OH, COME NOW, WINTERGREEN--
"Two Guns"
EDINBURGH
--HAS IT REALLY ALL COME TO THIS?
"MAN WALKS SLOWLY INTO DARKENED PUB."
HOW LONG'S IT BEEN--? EIGHT YEARS SINCE WE PULLED THAT WHORE OUT OF CAMBODIA--?
THEREABOUTS.
YET YOU NEVER CALL, YOU NEVER WRITE.
BEEN TIED UP.
OF COURSE.
DRINK WITH ME.
OPEN
ONE FOR YOU--
--ONE FOR OUR BOY.

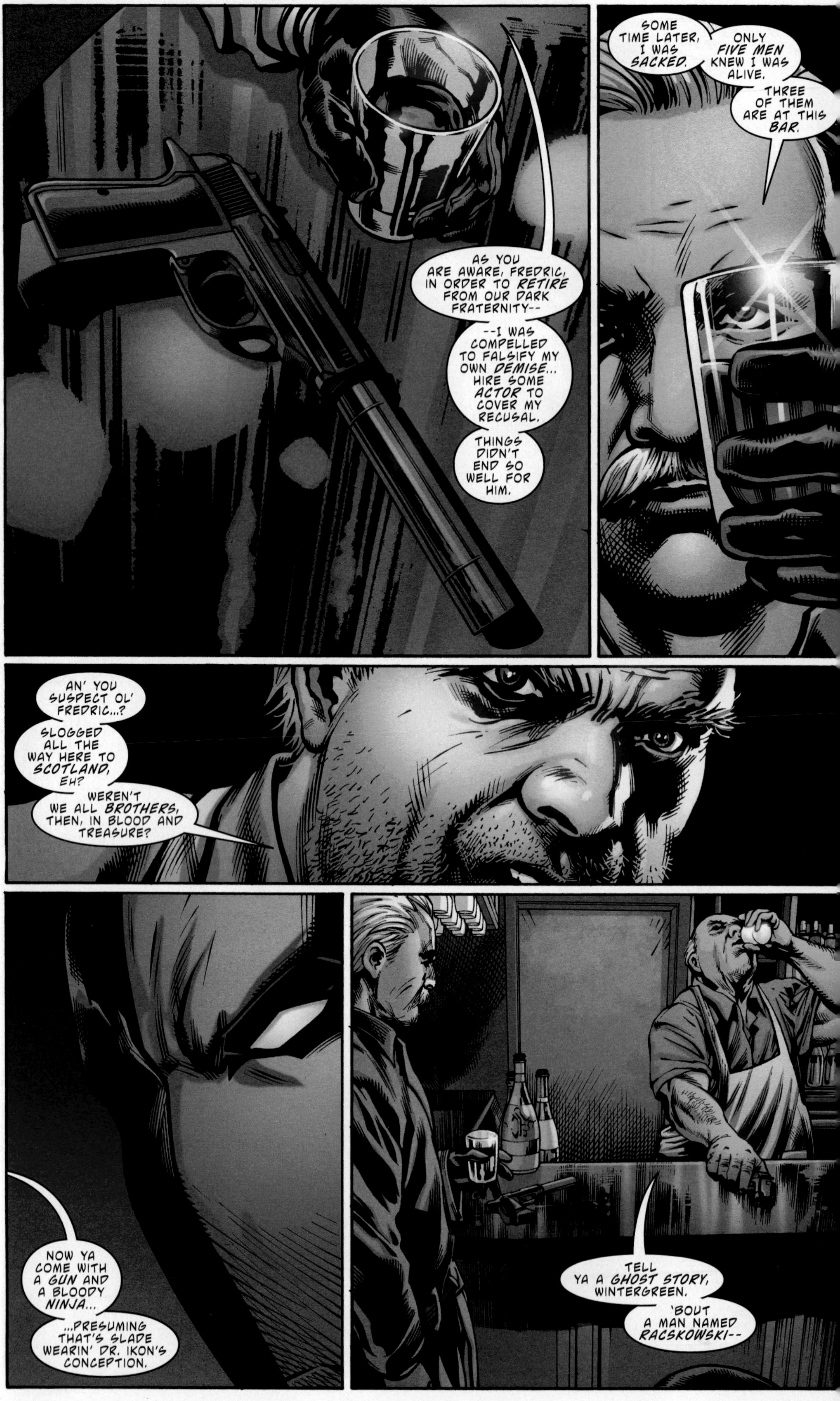
AS YOU ARE AWARE, FREDRIC, IN ORDER TO RETIRE FROM OUR DARK FRATERNITY--
--I WAS COMPELLED TO FALSIFY MY OWN DEMISE... HIRE SOME ACTOR TO COVER MY RECUSAL.
THINGS DIDN'T END SO WELL FOR HIM.
SOME TIME LATER, I WAS SACKED.
ONLY FIVE MEN KNEW I WAS ALIVE.
THREE OF THEM ARE AT THIS BAR.
AN' YOU SUSPECT OL' FREDRIC...?
SLOGGED ALL THE WAY HERE TO SCOTLAND, EH?
WEREN'T WE ALL BROTHERS, THEN, IN BLOOD AND TREASURE?
NOW YA COME WITH A GUN AND A BLOODY NINJA...
...PRESUMING THAT'S SLADE WEARIN' DR. IKON'S CONCEPTION.
TELL YA A GHOST STORY, WINTERGREEN.
'BOUT A MAN NAMED RACSKOWSKI--

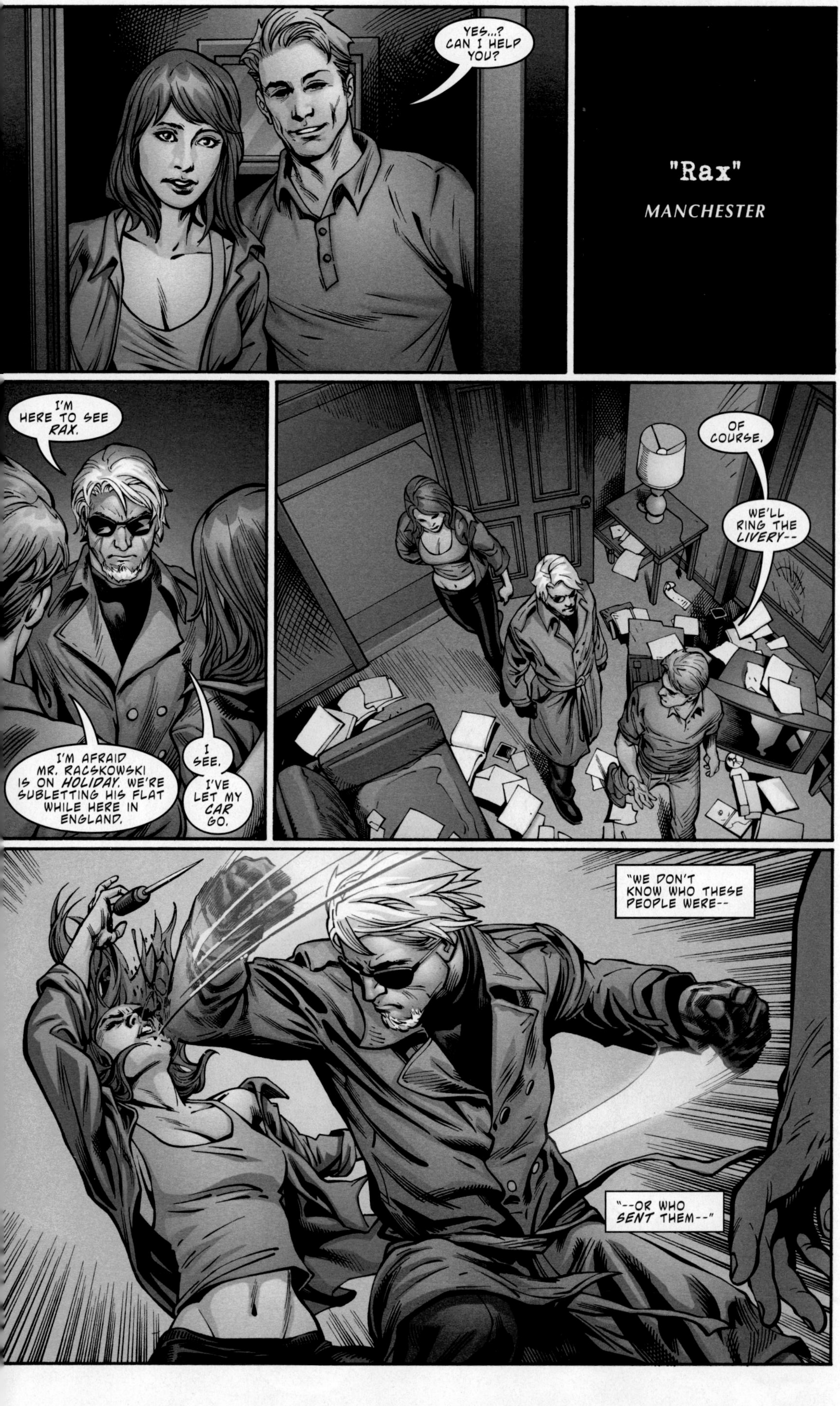
YES...? CAN I HELP YOU?
"Rax"
MANCHESTER
I'M HERE TO SEE RAX.
I'M AFRAID MR. RACSKOWSKI IS ON HOLIDAY. WE'RE SUBLETTING HIS FLAT WHILE HERE IN ENGLAND.
I SEE.
I'VE LET MY CAR GO.
OF COURSE.
WE'LL RING THE LIVERY--
"WE DON'T KNOW WHO THESE PEOPLE WERE--
"--OR WHO SENT THEM--"

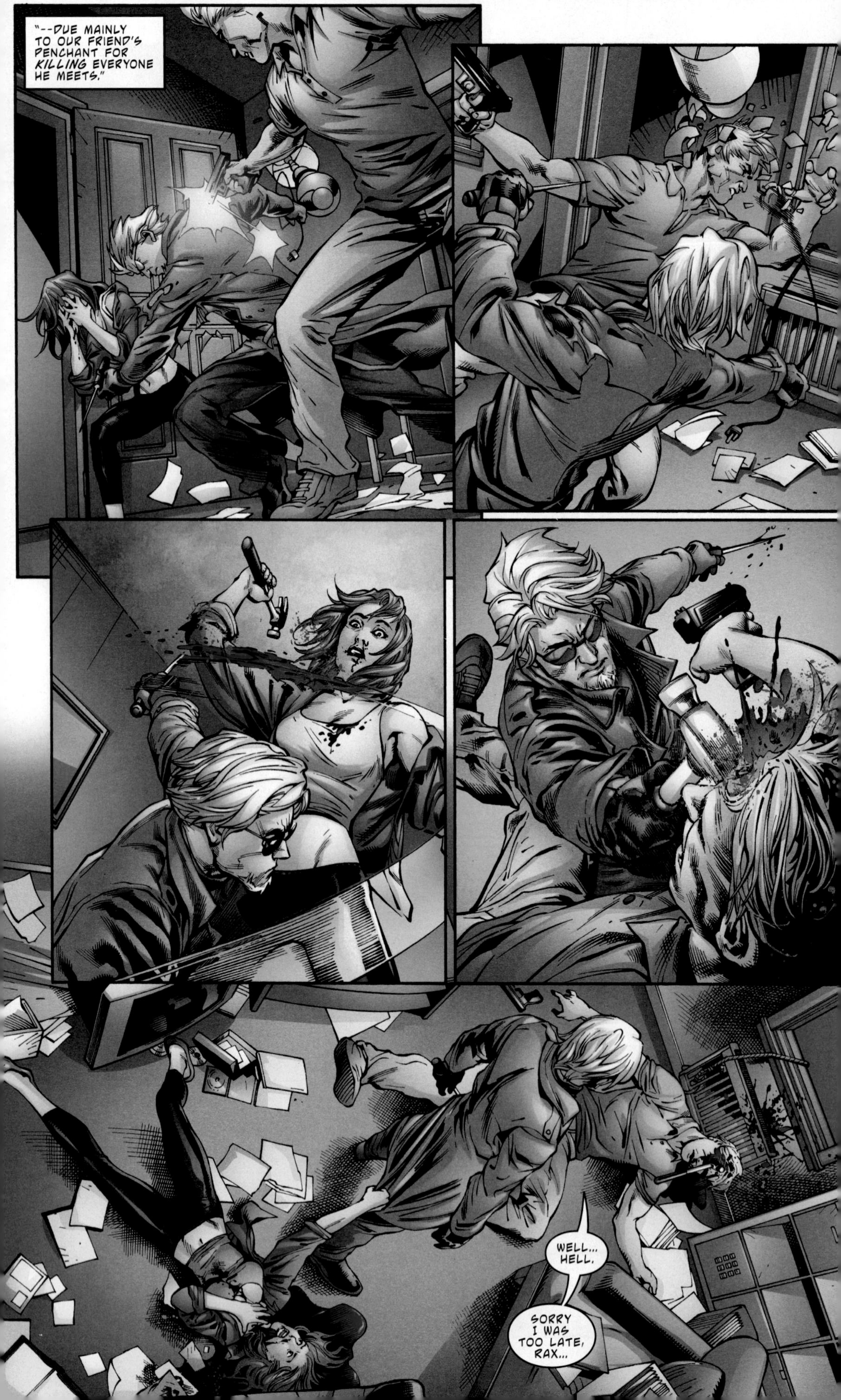
"--DUE MAINLY TO OUR FRIEND'S PENCHANT FOR *KILLING* EVERYONE HE MEETS."
WELL... HELL.
SORRY I WAS TOO LATE, RAX...

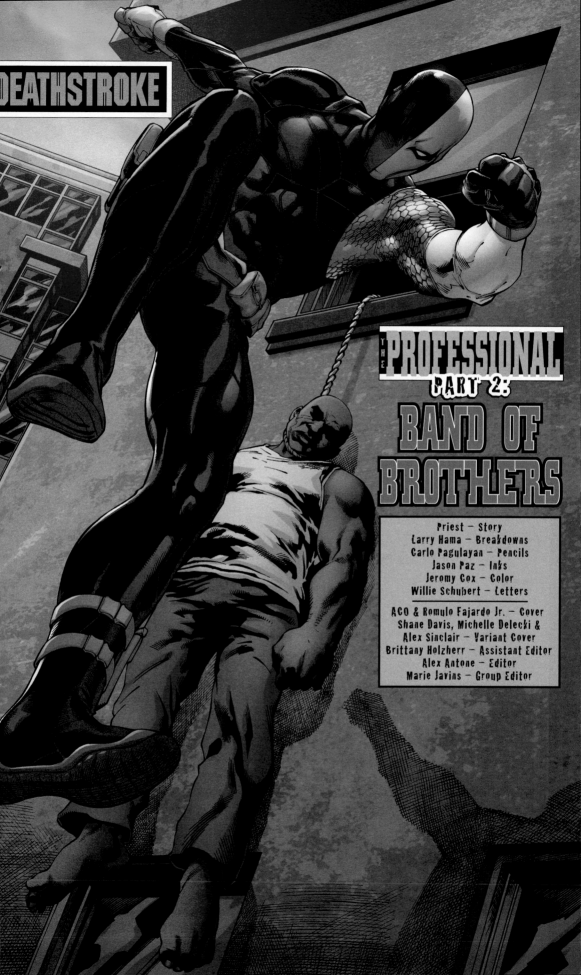

DEATHSTROKE

THE PROFESSIONAL PART 2:
BAND OF BROTHERS

Priest — Story
Larry Hama — Breakdowns
Carlo Pagulayan — Pencils
Jason Paz — Inks
Jeromy Cox — Color
Willie Schubert — Letters

ACO & Romulo Fajardo Jr. — Cover
Shane Davis, Michelle Delecki &
Alex Sinclair — Variant Cover
Brittany Holzherr — Assistant Editor
Alex Antone — Editor
Marie Javins — Group Editor

AND THEN THERE WERE FOUR.

WE THREE AND THE CANUCK.

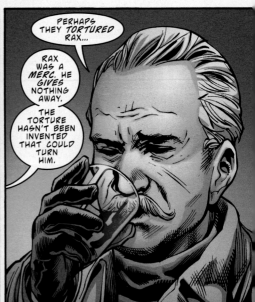

PERHAPS THEY *TORTURED* RAX...

RAX WAS A *MERC.* HE GIVES NOTHING AWAY.

THE TORTURE HASN'T BEEN INVENTED THAT COULD TURN HIM.

ISHERWOOD, ON THE OTHER HAND, IS A SPINELESS COWARD.

A GADGET FREAK...

AND YOU...?

ME? A *DEFINITE* SUSPECT.

THE *RECON* MAN...OUR FINAL MISSION, EIGHT YEARS GONE...

"Rose"
CAMBODIA

LILLIAN *WORTH.*

STRANGE NAME FOR *HMONG,* IDDIN' IT?

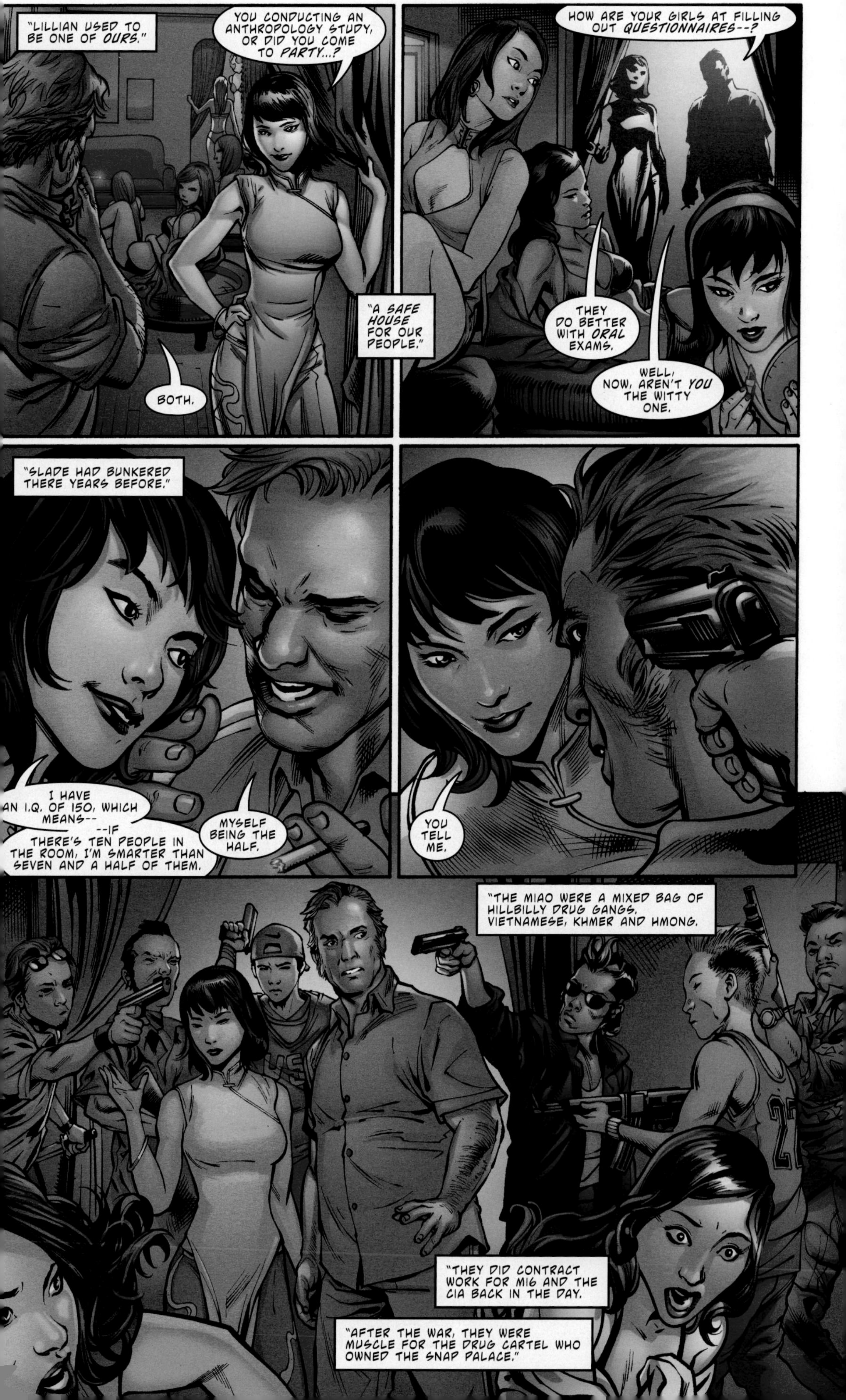
"LILLIAN USED TO BE ONE OF OURS."
YOU CONDUCTING AN ANTHROPOLOGY STUDY, OR DID YOU COME TO PARTY...?
BOTH.
"A SAFE HOUSE FOR OUR PEOPLE."
HOW ARE YOUR GIRLS AT FILLING OUT QUESTIONNAIRES--?
THEY DO BETTER WITH ORAL EXAMS.
WELL, NOW, AREN'T YOU THE WITTY ONE.
"SLADE HAD BUNKERED THERE YEARS BEFORE."
I HAVE AN I.Q. OF 150, WHICH MEANS--
--IF THERE'S TEN PEOPLE IN THE ROOM, I'M SMARTER THAN SEVEN AND A HALF OF THEM.
MYSELF BEING THE HALF.
YOU TELL ME.
"THE MIAO WERE A MIXED BAG OF HILLBILLY DRUG GANGS, VIETNAMESE, KHMER AND HMONG.
"THEY DID CONTRACT WORK FOR MI6 AND THE CIA BACK IN THE DAY.
"AFTER THE WAR, THEY WERE MUSCLE FOR THE DRUG CARTEL WHO OWNED THE SNAP PALACE."

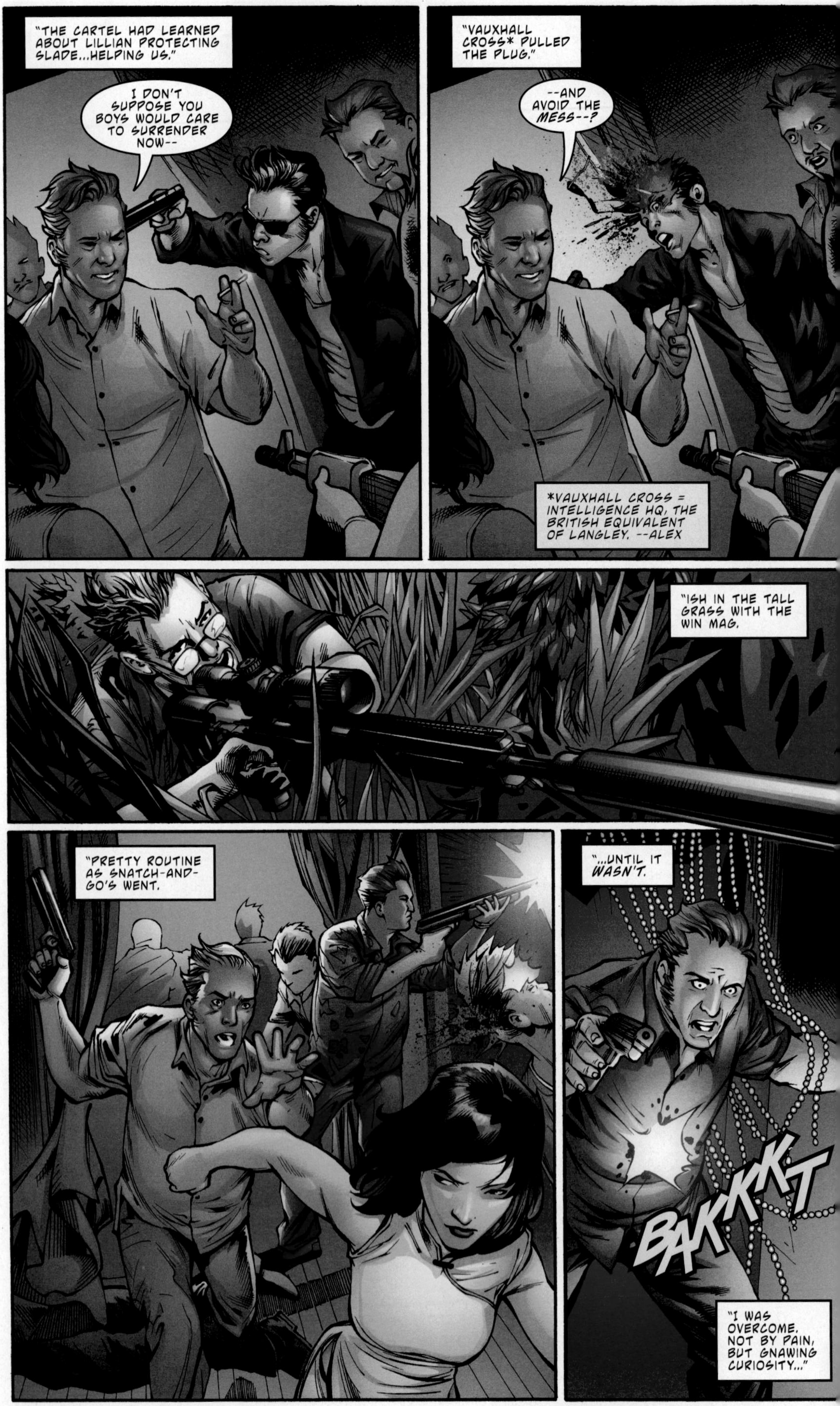
"THE CARTEL HAD LEARNED ABOUT LILLIAN PROTECTING SLADE...HELPING US."
I DON'T SUPPOSE YOU BOYS WOULD CARE TO SURRENDER NOW--
"VAUXHALL CROSS* PULLED THE PLUG."
--AND AVOID THE MESS--?
*VAUXHALL CROSS = INTELLIGENCE HQ, THE BRITISH EQUIVALENT OF LANGLEY. --ALEX
"ISH IN THE TALL GRASS WITH THE WIN MAG.
"PRETTY ROUTINE AS SNATCH-AND-GO'S WENT.
"...UNTIL IT WASN'T.
BAKKKKT
"I WAS OVERCOME. NOT BY PAIN, BUT GNAWING CURIOSITY..."

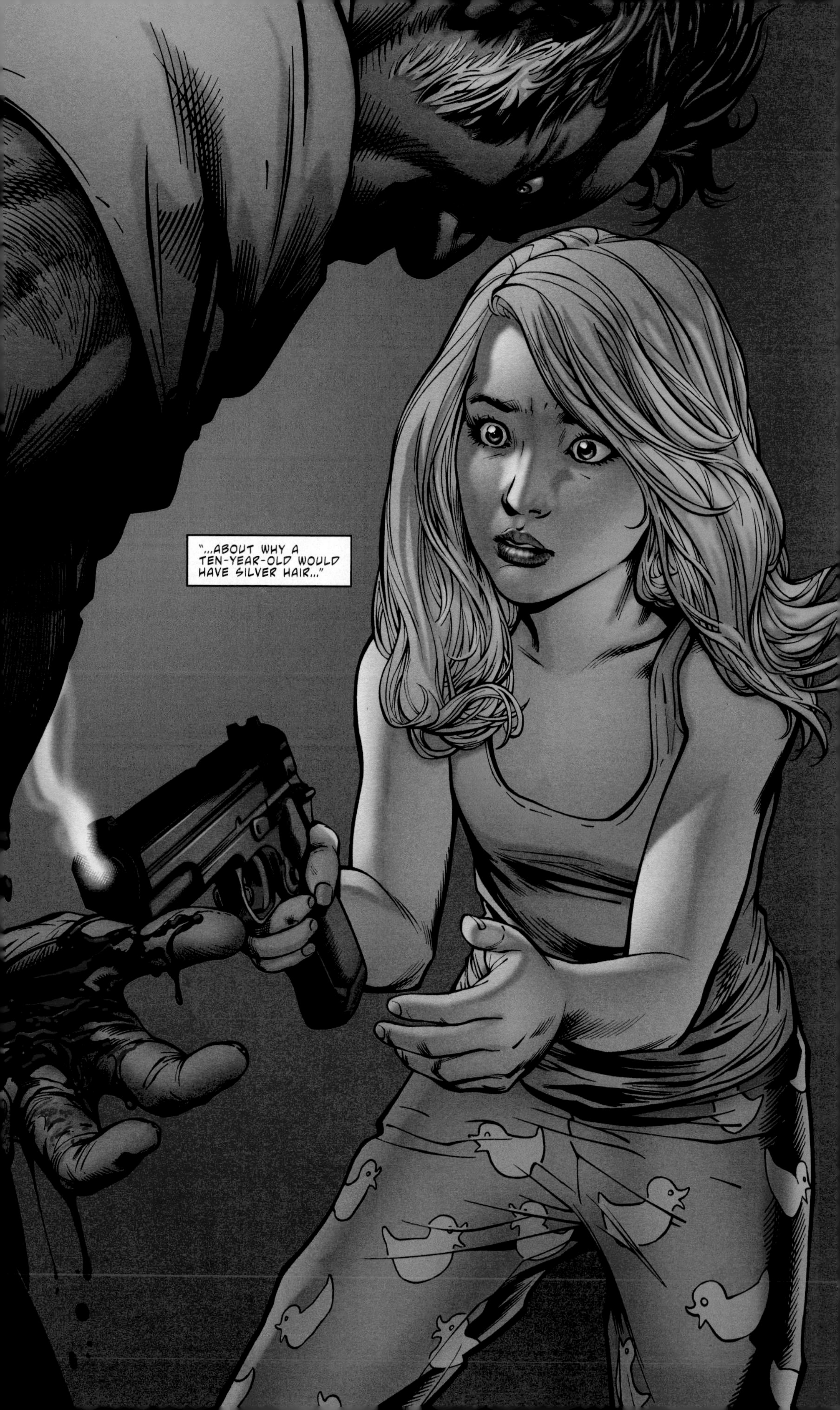
"...ABOUT WHY A TEN-YEAR-OLD WOULD HAVE SILVER HAIR..."

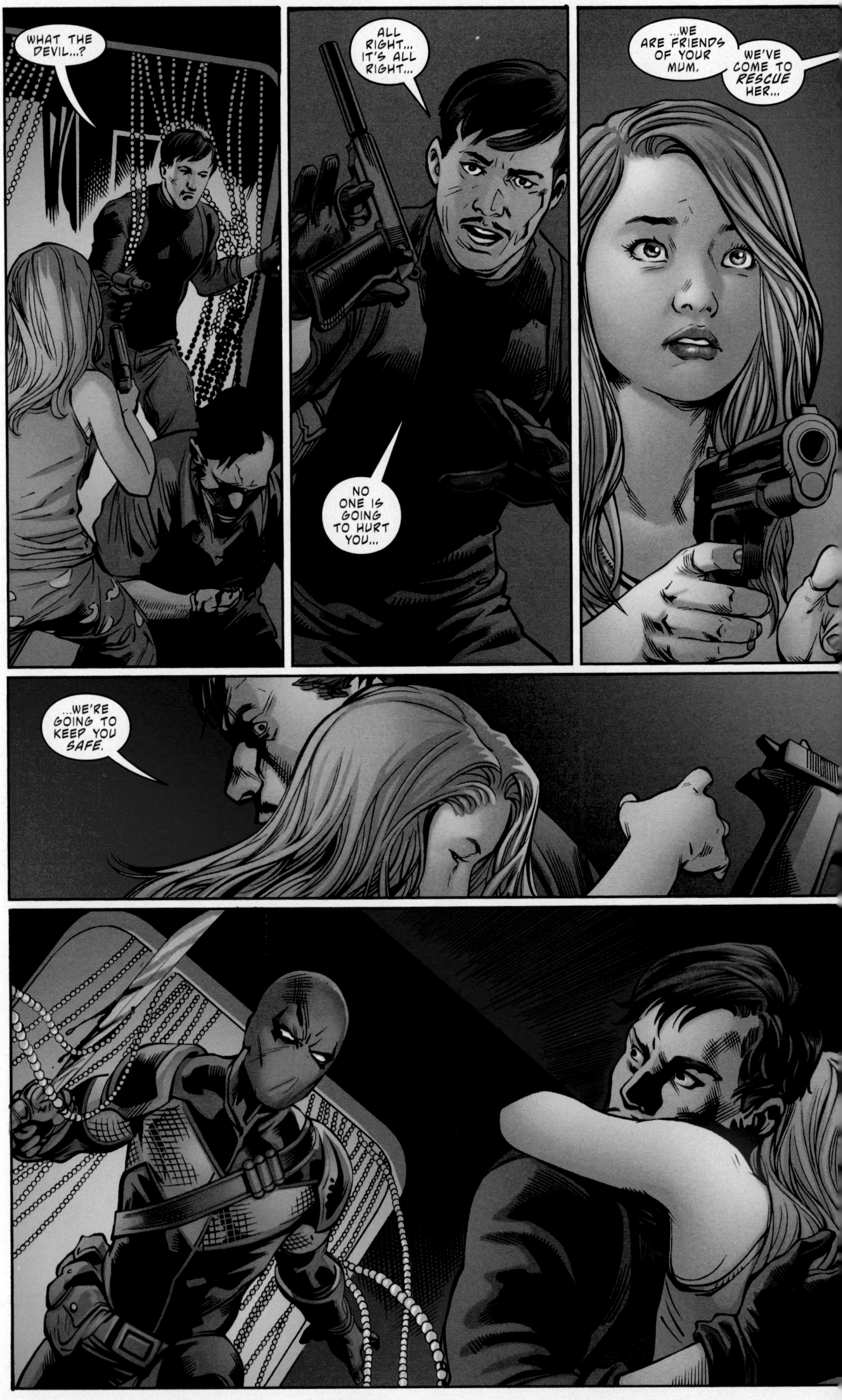
WHAT THE DEVIL...?
ALL RIGHT... IT'S ALL RIGHT...
NO ONE IS GOING TO HURT YOU...
...WE ARE FRIENDS OF YOUR MUM.
WE'VE COME TO RESCUE HER...
...WE'RE GOING TO KEEP YOU SAFE.

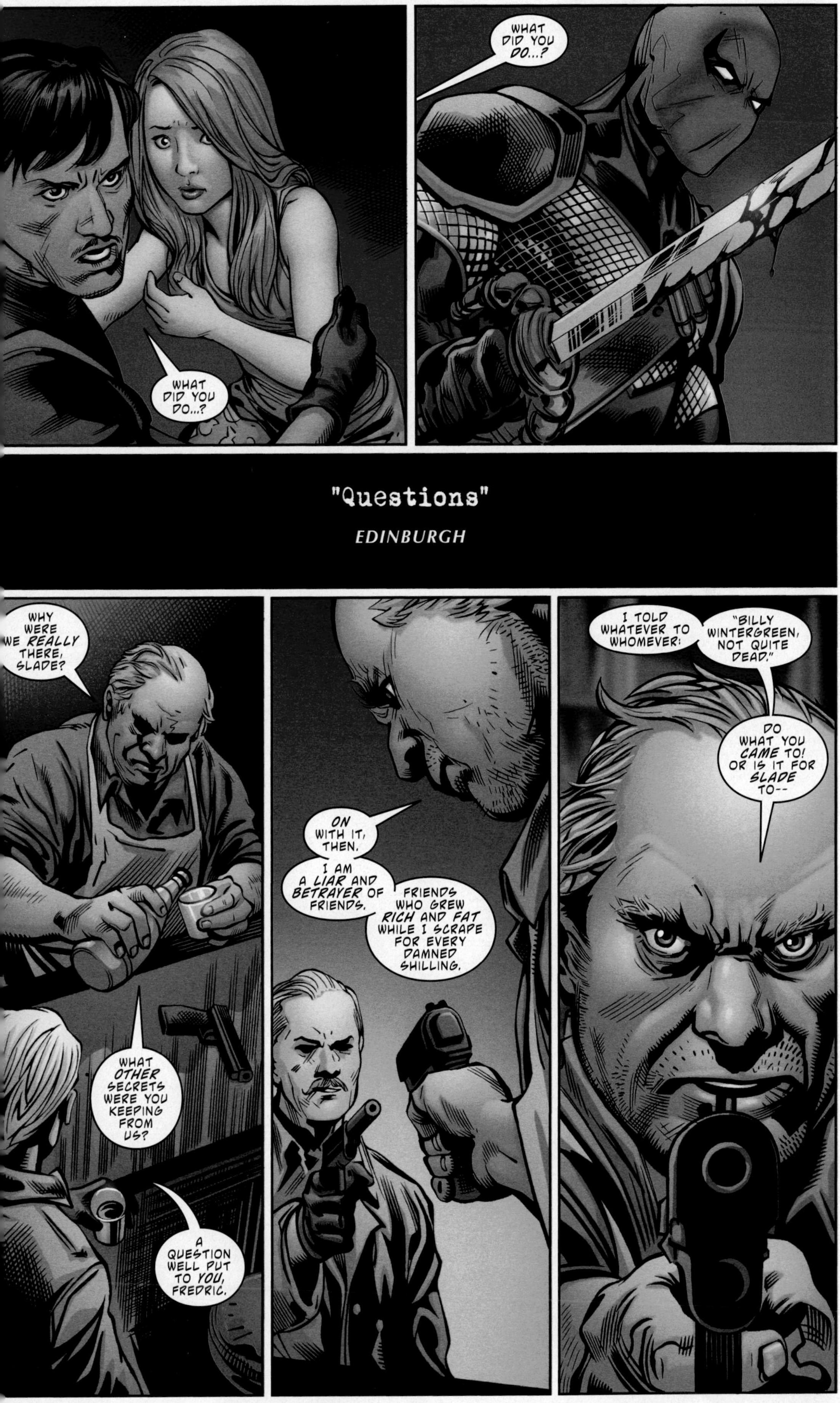
WHAT DID YOU DO...?
WHAT DID YOU DO...?
"Questions"
EDINBURGH
WHY WERE WE REALLY THERE, SLADE?
WHAT OTHER SECRETS WERE YOU KEEPING FROM US?
A QUESTION WELL PUT TO YOU, FREDRIC.
ON WITH IT, THEN.
I AM A LIAR AND BETRAYER OF FRIENDS.
FRIENDS WHO GREW RICH AND FAT WHILE I SCRAPE FOR EVERY DAMNED SHILLING.
I TOLD WHATEVER TO WHOMEVER:
"BILLY WINTERGREEN, NOT QUITE DEAD."
DO WHAT YOU CAME TO! OR IS IT FOR SLADE TO--

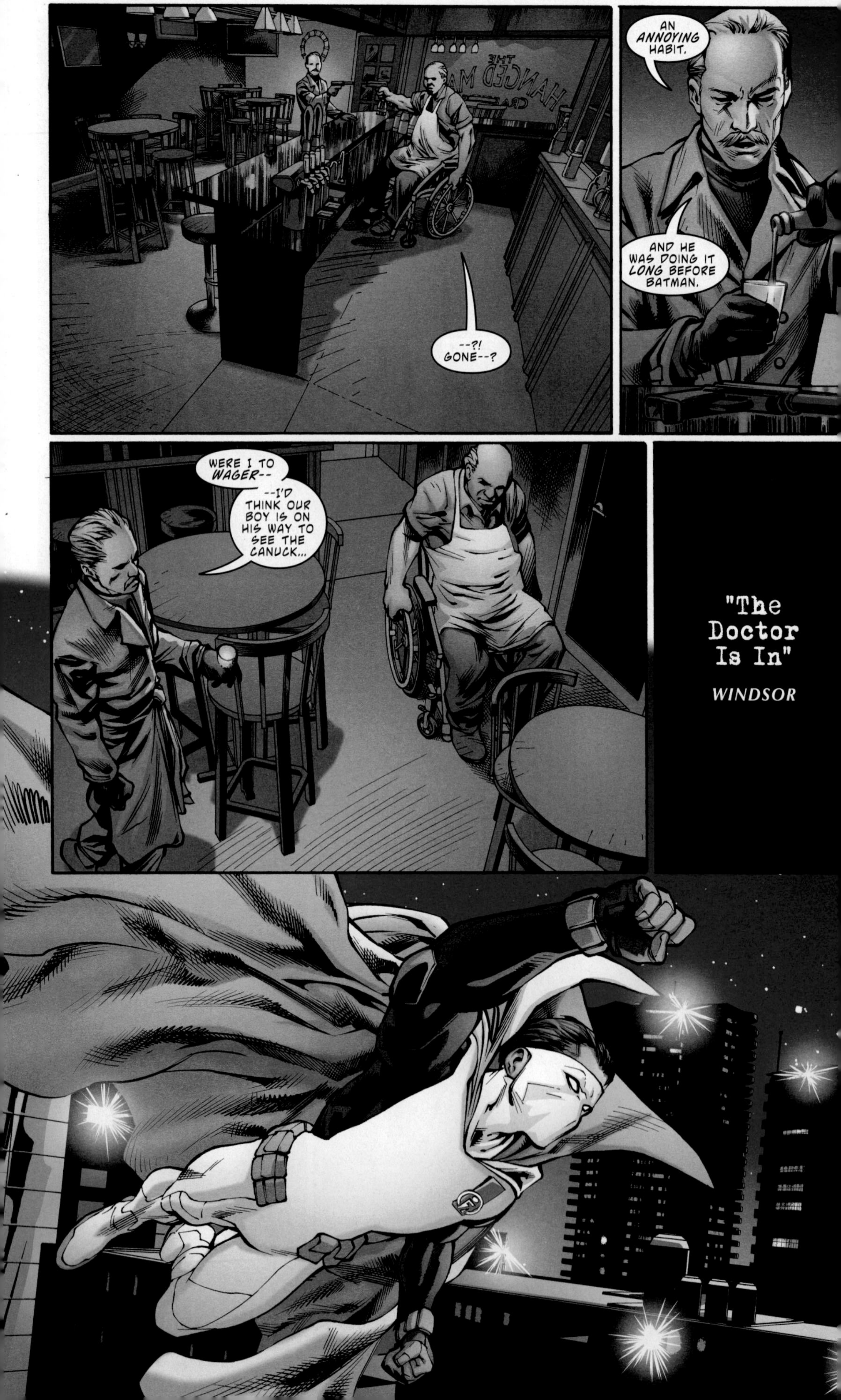
THE HANGED MAN
--?! GONE--?
AN ANNOYING HABIT.
AND HE WAS DOING IT LONG BEFORE BATMAN.
WERE I TO WAGER--
--I'D THINK OUR BOY IS ON HIS WAY TO SEE THE CANUCK...
"The Doctor Is In"
WINDSOR

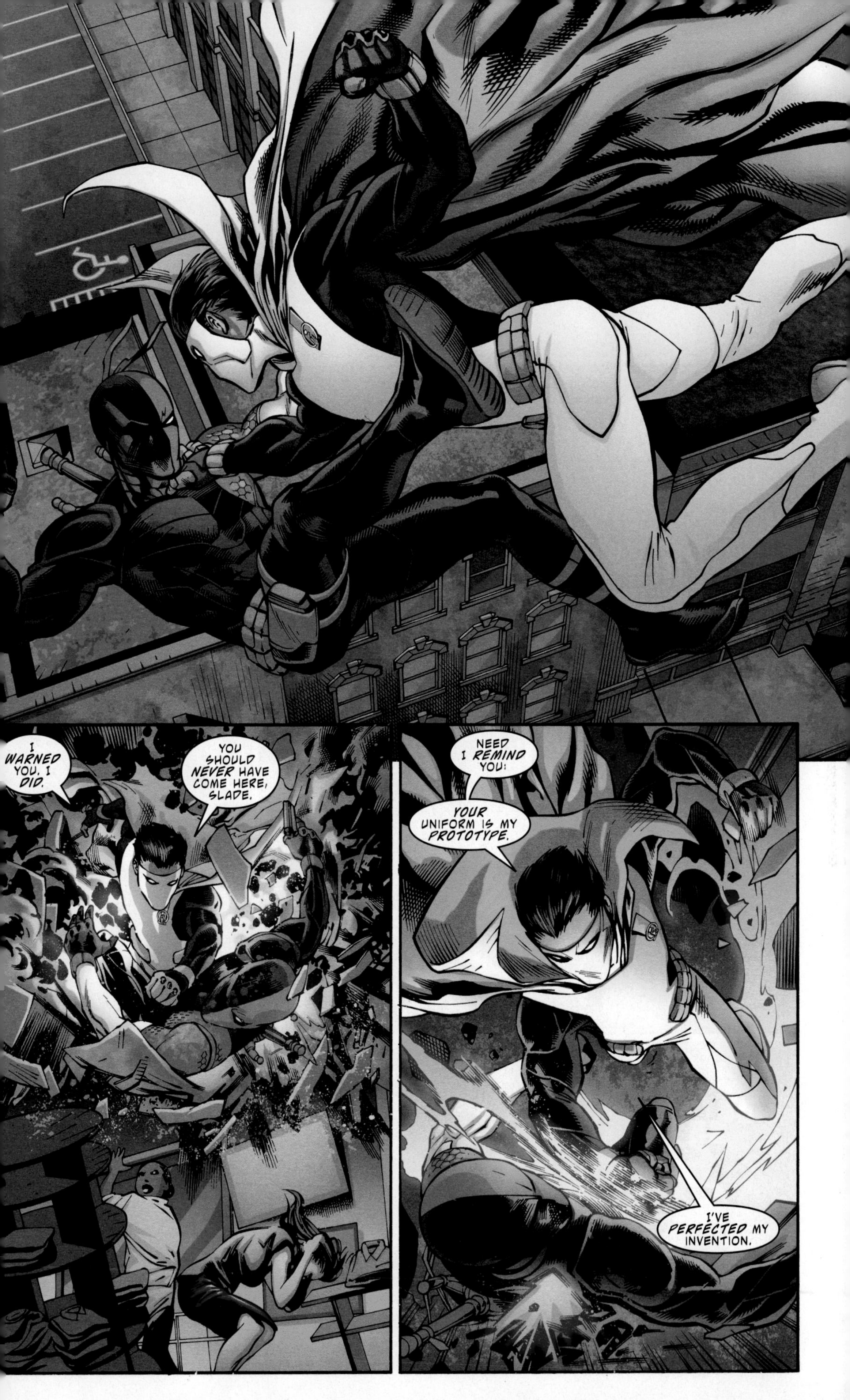
I WARNED YOU. I DID.
YOU SHOULD NEVER HAVE COME HERE, SLADE.
NEED I REMIND YOU:
YOUR UNIFORM IS MY PROTOTYPE.
I'VE PERFECTED MY INVENTION.

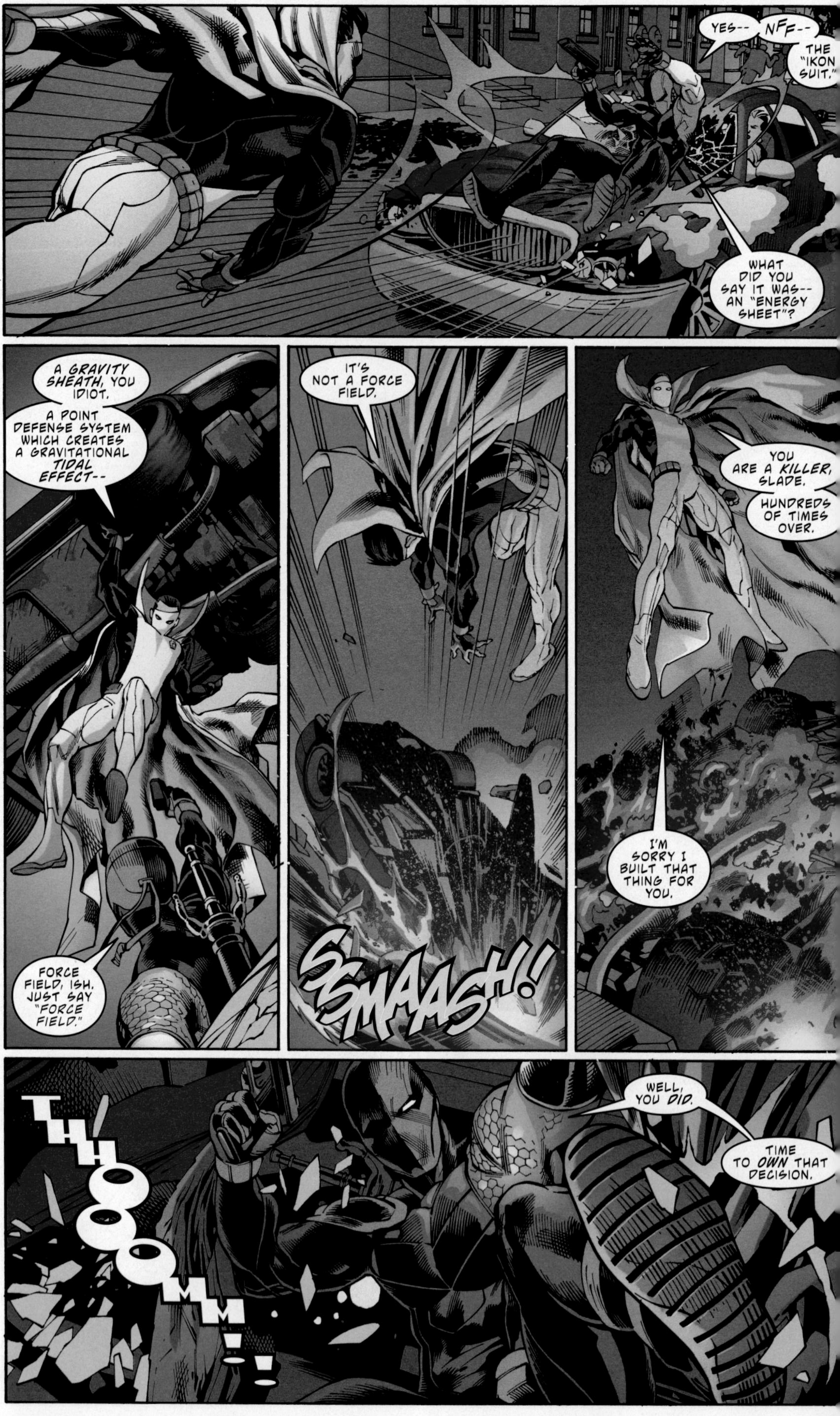

YES-- NFF--
THE "IKON SUIT."
WHAT DID YOU SAY IT WAS-- AN "ENERGY SHEET"?
A GRAVITY SHEATH, YOU IDIOT.
A POINT DEFENSE SYSTEM WHICH CREATES A GRAVITATIONAL TIDAL EFFECT--
FORCE FIELD, ISH. JUST SAY "FORCE FIELD."
IT'S NOT A FORCE FIELD.
SSMAASH!!
YOU ARE A KILLER, SLADE.
HUNDREDS OF TIMES OVER.
I'M SORRY I BUILT THAT THING FOR YOU.
THHOOOMMM!!
WELL, YOU DID.
TIME TO OWN THAT DECISION.

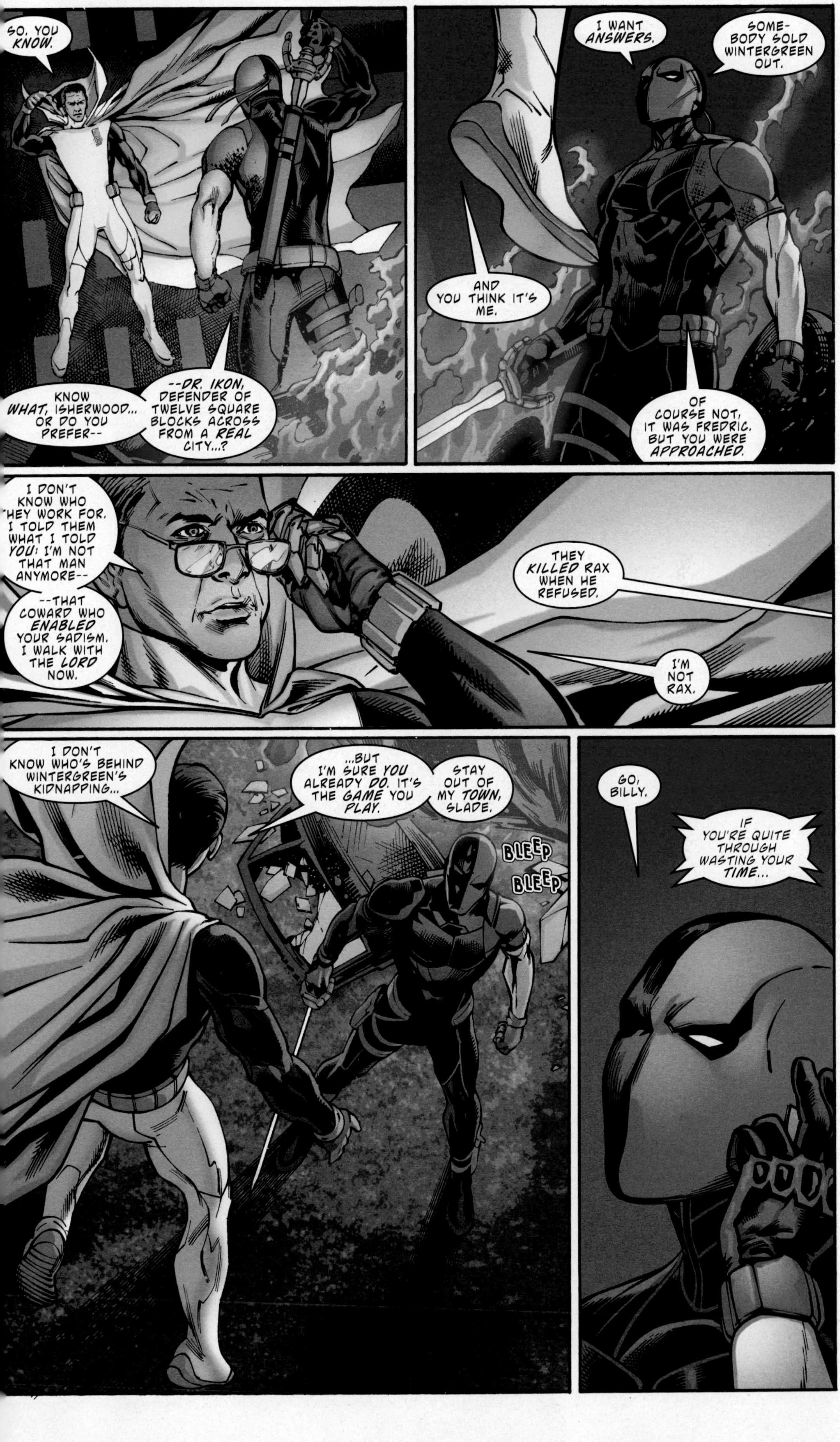
SO, YOU KNOW.
KNOW WHAT, ISHERWOOD... OR DO YOU PREFER--
--DR. IKON, DEFENDER OF TWELVE SQUARE BLOCKS ACROSS FROM A REAL CITY...?
I WANT ANSWERS.
SOME-BODY SOLD WINTERGREEN OUT.
AND YOU THINK IT'S ME.
OF COURSE NOT, IT WAS FREDRIC. BUT YOU WERE APPROACHED.
I DON'T KNOW WHO THEY WORK FOR. I TOLD THEM WHAT I TOLD YOU: I'M NOT THAT MAN ANYMORE--
--THAT COWARD WHO ENABLED YOUR SADISM. I WALK WITH THE LORD NOW.
THEY KILLED RAX WHEN HE REFUSED.
I'M NOT RAX.
I DON'T KNOW WHO'S BEHIND WINTERGREEN'S KIDNAPPING...
...BUT I'M SURE YOU ALREADY DO. IT'S THE GAME YOU PLAY.
STAY OUT OF MY TOWN, SLADE.
BLEEP
BLEEP
GO, BILLY.
IF YOU'RE QUITE THROUGH WASTING YOUR TIME...

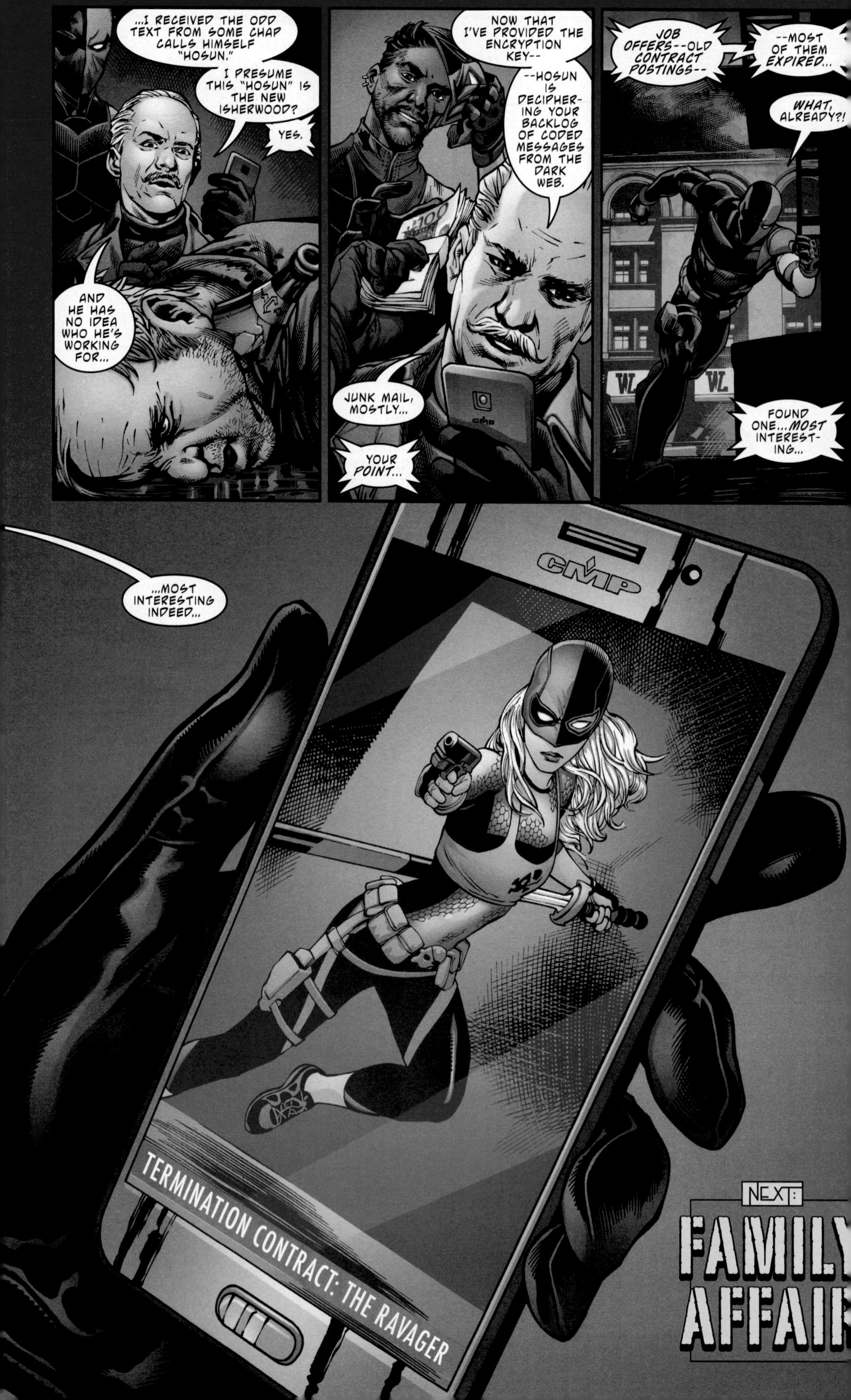

...I RECEIVED THE ODD TEXT FROM SOME CHAP CALLS HIMSELF "HOSUN."
I PRESUME THIS "HOSUN" IS THE NEW ISHERWOOD?
YES.
AND HE HAS NO IDEA WHO HE'S WORKING FOR...
NOW THAT I'VE PROVIDED THE ENCRYPTION KEY--
--HOSUN IS DECIPHERING YOUR BACKLOG OF CODED MESSAGES FROM THE DARK WEB.
JUNK MAIL, MOSTLY...
YOUR POINT...
JOB OFFERS--OLD CONTRACT POSTINGS--
--MOST OF THEM EXPIRED...
WHAT, ALREADY?!
FOUND ONE...MOST INTERESTING...
...MOST INTERESTING INDEED...
CMP
TERMINATION CONTRACT: THE RAVAGER
NEXT:
FAMILY AFFAIR

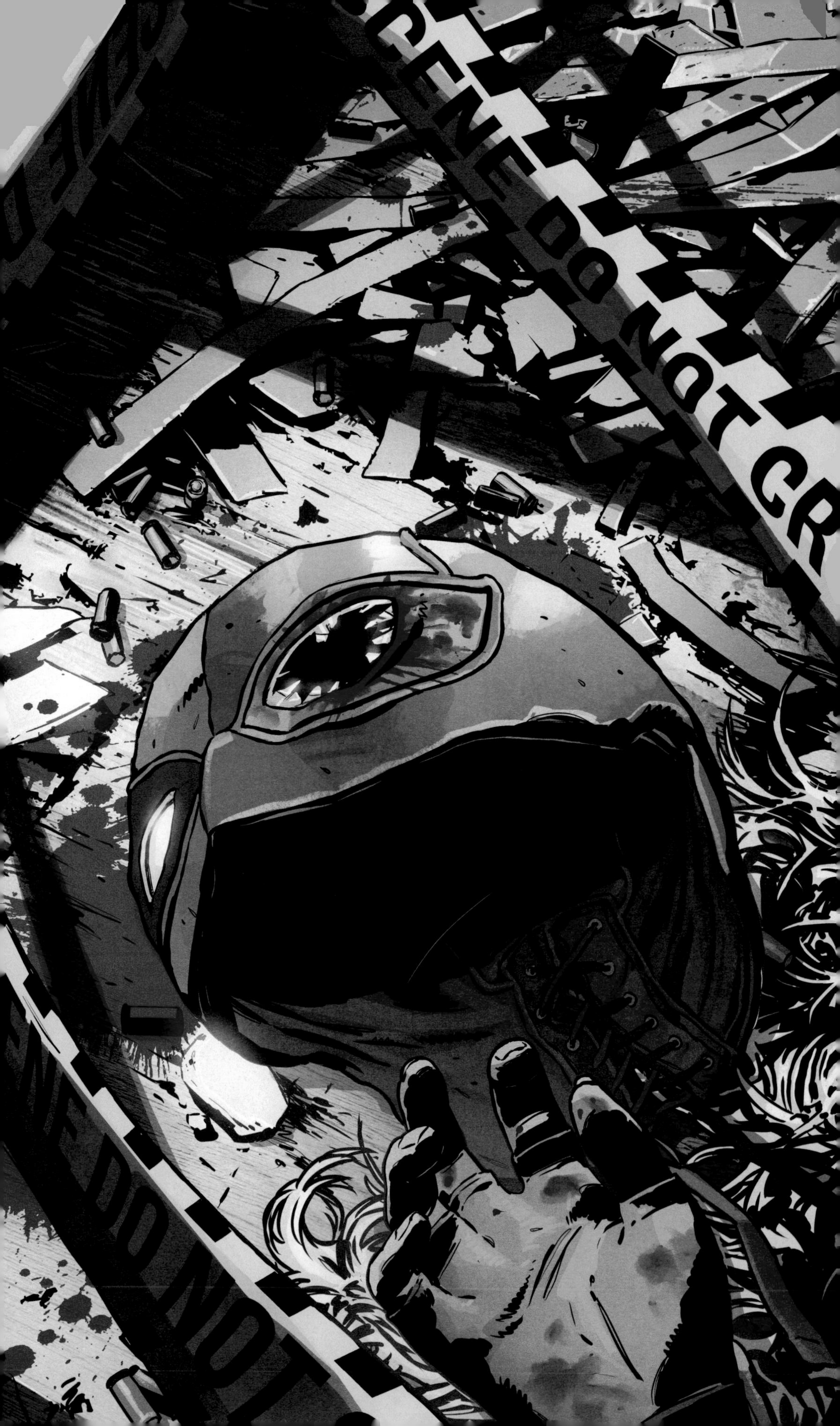
CENE DO NOT CR
ENE DO NOT

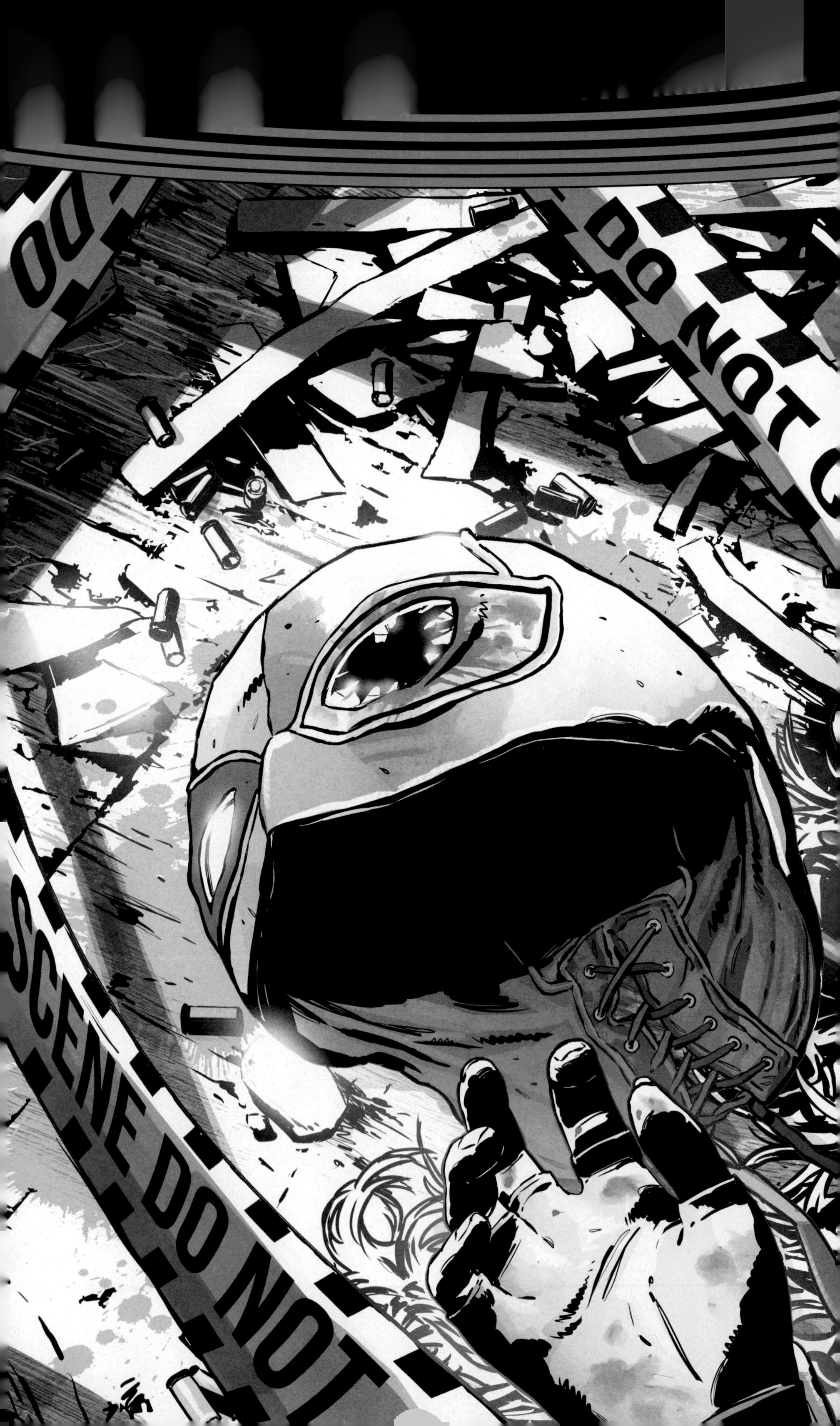
DO
DO NOT
SCENE DO NOT

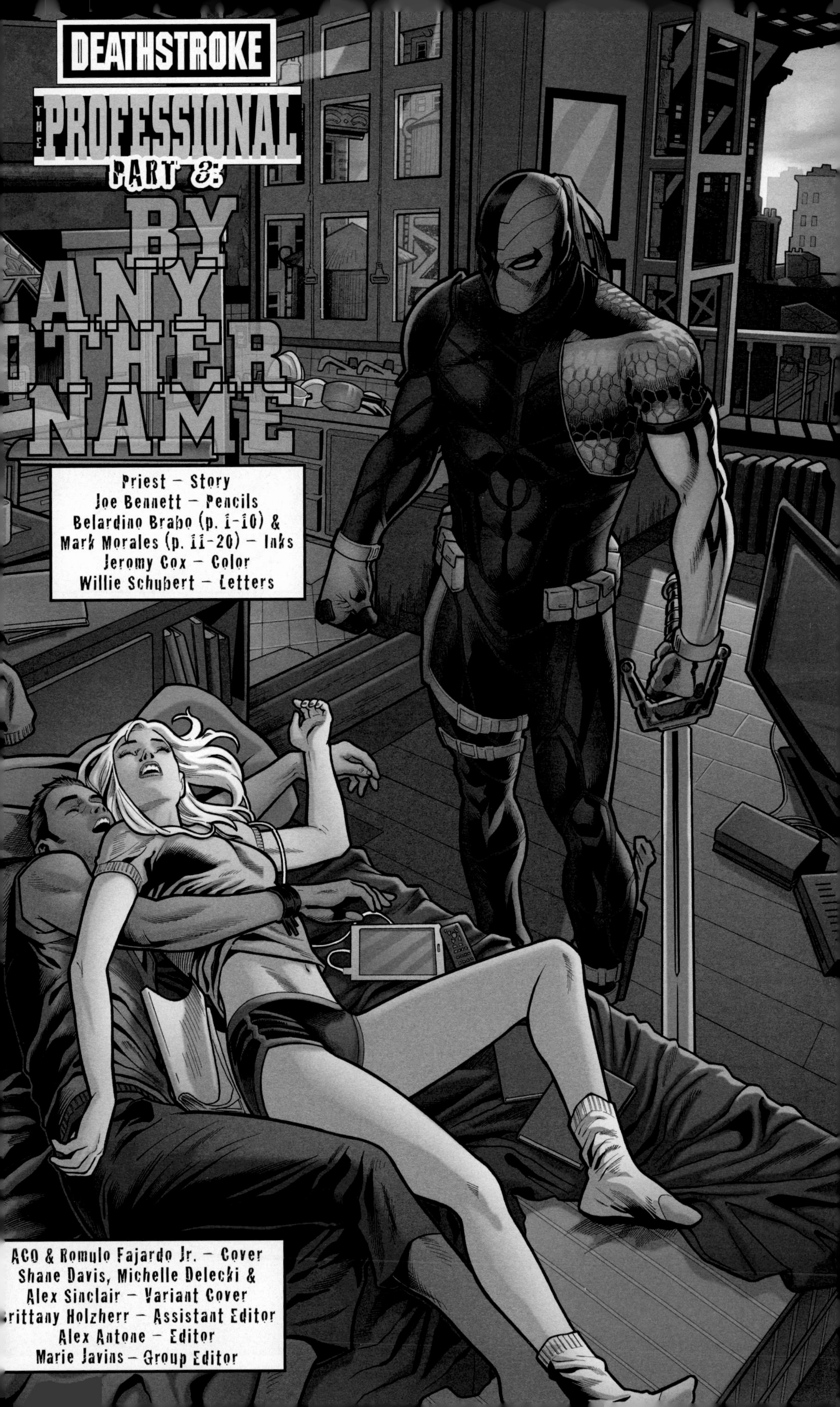

DEATHSTROKE
THE PROFESSIONAL
PART 8:
BY ANY OTHER NAME
Priest – Story
Joe Bennett – Pencils
Belardino Brabo (p. 1-10) &
Mark Morales (p. 11-20) – Inks
Jeromy Cox – Color
Willie Schubert – Letters
ACO & Romulo Fajardo Jr. – Cover
Shane Davis, Michelle Delecki &
Alex Sinclair – Variant Cover
Brittany Holzherr – Assistant Editor
Alex Antone – Editor
Marie Javins – Group Editor

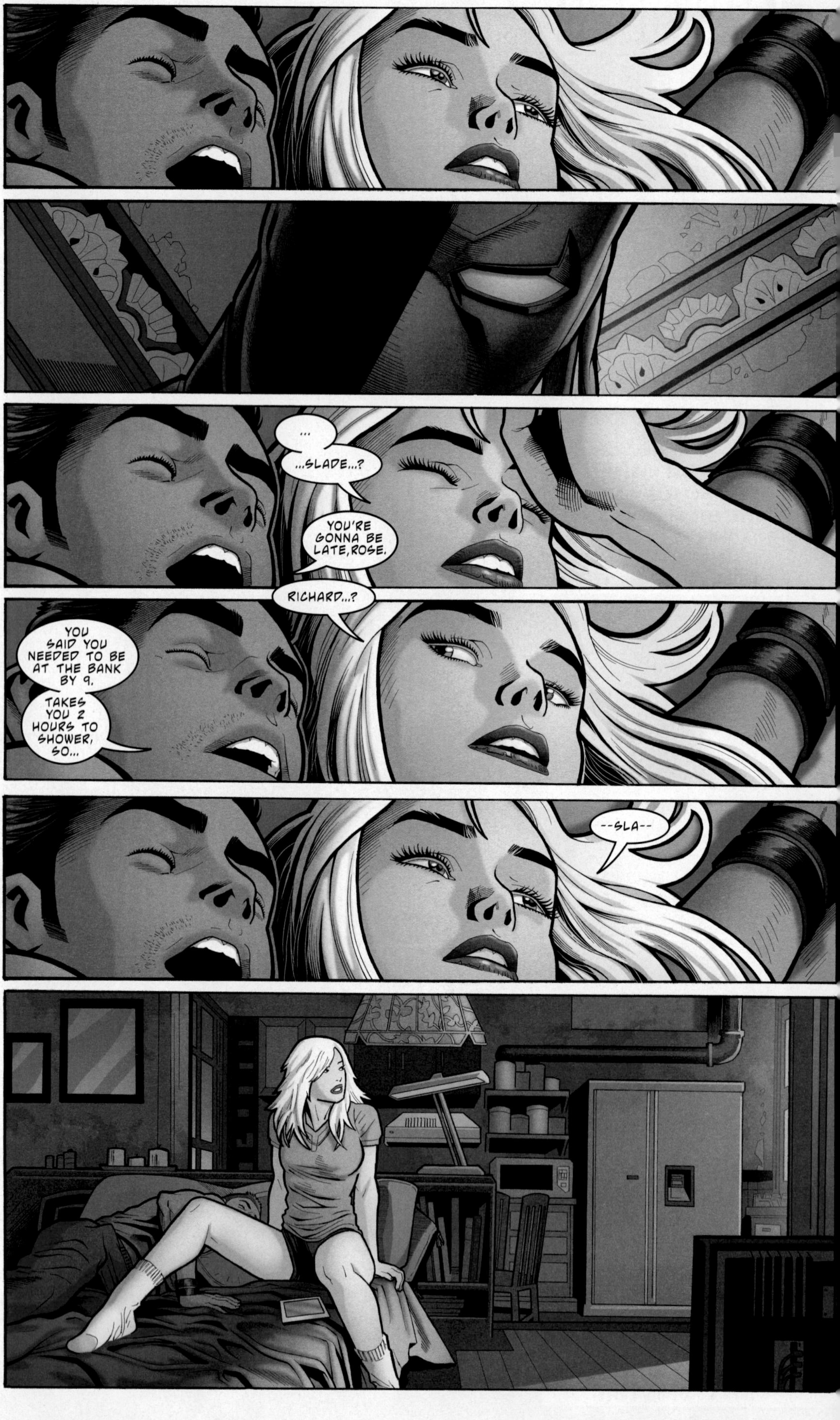

...
...SLADE...?
YOU'RE GONNA BE LATE, ROSE.
RICHARD...?
YOU SAID YOU NEEDED TO BE AT THE BANK BY 9.
TAKES YOU 2 HOURS TO SHOWER, SO...
--SLA--

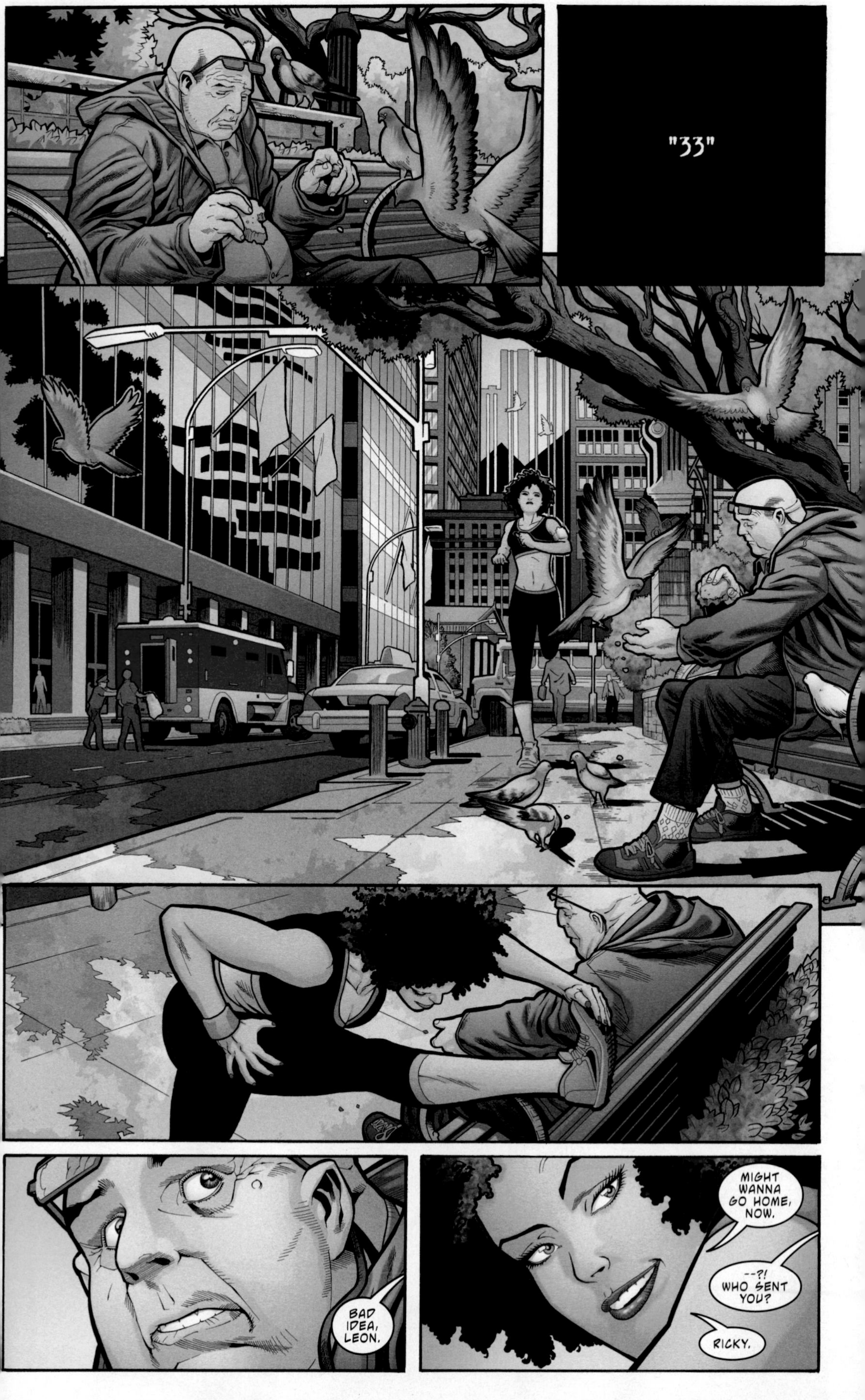
"33"
BAD IDEA, LEON.
MIGHT WANNA GO HOME, NOW.
--?! WHO SENT YOU?
RICKY.

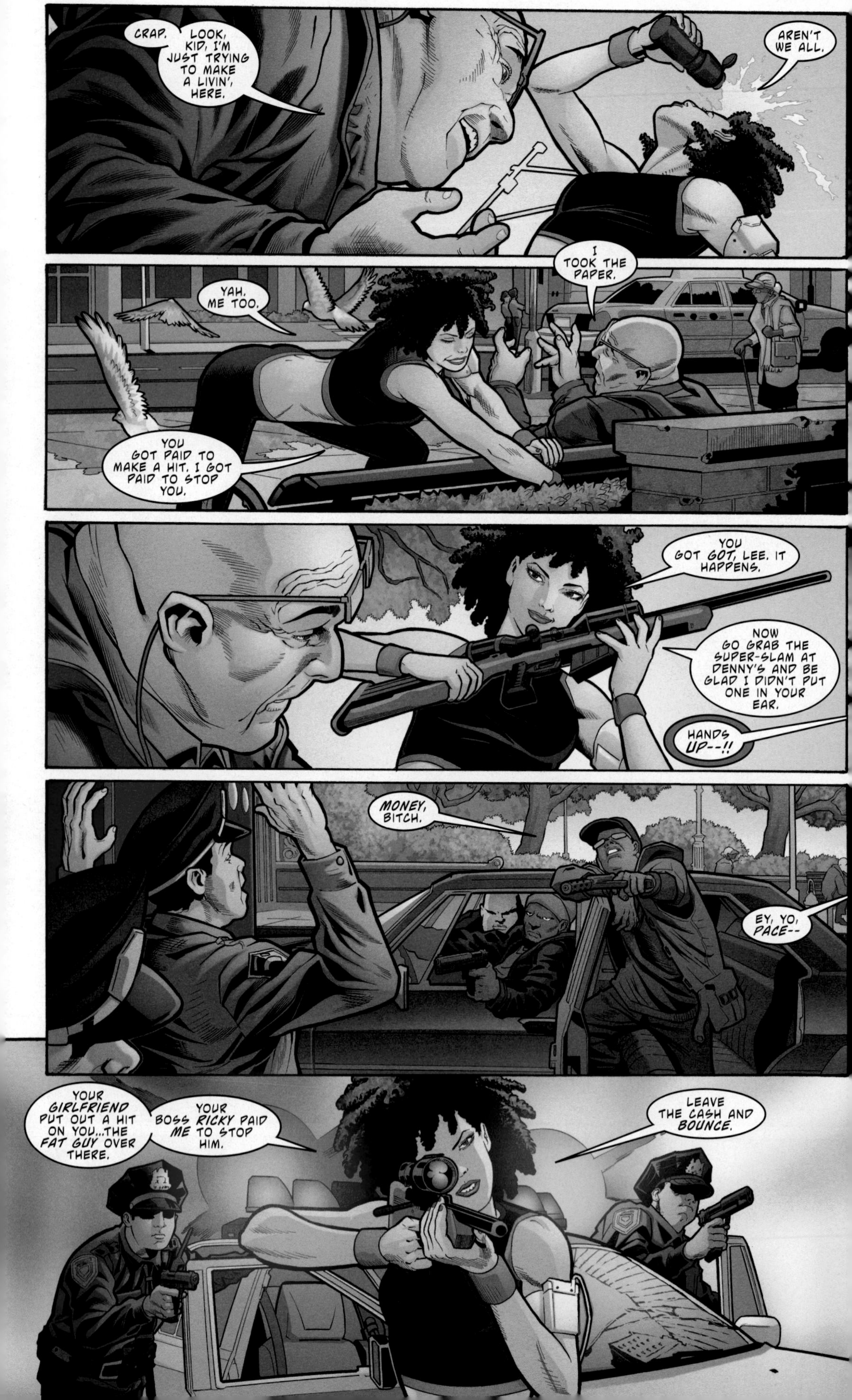
CRAP.
LOOK, KID, I'M JUST TRYING TO MAKE A LIVIN', HERE.
AREN'T WE ALL.
YAH. ME TOO.
I TOOK THE PAPER.
YOU GOT PAID TO MAKE A HIT. I GOT PAID TO STOP YOU.
YOU GOT *GOT*, LEE. IT HAPPENS.
NOW GO GRAB THE SUPER-SLAM AT DENNY'S AND BE GLAD I DIDN'T PUT ONE IN YOUR EAR.
HANDS *UP*--!!
MONEY, BITCH.
EY, YO, *PACE*--
YOUR *GIRLFRIEND* PUT OUT A HIT ON YOU...THE *FAT GUY* OVER THERE.
YOUR BOSS *RICKY* PAID *ME* TO STOP HIM.
LEAVE THE CASH AND *BOUNCE*.

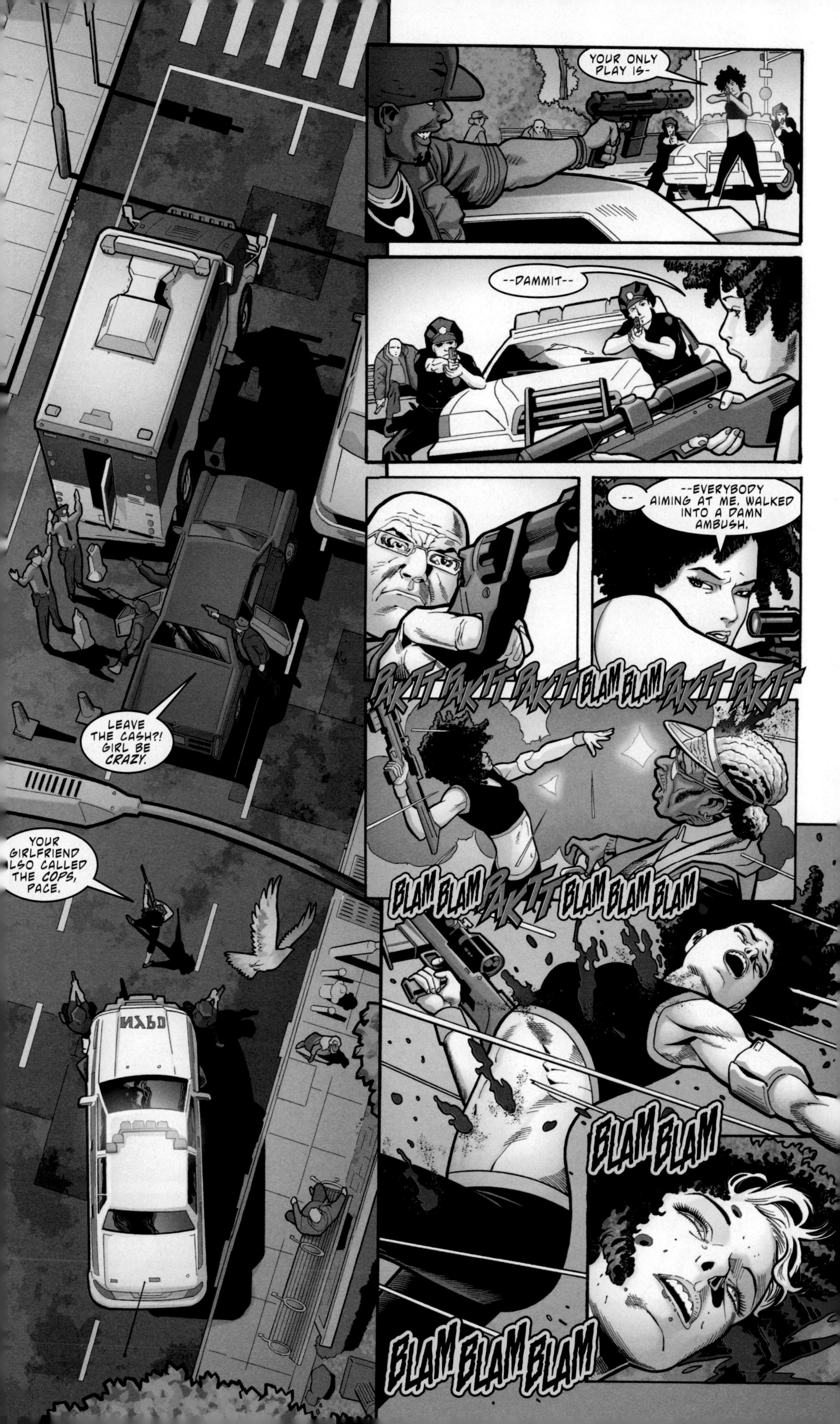
LEAVE THE CASH?! GIRL BE CRAZY.
YOUR GIRLFRIEND ALSO CALLED THE COPS, PACE.
NYPD
YOUR ONLY PLAY IS-
--DAMMIT--
--EVERYBODY AIMING AT ME. WALKED INTO A DAMN AMBUSH.
PAKTT PAKTT PAKTT BLAM BLAM PAKTT PAKTT
BLAM BLAM PAKTT BLAM BLAM BLAM
BLAM BLAM
BLAM BLAM BLAM

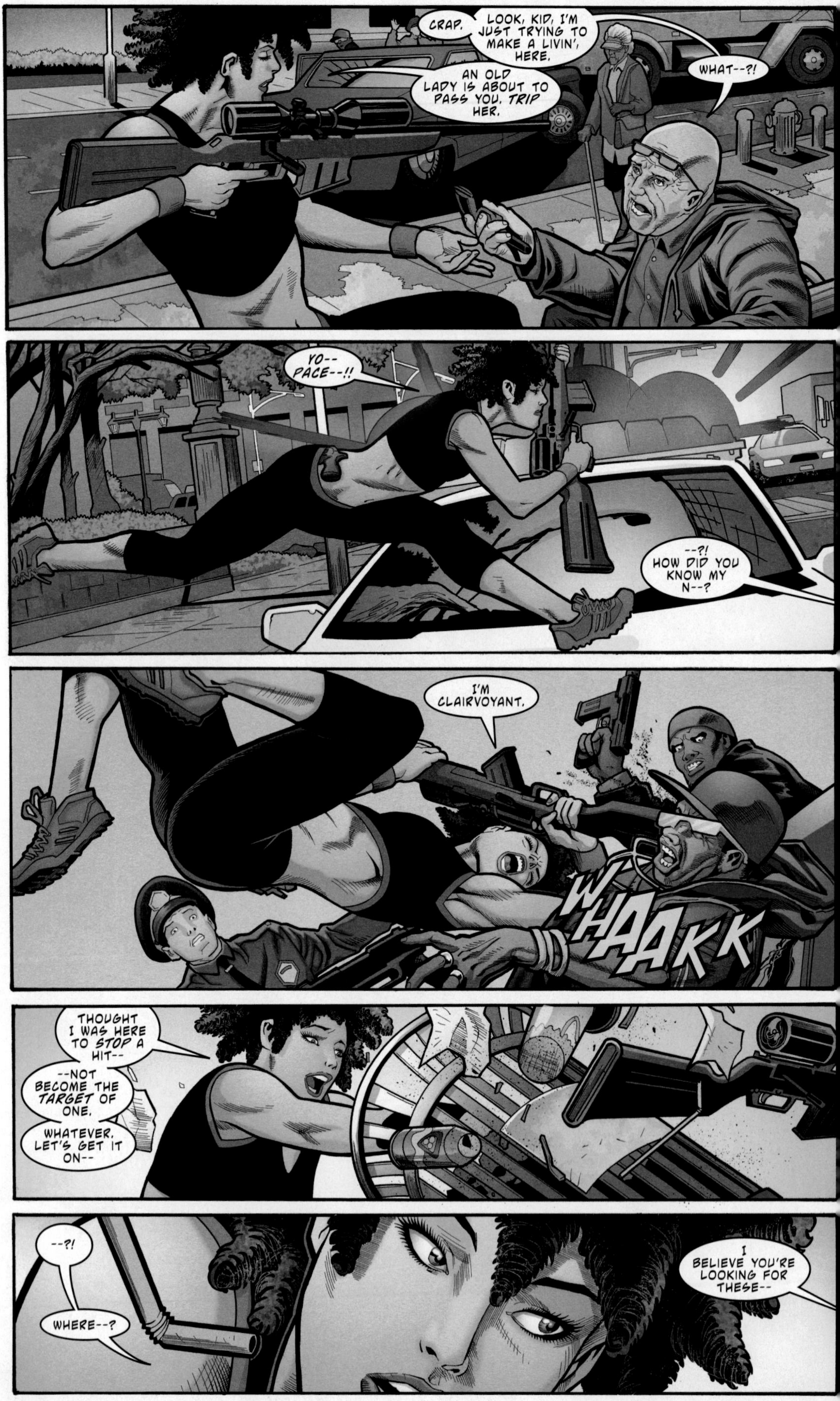
CRAP.
LOOK, KID, I'M JUST TRYING TO MAKE A LIVIN', HERE.
AN OLD LADY IS ABOUT TO PASS YOU. *TRIP* HER.
WHAT--?!
YO-- *PACE*--!!
--?! HOW DID YOU KNOW MY N--?
I'M CLAIRVOYANT.
WHAAKK
THOUGHT I WAS HERE TO *STOP* A HIT--
--NOT BECOME THE *TARGET* OF ONE.
WHATEVER. LET'S GET IT ON--
--?!
WHERE--?
I BELIEVE YOU'RE LOOKING FOR THESE--

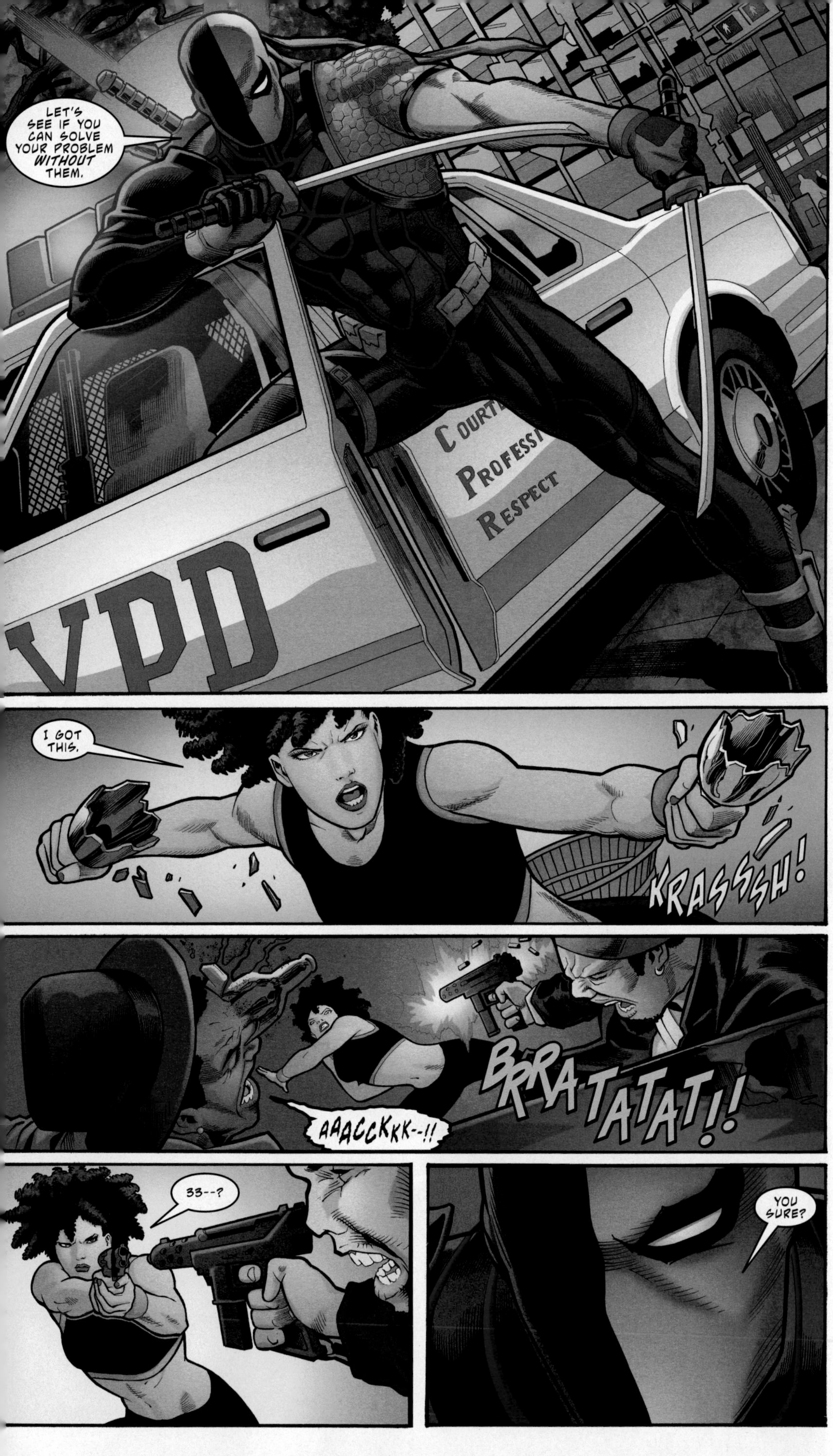
LET'S SEE IF YOU CAN SOLVE YOUR PROBLEM WITHOUT THEM.
COURTE
PROFESSI
RESPECT
YPD
I GOT THIS.
KRASSSH!
BRRATATATAT!!
AAACCKKK--!!
33--?
YOU SURE?

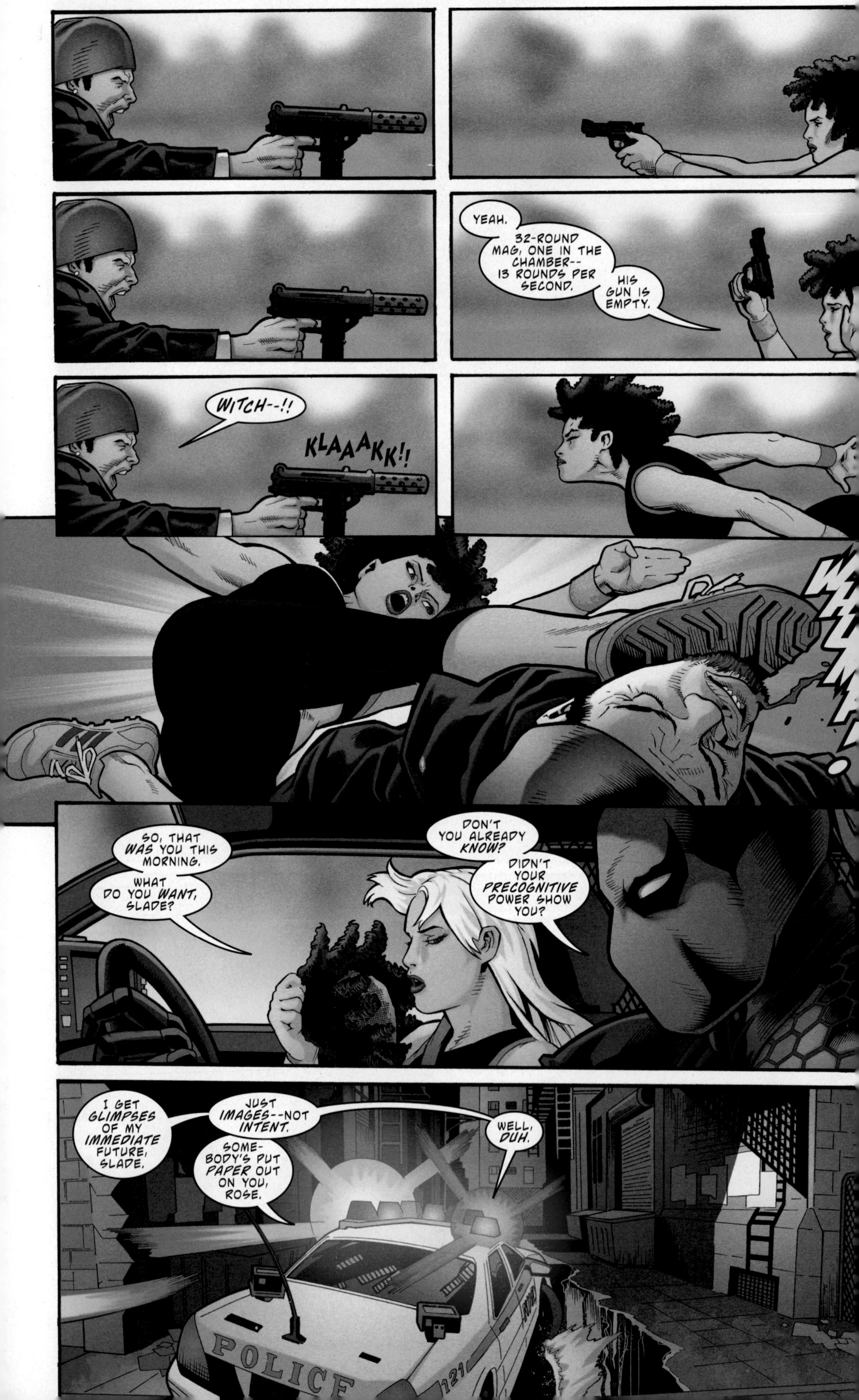

YEAH.
32-ROUND MAG, ONE IN THE CHAMBER-- 13 ROUNDS PER SECOND.
HIS GUN IS EMPTY.
WITCH--!!
KLAAAKK!!
SO, THAT WAS YOU THIS MORNING.
WHAT DO YOU WANT, SLADE?
DON'T YOU ALREADY KNOW?
DIDN'T YOUR PRECOGNITIVE POWER SHOW YOU?
I GET GLIMPSES OF MY IMMEDIATE FUTURE, SLADE.
JUST IMAGES--NOT INTENT.
WELL, DUH.
SOME-BODY'S PUT PAPER OUT ON YOU, ROSE.
POLICE

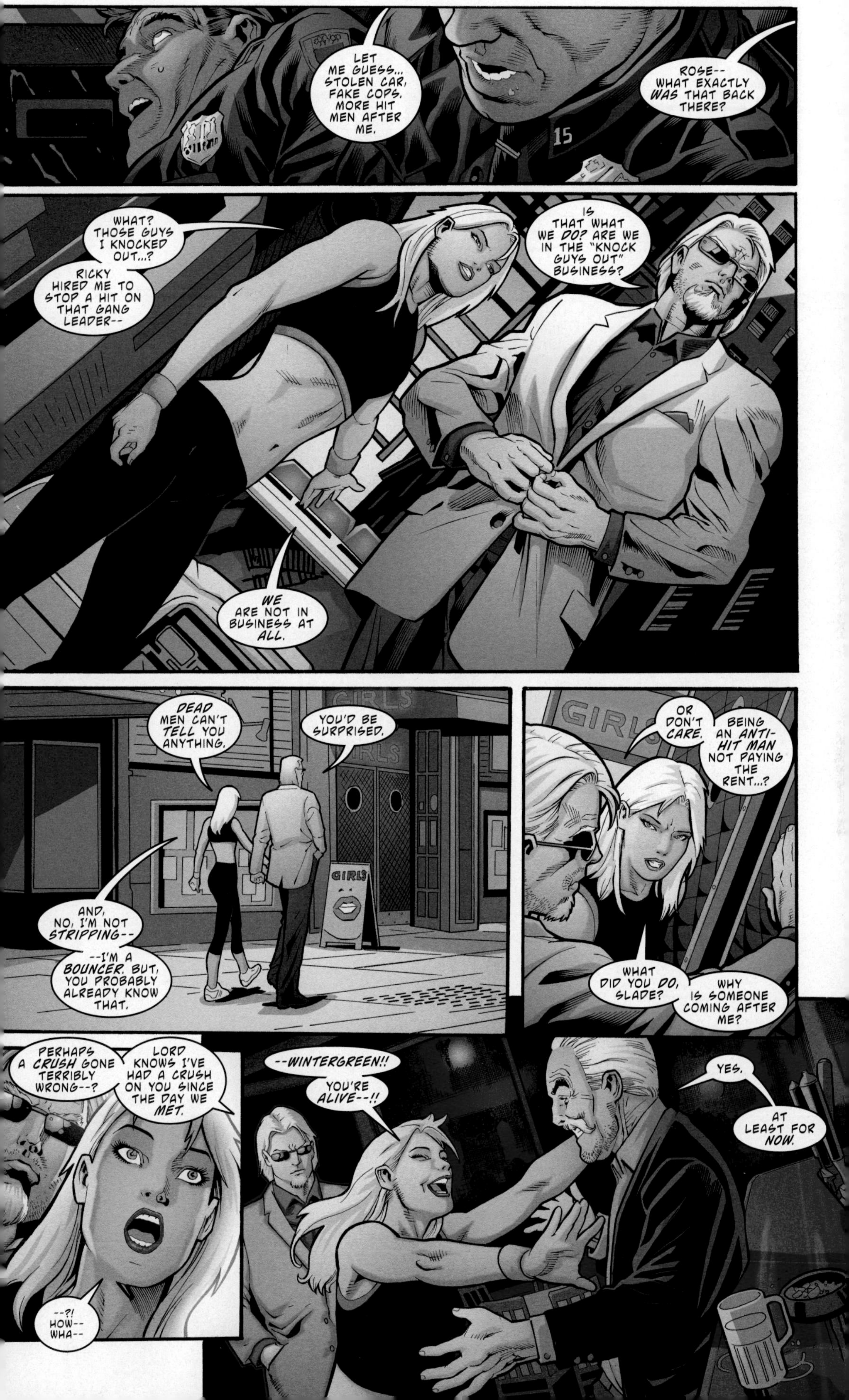
LET ME GUESS... STOLEN CAR, FAKE COPS, MORE HIT MEN AFTER ME.
ROSE-- WHAT EXACTLY WAS THAT BACK THERE?
15
WHAT? THOSE GUYS I KNOCKED OUT...?
RICKY HIRED ME TO STOP A HIT ON THAT GANG LEADER--
IS THAT WHAT WE DO? ARE WE IN THE "KNOCK GUYS OUT" BUSINESS?
WE ARE NOT IN BUSINESS AT ALL.
DEAD MEN CAN'T TELL YOU ANYTHING.
YOU'D BE SURPRISED.
GIRLS
AND, NO, I'M NOT STRIPPING--
--I'M A BOUNCER. BUT, YOU PROBABLY ALREADY KNOW THAT.
OR DON'T CARE.
BEING AN ANTI-HIT MAN NOT PAYING THE RENT...?
WHAT DID YOU DO, SLADE?
WHY IS SOMEONE COMING AFTER ME?
PERHAPS A CRUSH GONE TERRIBLY WRONG--?
LORD KNOWS I'VE HAD A CRUSH ON YOU SINCE THE DAY WE MET.
--?! HOW-- WHA--
--WINTERGREEN!!
YOU'RE ALIVE--!!
YES.
AT LEAST FOR NOW.

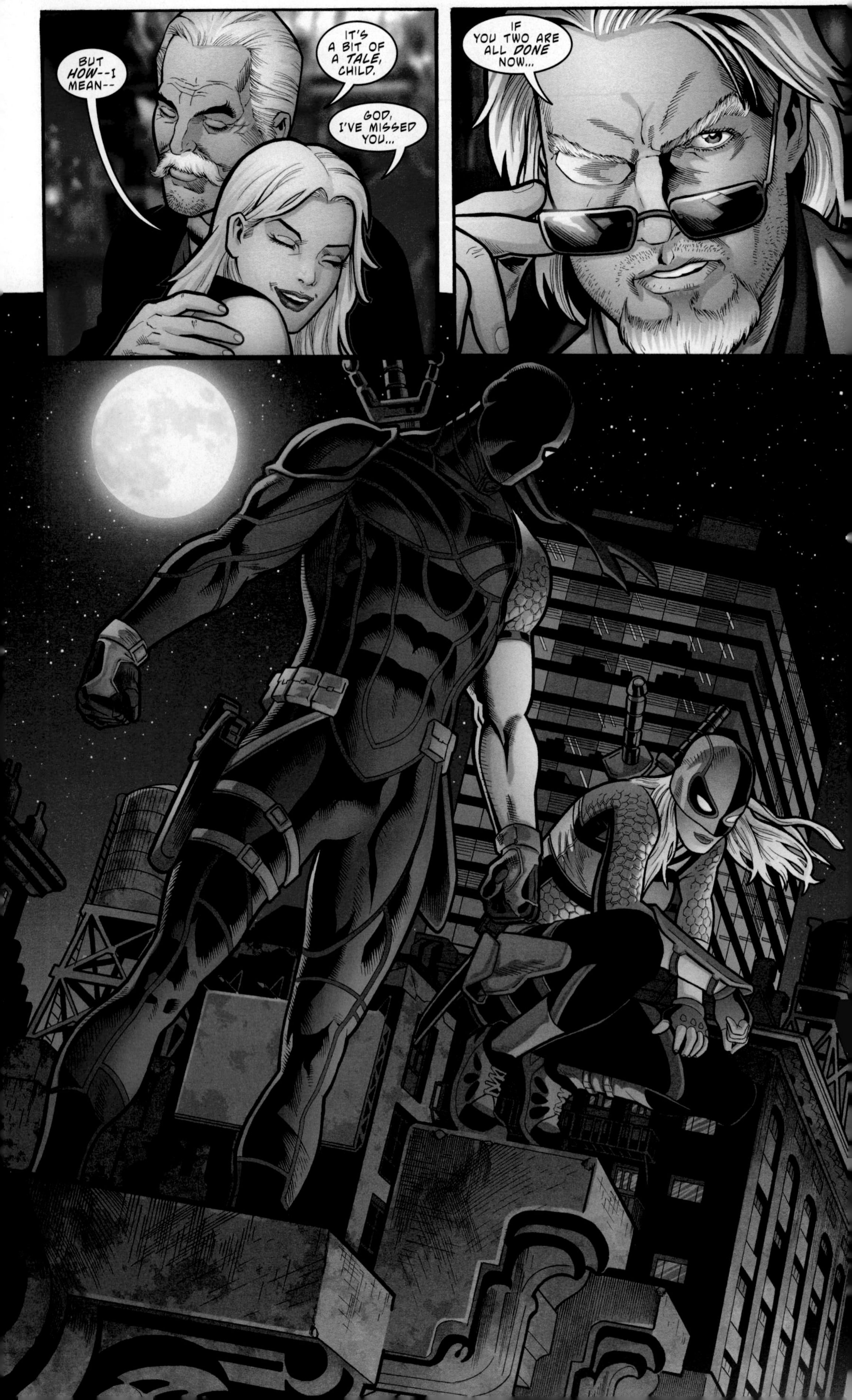
BUT HOW--I MEAN--
IT'S A BIT OF A TALE, CHILD.
GOD, I'VE MISSED YOU...
IF YOU TWO ARE ALL DONE NOW...

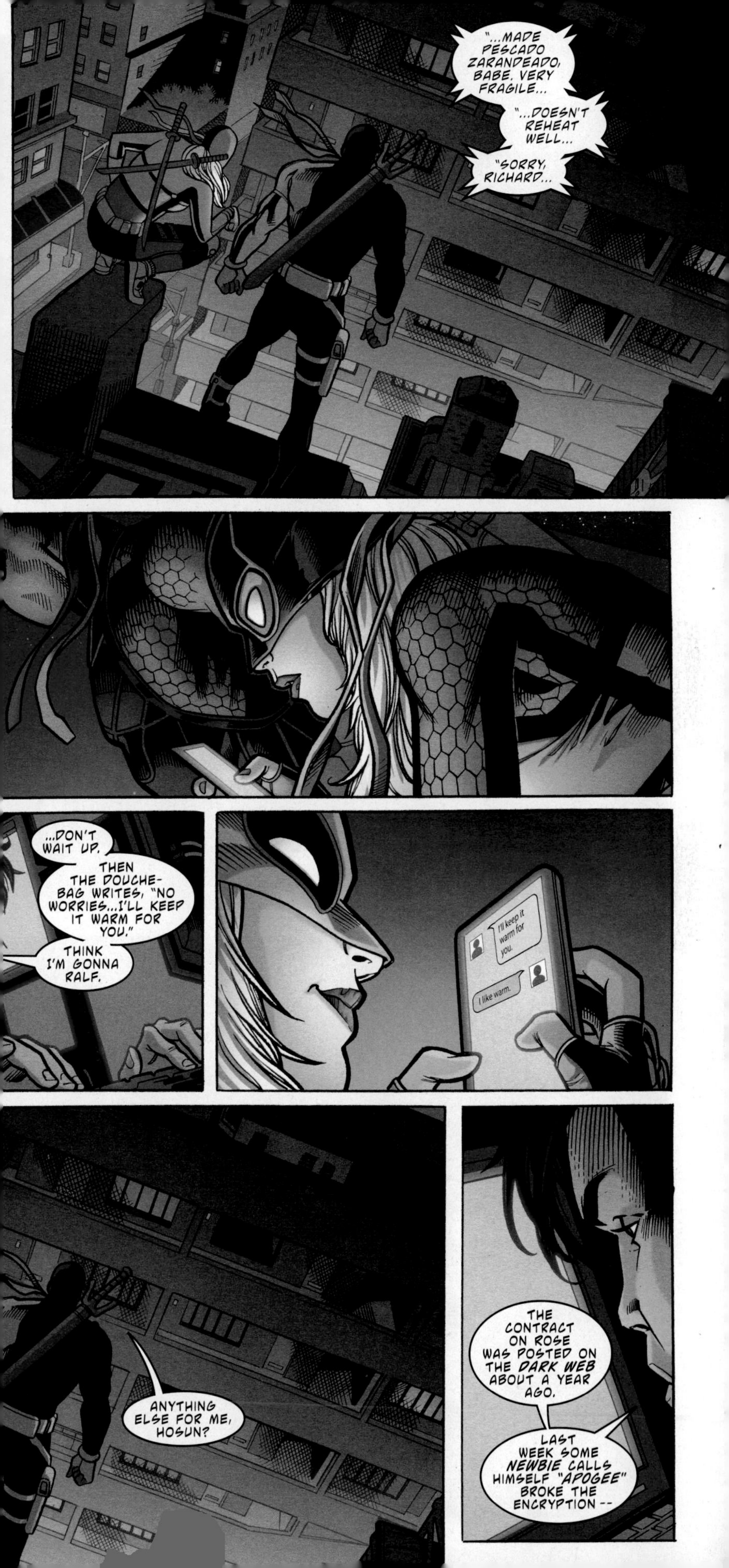
"...MADE PESCADO ZARANDEADO, BABE. VERY FRAGILE...
"...DOESN'T REHEAT WELL...
"SORRY, RICHARD...
...DON'T WAIT UP.
THEN THE DOUCHE-BAG WRITES, "NO WORRIES...I'LL KEEP IT WARM FOR YOU."
THINK I'M GONNA RALF.
I'll keep it warm for you.
I like warm.
ANYTHING ELSE FOR ME, HOSUN?
THE CONTRACT ON ROSE WAS POSTED ON THE DARK WEB ABOUT A YEAR AGO.
LAST WEEK SOME NEWBIE CALLS HIMSELF "APOGEE" BROKE THE ENCRYPTION --

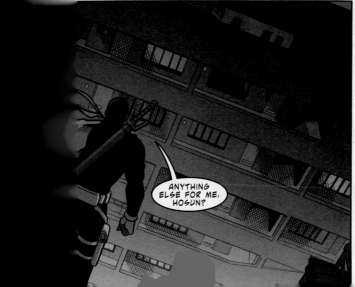

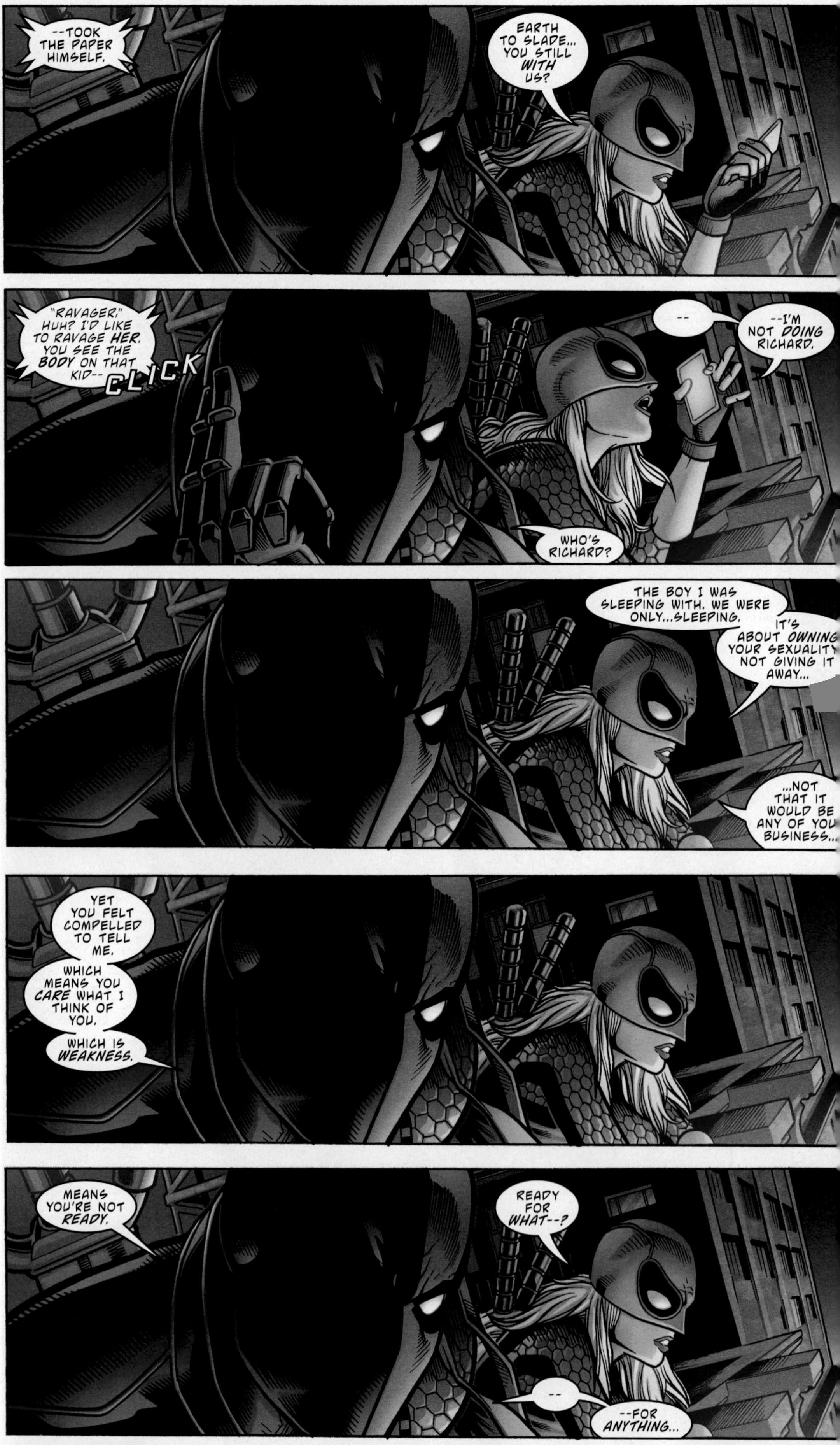
--TOOK THE PAPER HIMSELF.
EARTH TO SLADE... YOU STILL WITH US?
"RAVAGER," HUH? I'D LIKE TO RAVAGE HER. YOU SEE THE BODY ON THAT KID--
CLICK
--
--I'M NOT DOING RICHARD.
WHO'S RICHARD?
THE BOY I WAS SLEEPING WITH. WE WERE ONLY...SLEEPING.
IT'S ABOUT OWNING YOUR SEXUALITY NOT GIVING IT AWAY...
...NOT THAT IT WOULD BE ANY OF YOUR BUSINESS...
YET YOU FELT COMPELLED TO TELL ME.
WHICH MEANS YOU CARE WHAT I THINK OF YOU.
WHICH IS WEAKNESS.
MEANS YOU'RE NOT READY.
READY FOR WHAT--?
--
--FOR ANYTHING...

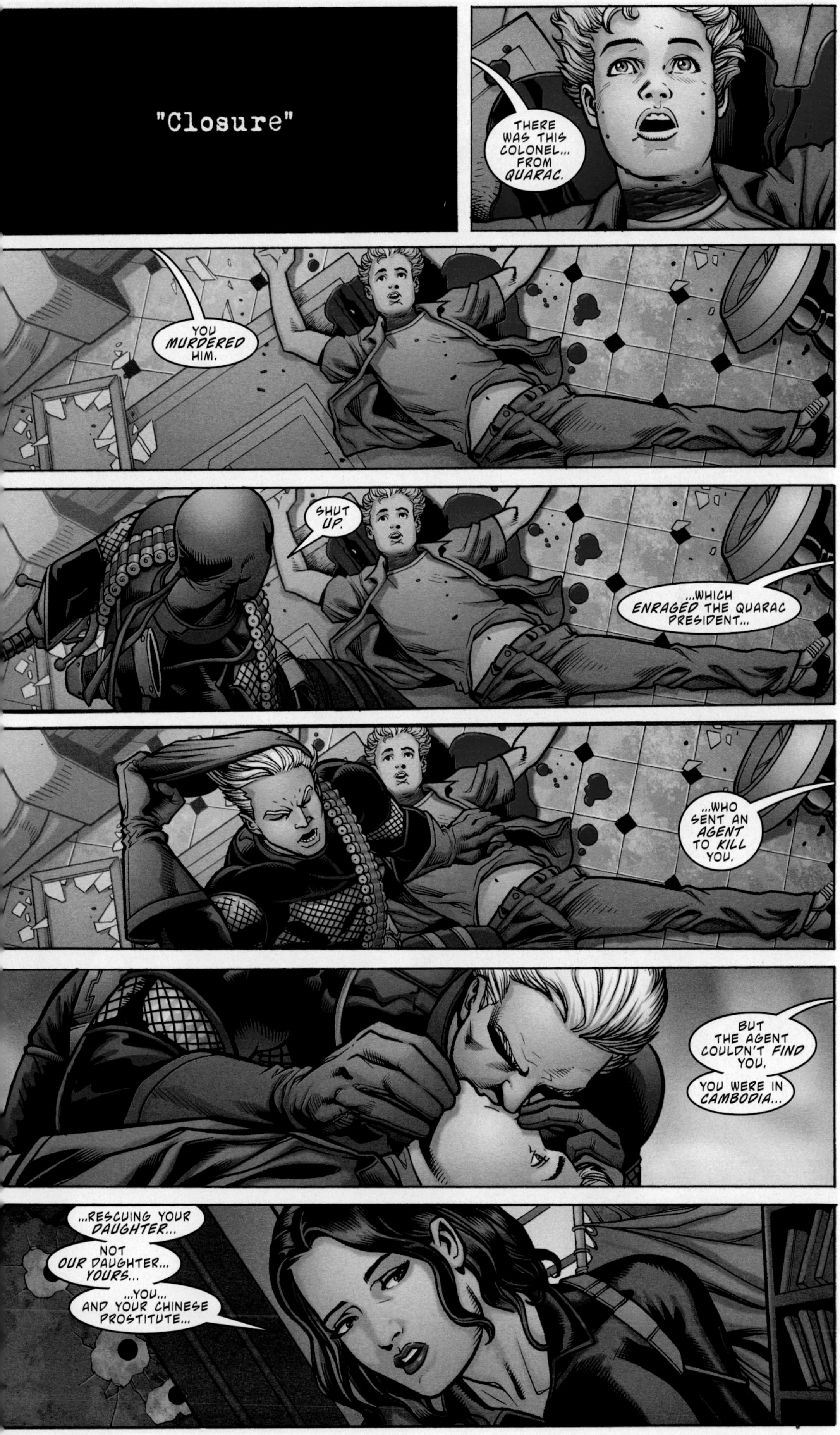
"Closure"
THERE WAS THIS COLONEL... FROM QUARAC.
YOU MURDERED HIM.
SHUT UP.
...WHICH ENRAGED THE QUARAC PRESIDENT...
...WHO SENT AN AGENT TO KILL YOU.
BUT THE AGENT COULDN'T FIND YOU.
YOU WERE IN CAMBODIA...
...RESCUING YOUR DAUGHTER...
NOT OUR DAUGHTER... YOURS...
...YOU...
AND YOUR CHINESE PROSTITUTE...

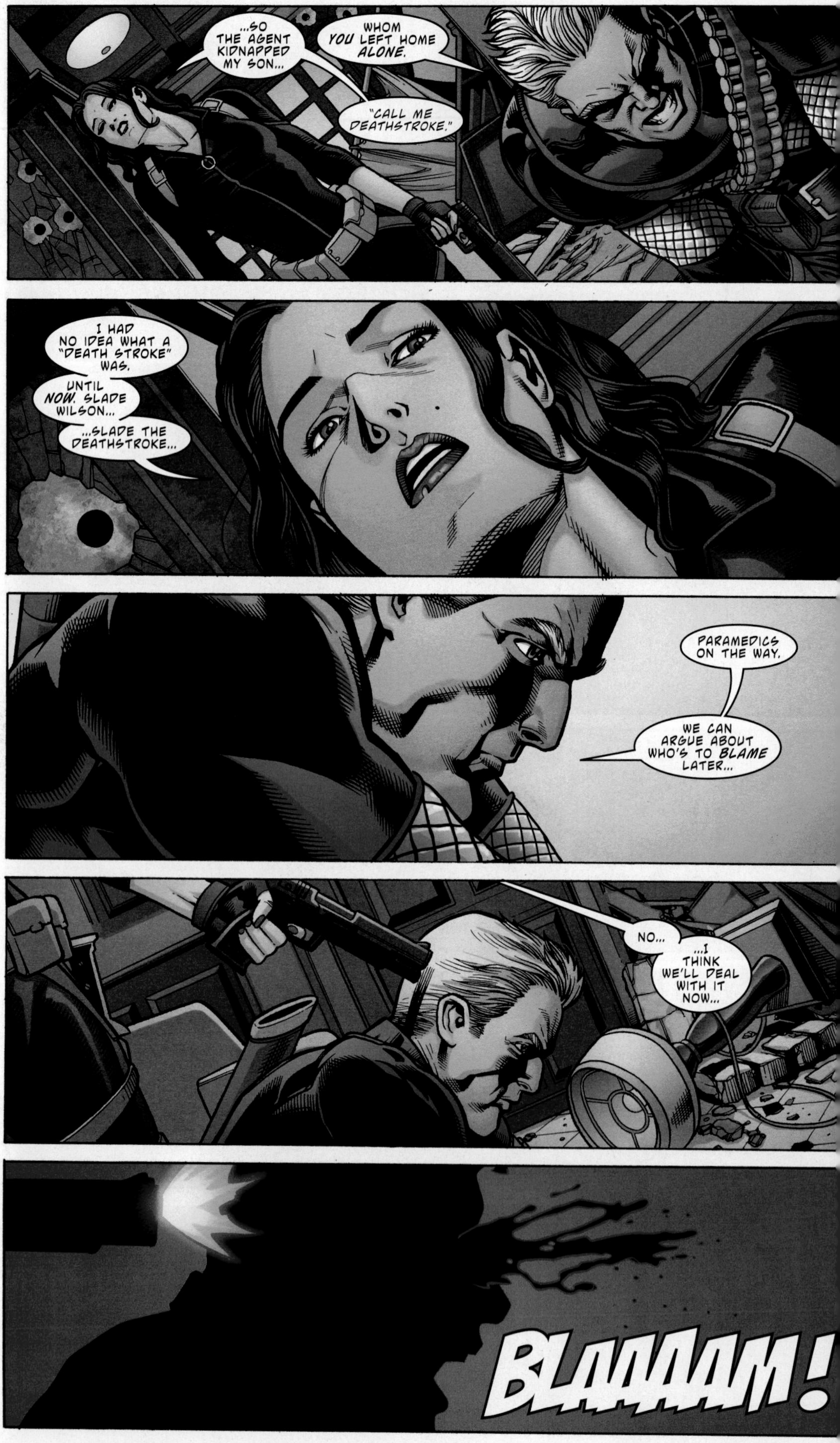
...SO THE AGENT KIDNAPPED MY SON...
WHOM YOU LEFT HOME ALONE.
"CALL ME DEATHSTROKE."
I HAD NO IDEA WHAT A "DEATH STROKE" WAS.
UNTIL NOW. SLADE WILSON...
...SLADE THE DEATHSTROKE...
PARAMEDICS ON THE WAY.
WE CAN ARGUE ABOUT WHO'S TO BLAME LATER...
NO...
...I THINK WE'LL DEAL WITH IT NOW...
BLAAAAM!

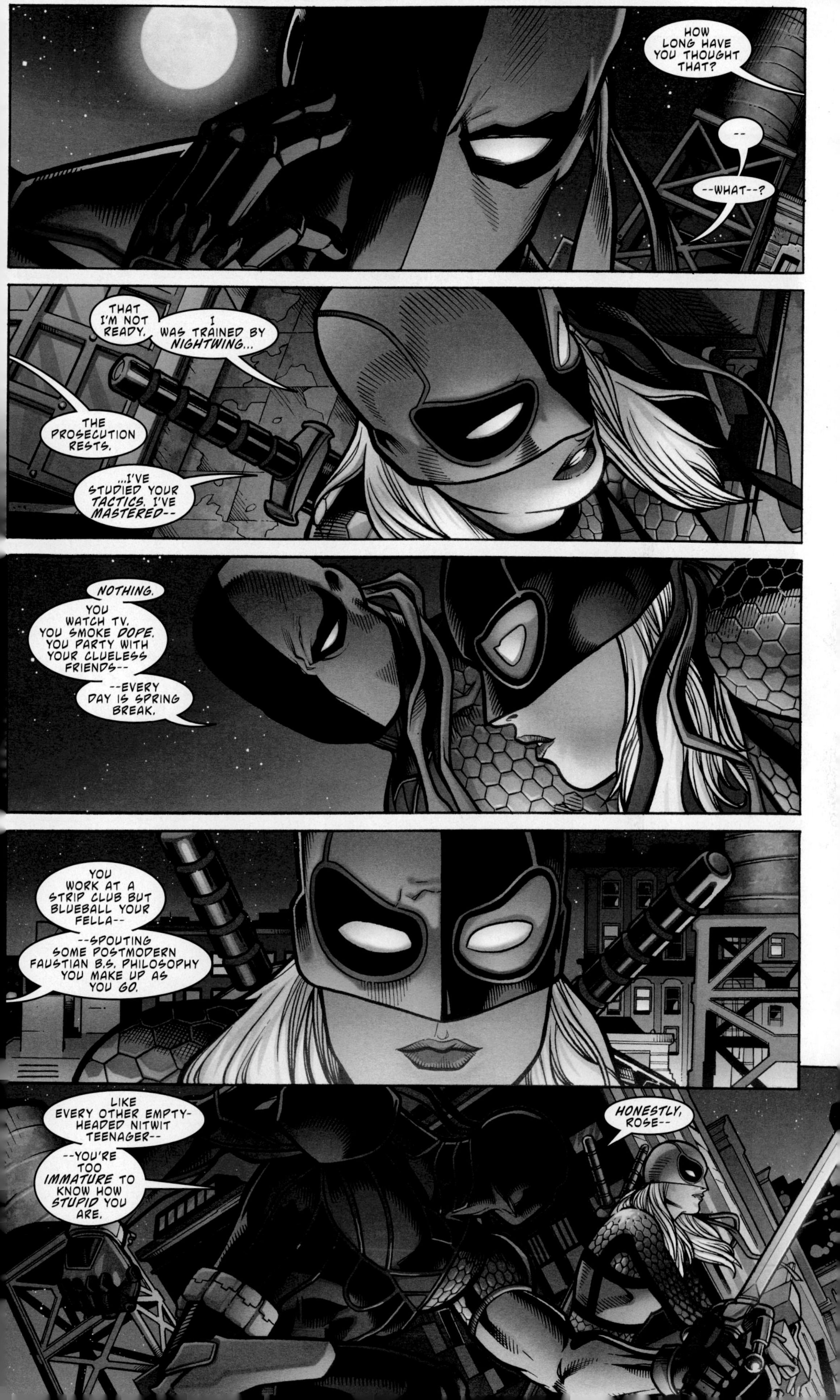
HOW LONG HAVE YOU THOUGHT THAT?
--
--WHAT--?
THAT I'M NOT READY.
I WAS TRAINED BY NIGHTWING...
THE PROSECUTION RESTS.
...I'VE STUDIED YOUR TACTICS. I'VE MASTERED--
NOTHING.
YOU WATCH TV. YOU SMOKE DOPE. YOU PARTY WITH YOUR CLUELESS FRIENDS--
--EVERY DAY IS SPRING BREAK.
YOU WORK AT A STRIP CLUB BUT BLUEBALL YOUR FELLA--
--SPOUTING SOME POSTMODERN FAUSTIAN B.S. PHILOSOPHY YOU MAKE UP AS YOU GO.
LIKE EVERY OTHER EMPTY-HEADED NITWIT TEENAGER--
--YOU'RE TOO IMMATURE TO KNOW HOW STUPID YOU ARE.
HONESTLY, ROSE--

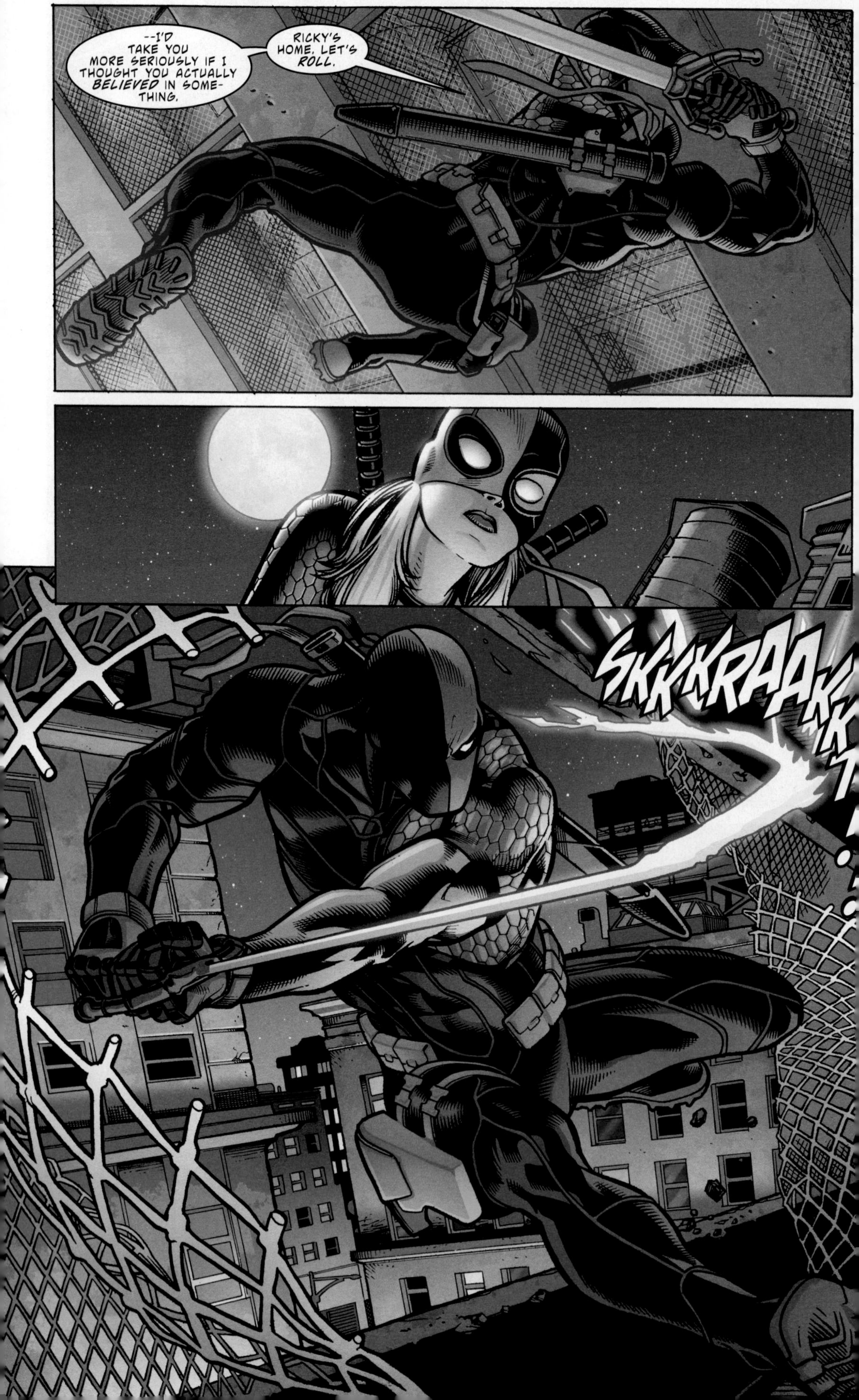
--I'D TAKE YOU MORE SERIOUSLY IF I THOUGHT YOU ACTUALLY BELIEVED IN SOME-THING.
RICKY'S HOME. LET'S ROLL.
SKKKRAAKK

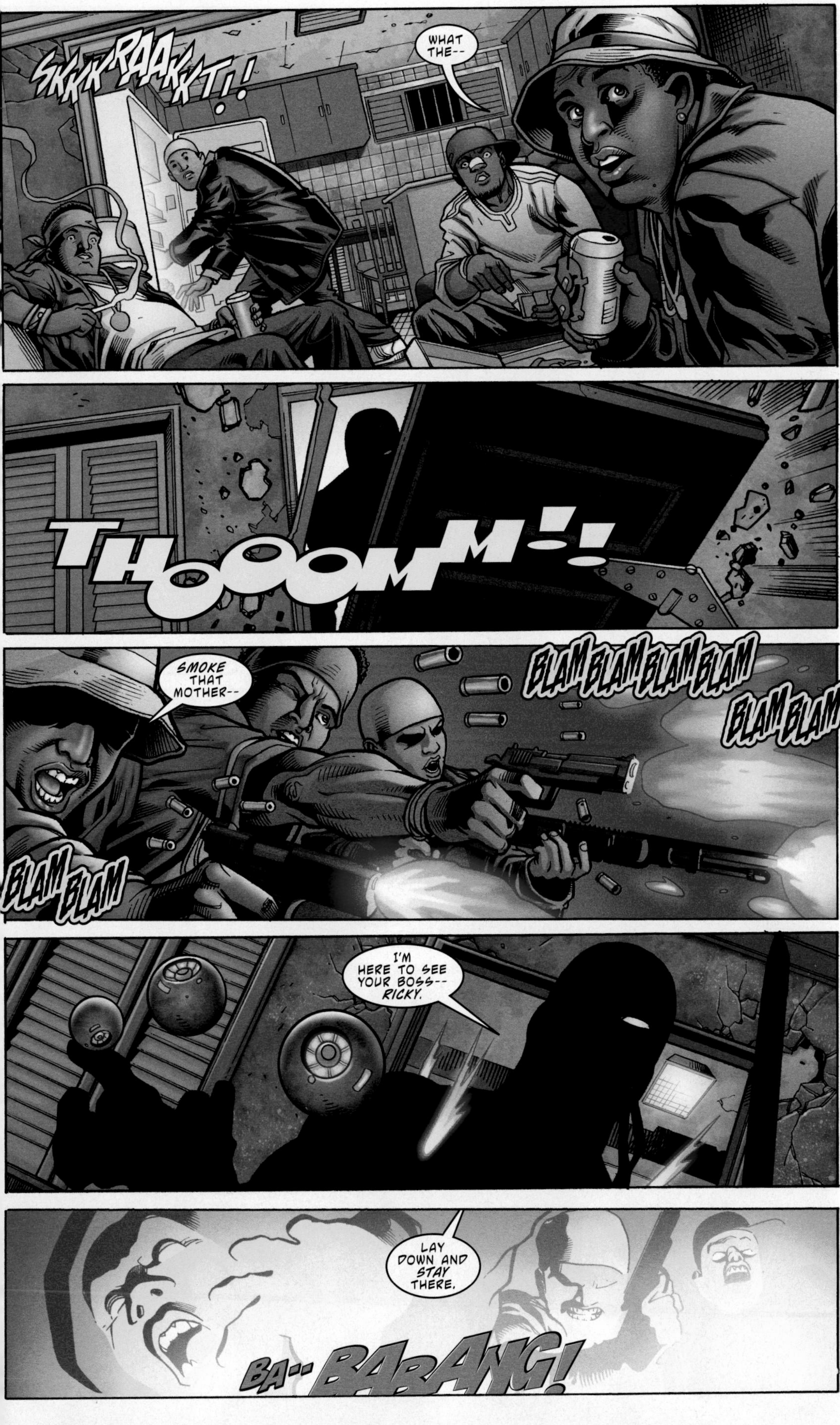
SKKKRAAKKT!!
WHAT THE--
THOOOOMM!!
SMOKE THAT MOTHER--
BLAMBLAMBLAMBLAM
BLAMBLAM
BLAM BLAM
I'M HERE TO SEE YOUR BOSS-- RICKY.
LAY DOWN AND STAY THERE.
BA-- BABANG!

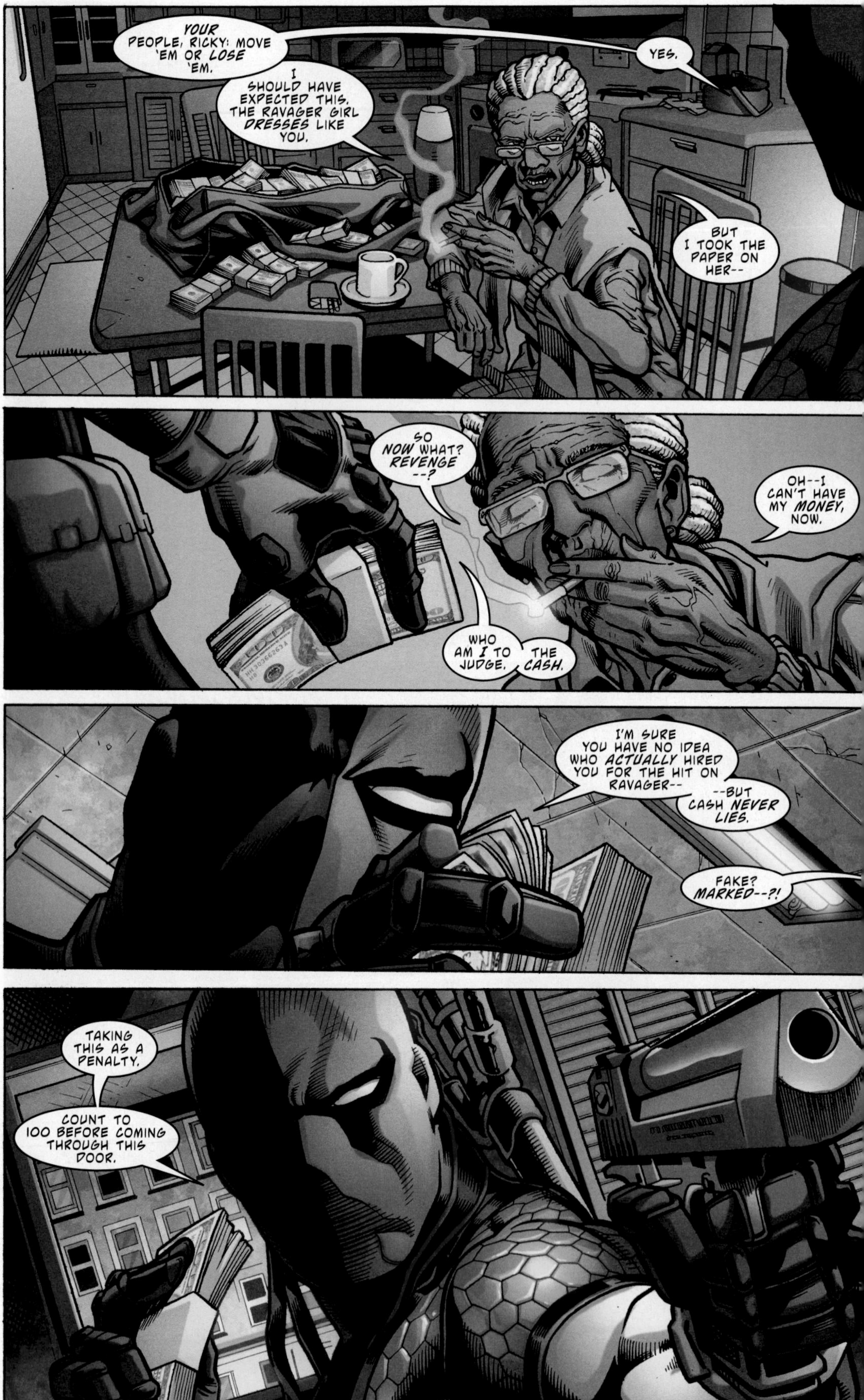
YOUR PEOPLE, RICKY: MOVE 'EM OR LOSE 'EM.
YES.
I SHOULD HAVE EXPECTED THIS. THE RAVAGER GIRL DRESSES LIKE YOU.
BUT I TOOK THE PAPER ON HER--
SO NOW WHAT? REVENGE--?
OH--I CAN'T HAVE MY MONEY, NOW.
WHO AM I TO JUDGE.
THE CASH.
I'M SURE YOU HAVE NO IDEA WHO ACTUALLY HIRED YOU FOR THE HIT ON RAVAGER--
--BUT CASH NEVER LIES.
FAKE? MARKED--?!
TAKING THIS AS A PENALTY.
COUNT TO 100 BEFORE COMING THROUGH THIS DOOR.

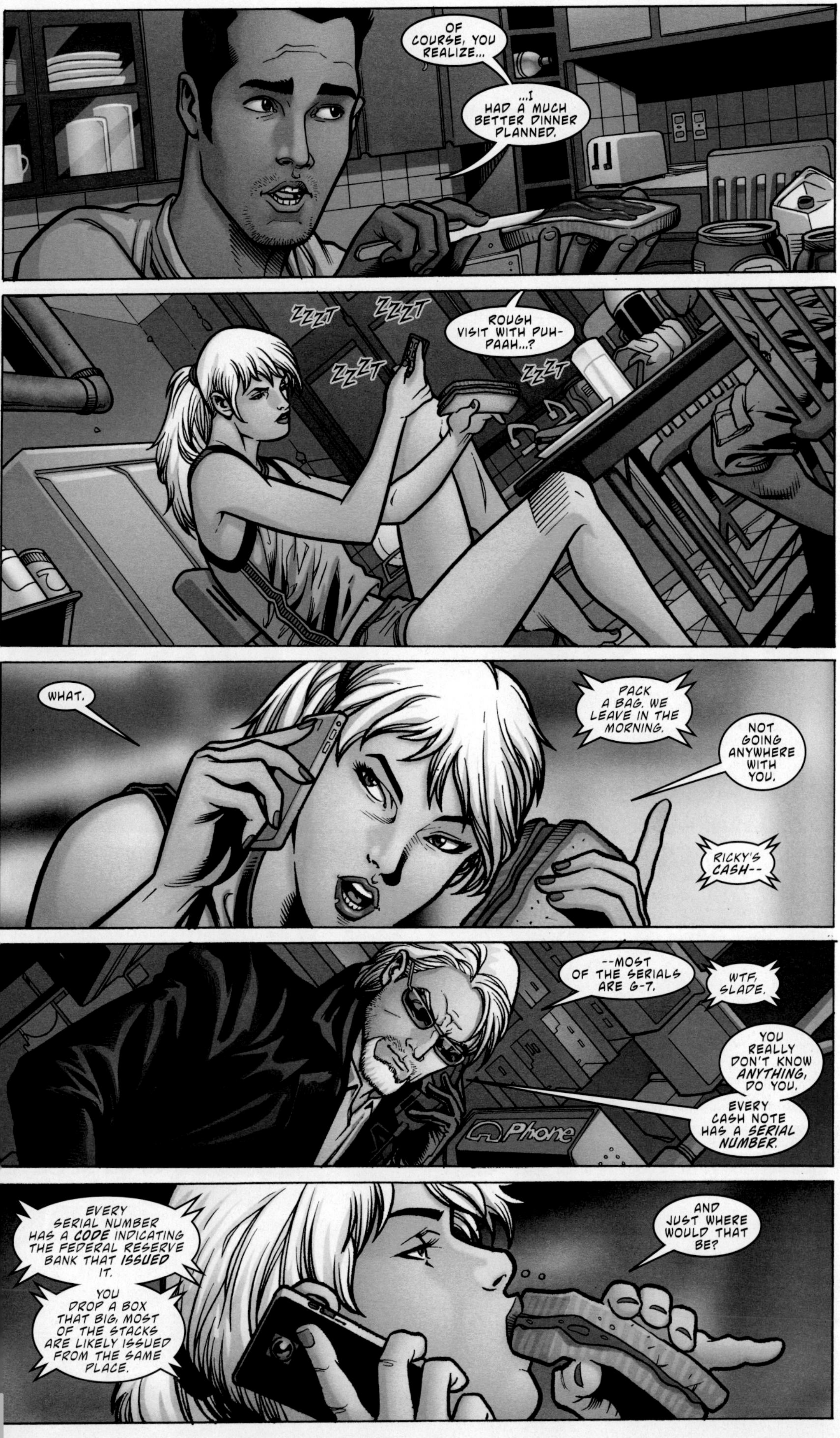
OF COURSE, YOU REALIZE...
...I HAD A MUCH BETTER DINNER PLANNED.
ZZZT
ZZZT
ZZZT
ZZZT
ROUGH VISIT WITH PUH-PAAH...?
WHAT.
PACK A BAG. WE LEAVE IN THE MORNING.
NOT GOING ANYWHERE WITH YOU.
RICKY'S CASH--
--MOST OF THE SERIALS ARE G-7.
WTF, SLADE.
YOU REALLY DON'T KNOW ANYTHING, DO YOU.
EVERY CASH NOTE HAS A SERIAL NUMBER.
Phone
EVERY SERIAL NUMBER HAS A CODE INDICATING THE FEDERAL RESERVE BANK THAT ISSUED IT.
YOU DROP A BOX THAT BIG, MOST OF THE STACKS ARE LIKELY ISSUED FROM THE SAME PLACE.
AND JUST WHERE WOULD THAT BE?

LOOK IT UP. LEARN SOMETHING.

BEHIND THE JAVITS CENTER, ELEVEN HUNDRED.

WELL, SLADE, IT'S OFFICIAL:

YOU'VE LOST YOUR BLOODY MIND.

MOST SANE PARENTS, WISHING TO SPEND TIME WITH THEIR KIDS, HANDLE THINGS THE PROPER WAY:

BRIBERY.

"EVAN DOSLETTER--?"

CALCULUS TEACHER AT MIDLAND HIGH SCHOOL IN WHEREVER WISCONSIN.

HE'LL NEVER KNOW.

SLADE...

EVAN J. DOSLETTER
325 West 9th Street
Belgium, WI 53004
ORGAN DONOR

...THERE ARE ANY NUMBER OF WAYS I COULD GET YOU INTO GOTHAM CITY UNNOTICED.

A CROSS-COUNTRY DRIVE IN AN OLD BANGER DISGUISED AS FRED FLINTSTONE ISN'T ONE OF THEM.

SOMEONE'S AFTER ROSE, WINTERGREEN, SOMEONE WITH MONEY AND RESOURCES.

I SMELL A BAT...

NEXT: BAT TRAP

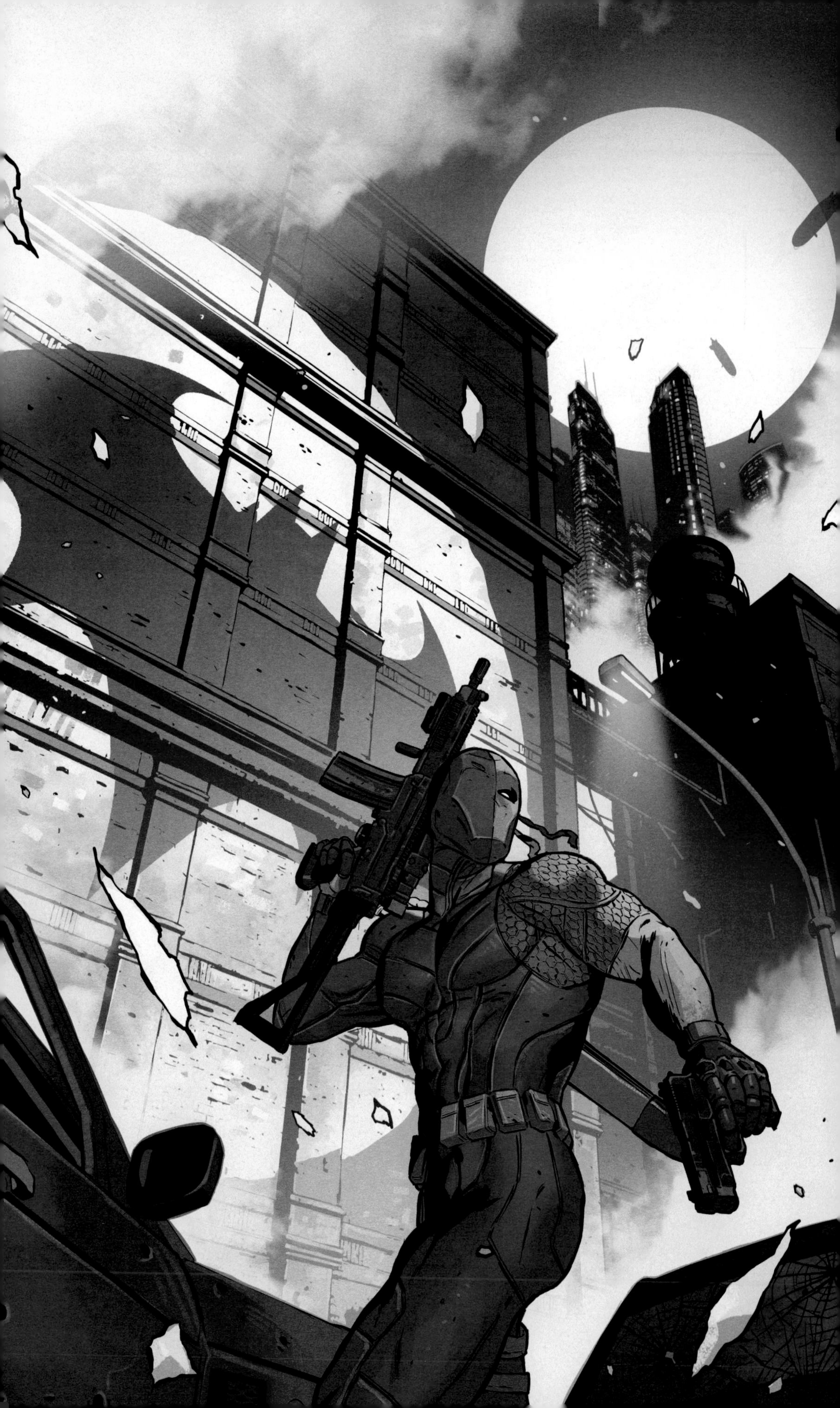

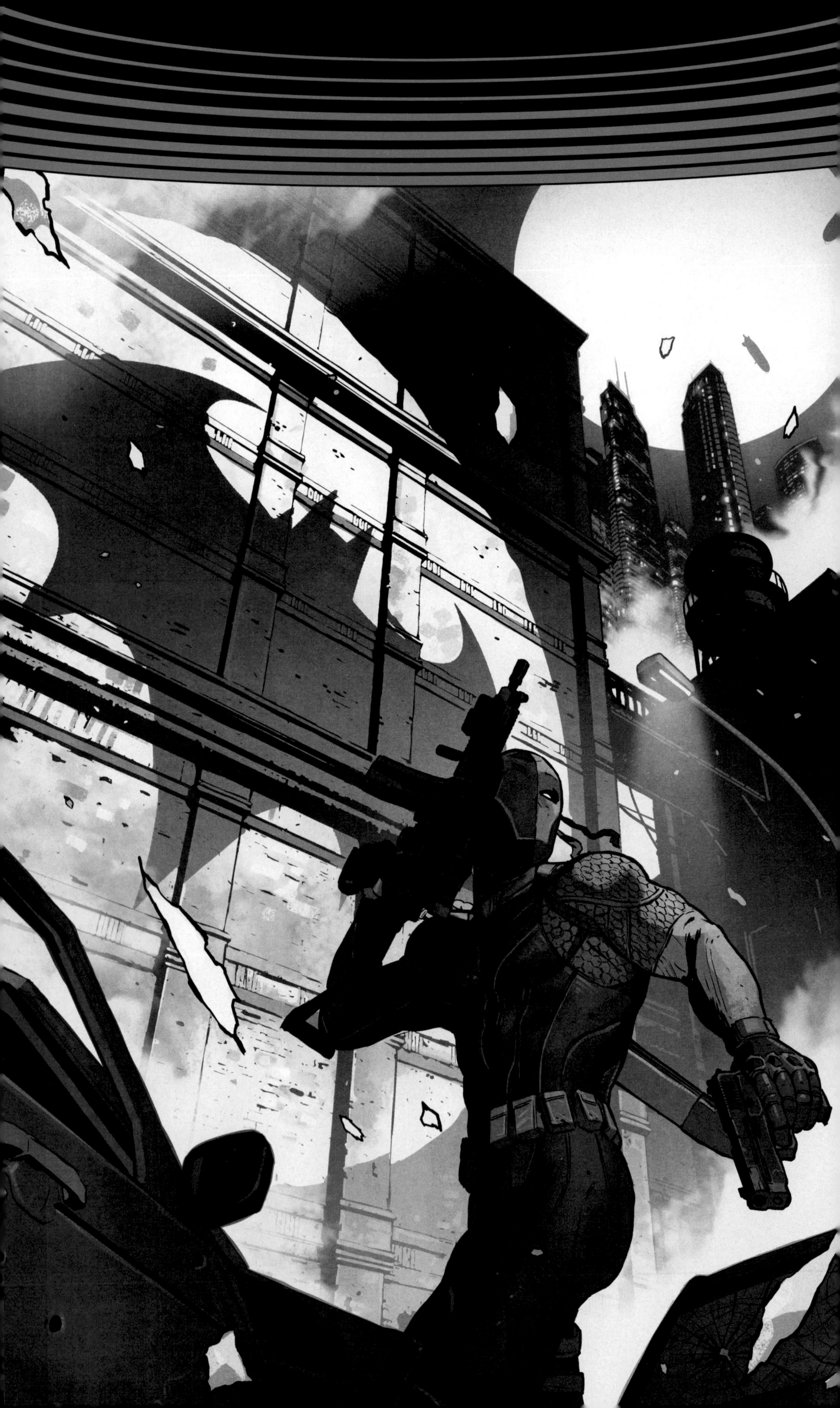

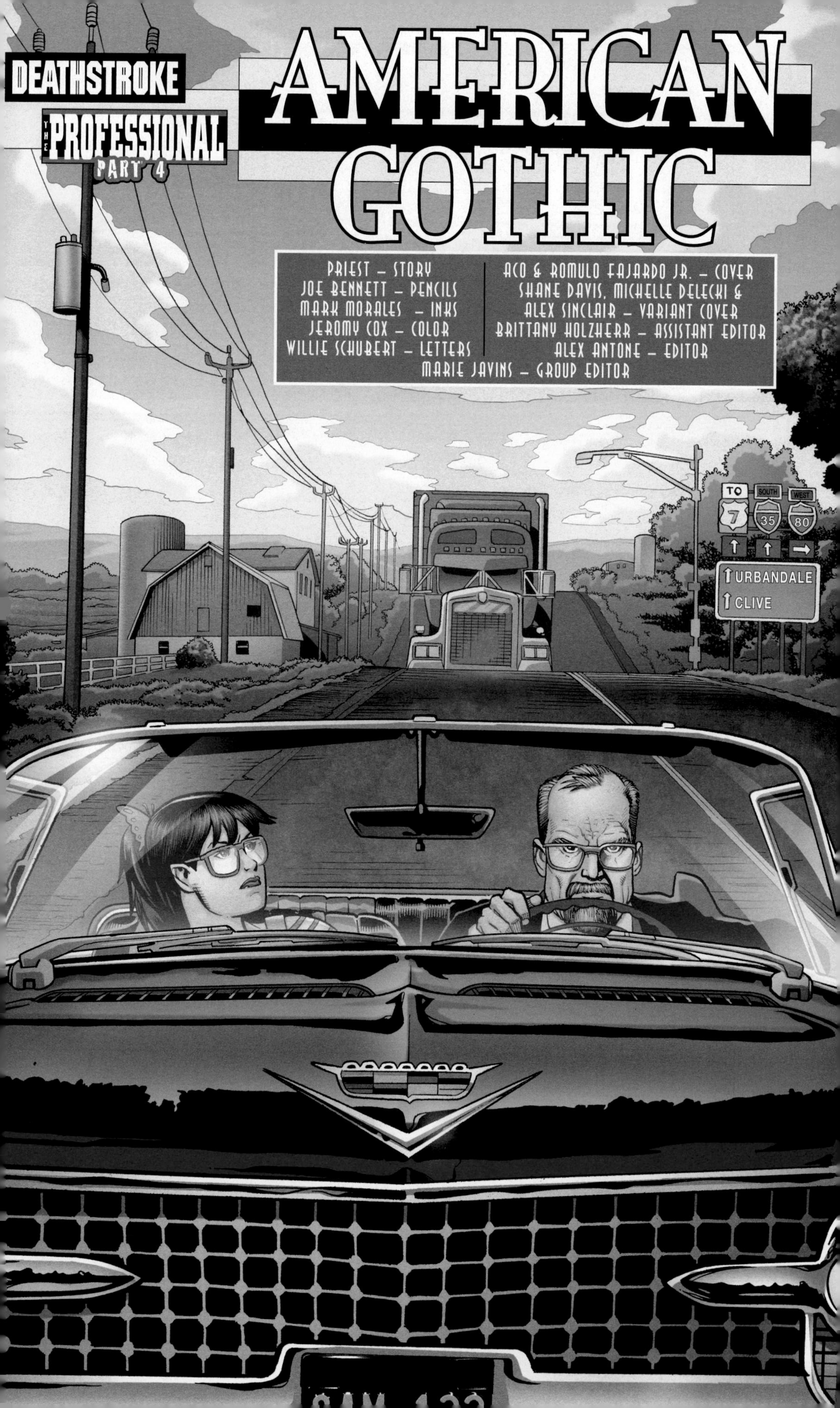

DEATHSTROKE
THE PROFESSIONAL
PART 4
AMERICAN GOTHIC
PRIEST – STORY
JOE BENNETT – PENCILS
MARK MORALES – INKS
JEROMY COX – COLOR
WILLIE SCHUBERT – LETTERS
ACO & ROMULO FAJARDO JR. – COVER
SHANE DAVIS, MICHELLE DELECKI &
ALEX SINCLAIR – VARIANT COVER
BRITTANY HOLZHERR – ASSISTANT EDITOR
ALEX ANTONE – EDITOR
MARIE JAVINS – GROUP EDITOR
TO 7
SOUTH 35
WEST 80
URBANDALE
CLIVE

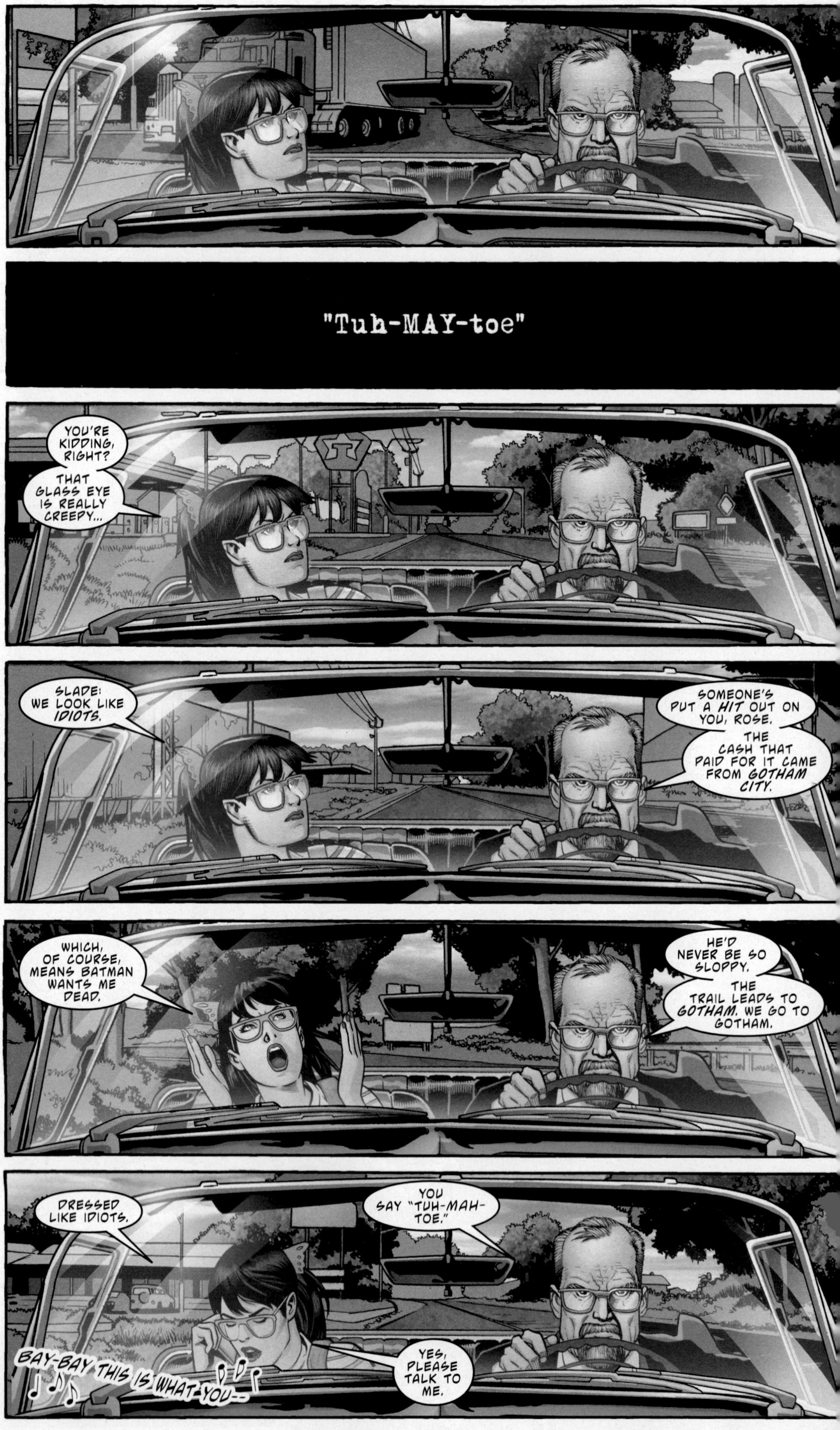

"Tuh-MAY-toe"
YOU'RE KIDDING, RIGHT?
THAT GLASS EYE IS REALLY CREEPY...
SLADE: WE LOOK LIKE IDIOTS.
SOMEONE'S PUT A HIT OUT ON YOU, ROSE.
THE CASH THAT PAID FOR IT CAME FROM GOTHAM CITY.
WHICH, OF COURSE, MEANS BATMAN WANTS ME DEAD.
HE'D NEVER BE SO SLOPPY.
THE TRAIL LEADS TO GOTHAM. WE GO TO GOTHAM.
DRESSED LIKE IDIOTS.
YOU SAY "TUH-MAH-TOE."
BAY-BAY THIS IS WHAT YOU--
YES, PLEASE TALK TO ME.

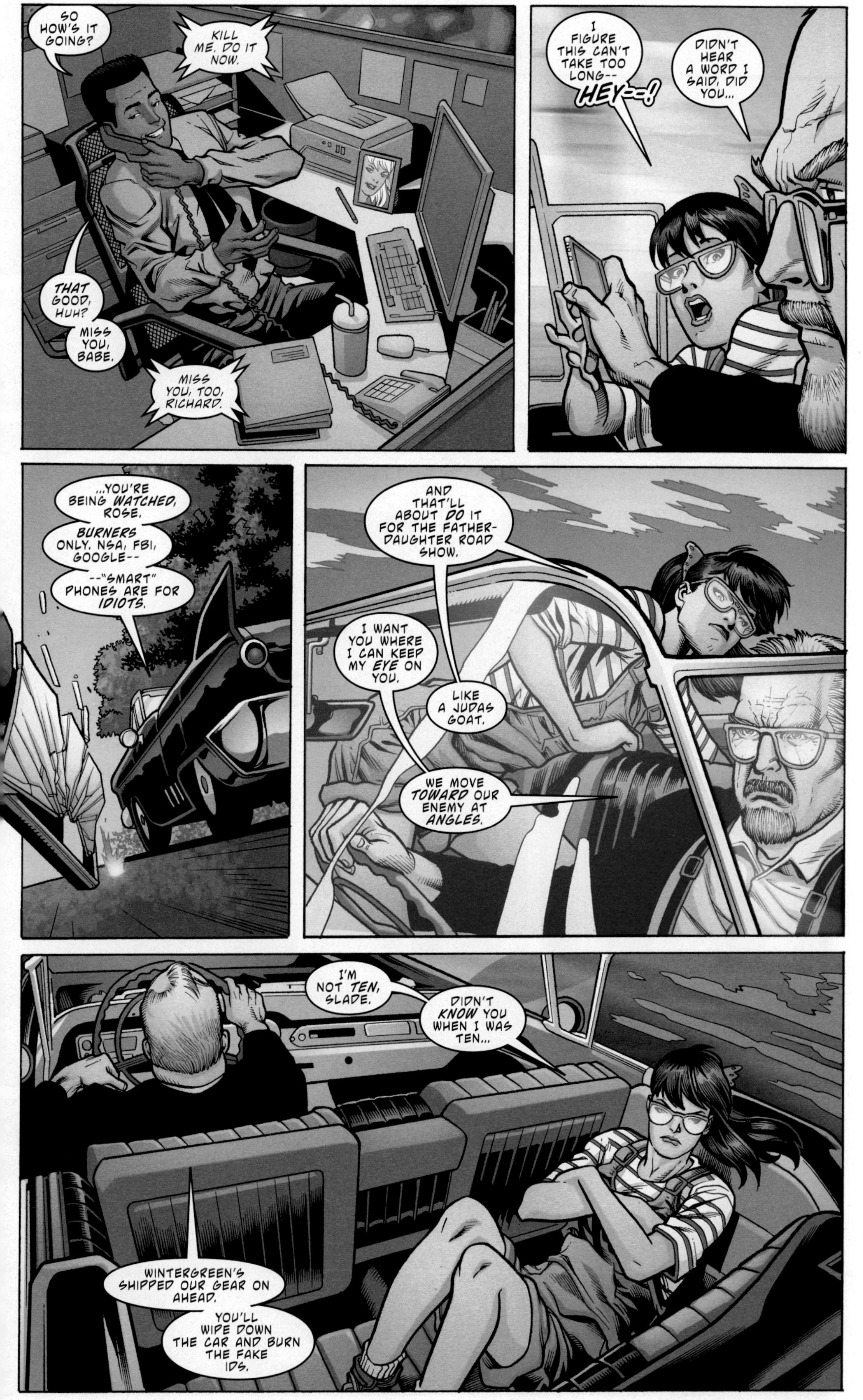
SO HOW'S IT GOING?
KILL ME. DO IT NOW.
THAT GOOD, HUH?
MISS YOU, BABE.
MISS YOU, TOO, RICHARD.
I FIGURE THIS CAN'T TAKE TOO LONG-- HEY--!
DIDN'T HEAR A WORD I SAID, DID YOU...
...YOU'RE BEING WATCHED, ROSE.
BURNERS ONLY. NSA, FBI, GOOGLE--
--"SMART" PHONES ARE FOR IDIOTS.
AND THAT'LL ABOUT DO IT FOR THE FATHER-DAUGHTER ROAD SHOW.
I WANT YOU WHERE I CAN KEEP MY EYE ON YOU.
LIKE A JUDAS GOAT.
WE MOVE TOWARD OUR ENEMY AT ANGLES.
I'M NOT TEN, SLADE.
DIDN'T KNOW YOU WHEN I WAS TEN...
WINTERGREEN'S SHIPPED OUR GEAR ON AHEAD.
YOU'LL WIPE DOWN THE CAR AND BURN THE FAKE IDS.

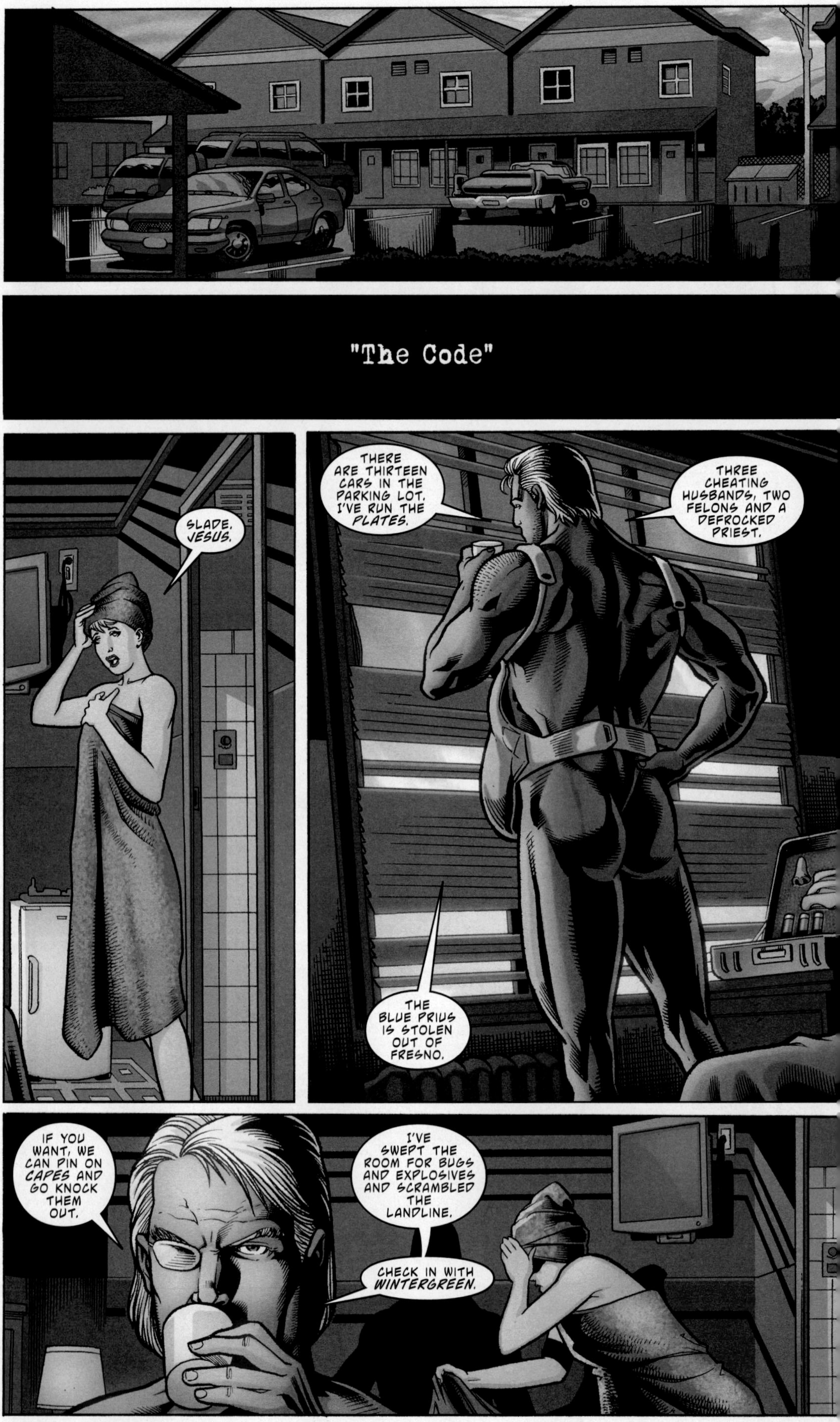
"The Code"
SLADE. JESUS.
THERE ARE THIRTEEN CARS IN THE PARKING LOT. I'VE RUN THE PLATES.
THREE CHEATING HUSBANDS, TWO FELONS AND A DEFROCKED PRIEST.
THE BLUE PRIUS IS STOLEN OUT OF FRESNO.
IF YOU WANT, WE CAN PIN ON CAPES AND GO KNOCK THEM OUT.
I'VE SWEPT THE ROOM FOR BUGS AND EXPLOSIVES AND SCRAMBLED THE LANDLINE.
CHECK IN WITH WINTERGREEN.

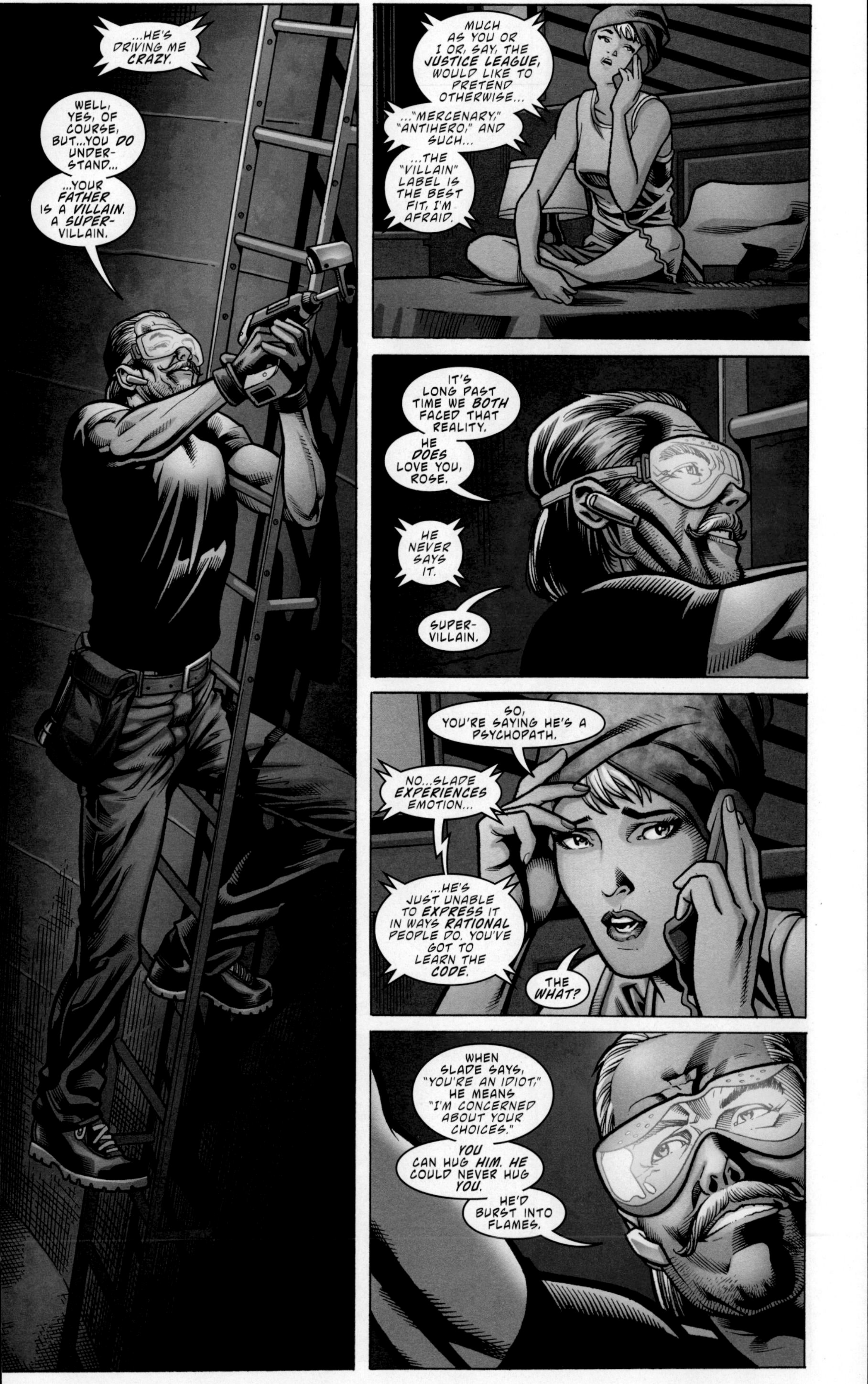
...HE'S DRIVING ME CRAZY.
WELL, YES, OF COURSE, BUT...YOU DO UNDER-STAND...
...YOUR FATHER IS A VILLAIN. A SUPER-VILLAIN.
MUCH AS YOU OR I OR, SAY, THE JUSTICE LEAGUE, WOULD LIKE TO PRETEND OTHERWISE...
..."MERCENARY," "ANTIHERO," AND SUCH...
...THE "VILLAIN" LABEL IS THE BEST FIT, I'M AFRAID.
IT'S LONG PAST TIME WE BOTH FACED THAT REALITY.
HE DOES LOVE YOU, ROSE.
HE NEVER SAYS IT.
SUPER-VILLAIN.
SO, YOU'RE SAYING HE'S A PSYCHOPATH.
NO...SLADE EXPERIENCES EMOTION...
...HE'S JUST UNABLE TO EXPRESS IT IN WAYS RATIONAL PEOPLE DO. YOU'VE GOT TO LEARN THE CODE.
THE WHAT?
WHEN SLADE SAYS, "YOU'RE AN IDIOT," HE MEANS "I'M CONCERNED ABOUT YOUR CHOICES."
YOU CAN HUG HIM. HE COULD NEVER HUG YOU.
HE'D BURST INTO FLAMES.

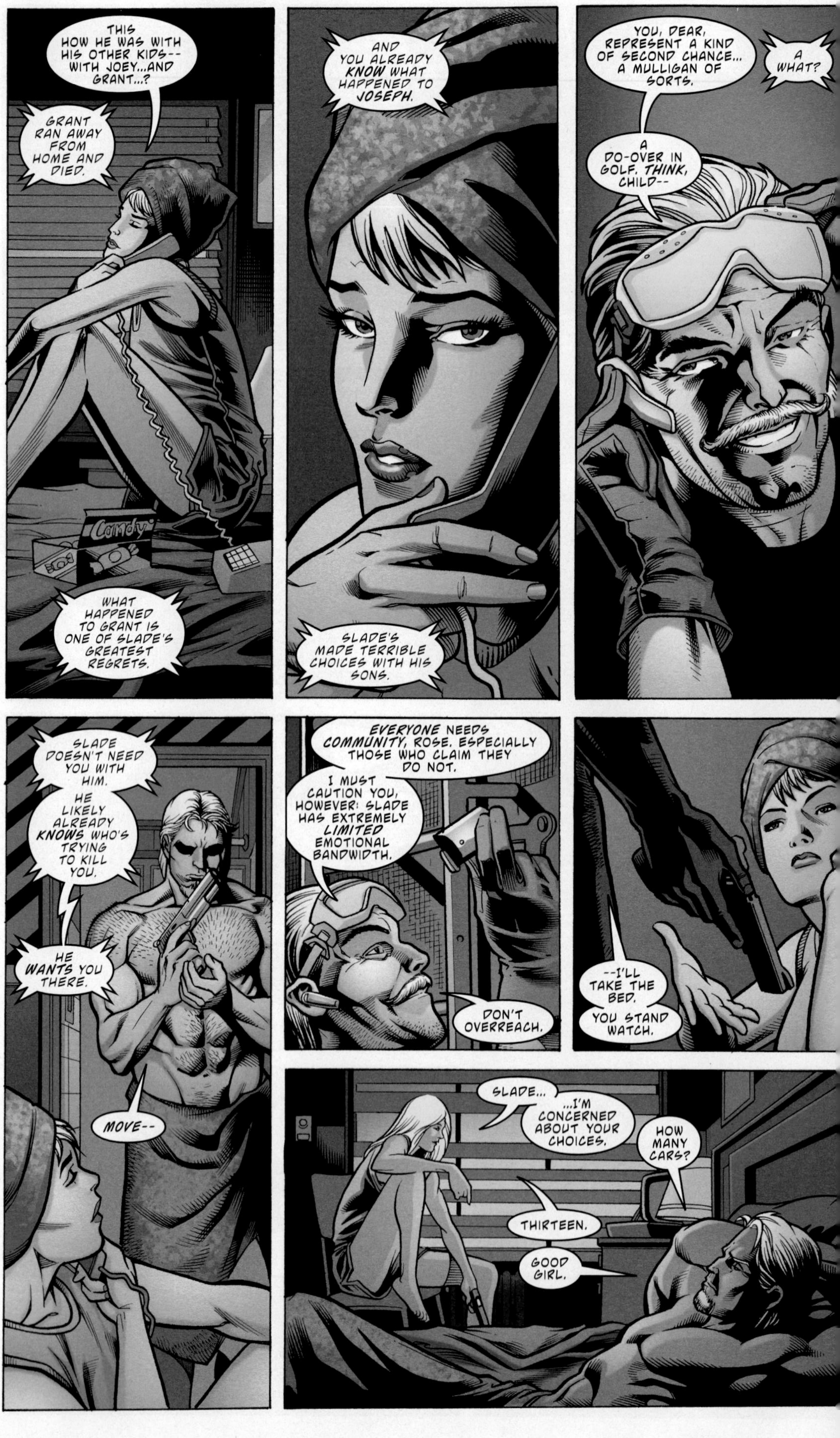

THIS HOW HE WAS WITH HIS OTHER KIDS-- WITH JOEY...AND GRANT...?
GRANT RAN AWAY FROM HOME AND DIED.
WHAT HAPPENED TO GRANT IS ONE OF SLADE'S GREATEST REGRETS.
AND YOU ALREADY KNOW WHAT HAPPENED TO JOSEPH.
SLADE'S MADE TERRIBLE CHOICES WITH HIS SONS.
YOU, DEAR, REPRESENT A KIND OF SECOND CHANCE... A MULLIGAN OF SORTS.
A WHAT?
A DO-OVER IN GOLF. THINK, CHILD--
SLADE DOESN'T NEED YOU WITH HIM.
HE LIKELY ALREADY KNOWS WHO'S TRYING TO KILL YOU.
HE WANTS YOU THERE.
MOVE--
EVERYONE NEEDS COMMUNITY, ROSE, ESPECIALLY THOSE WHO CLAIM THEY DO NOT.
I MUST CAUTION YOU, HOWEVER: SLADE HAS EXTREMELY LIMITED EMOTIONAL BANDWIDTH.
DON'T OVERREACH.
--I'LL TAKE THE BED.
YOU STAND WATCH.
SLADE...
...I'M CONCERNED ABOUT YOUR CHOICES.
HOW MANY CARS?
THIRTEEN.
GOOD GIRL.

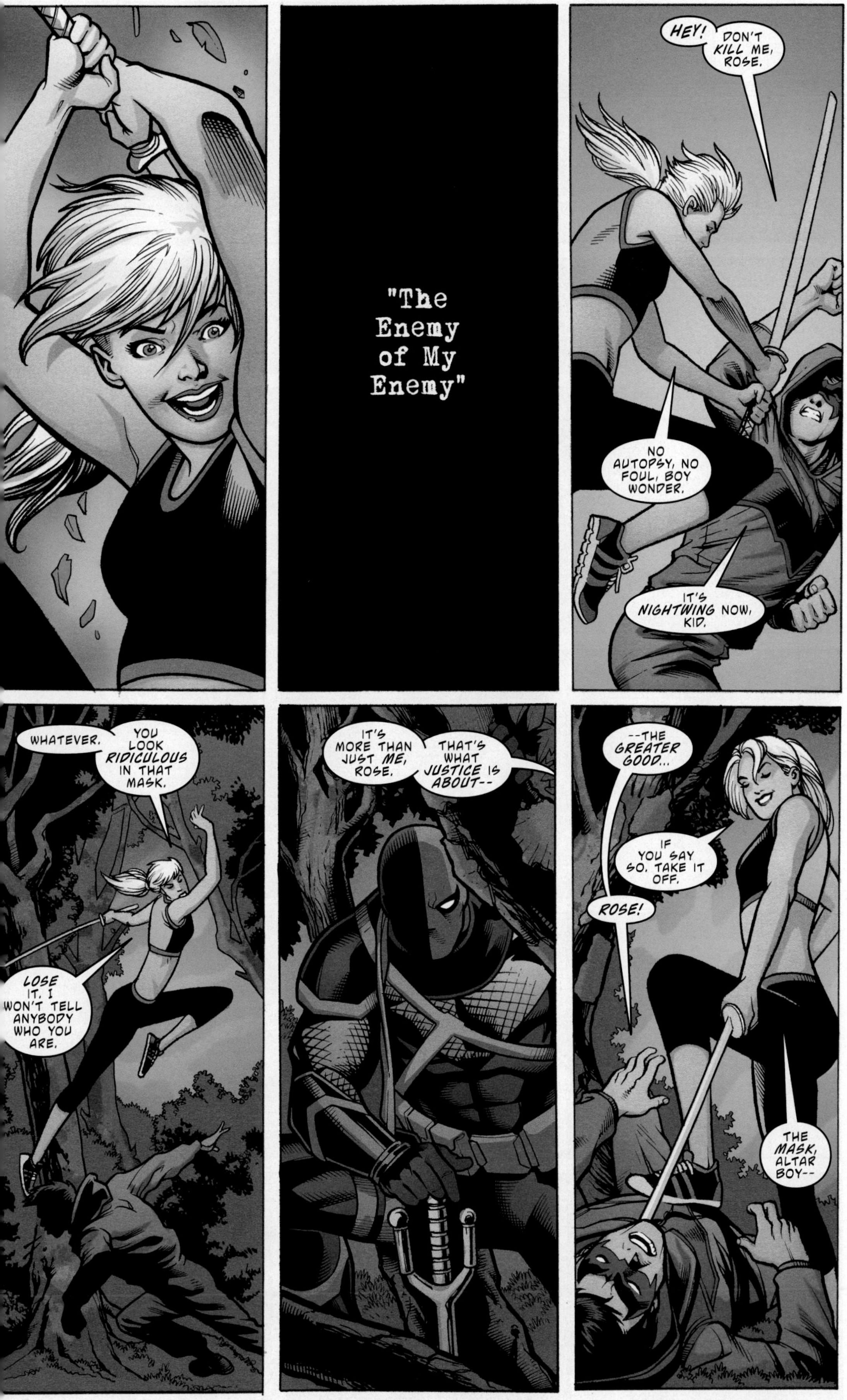
"The Enemy of My Enemy"
HEY!
DON'T KILL ME, ROSE.
NO AUTOPSY, NO FOUL, BOY WONDER.
IT'S NIGHTWING NOW, KID.
WHATEVER.
YOU LOOK RIDICULOUS IN THAT MASK.
LOSE IT. I WON'T TELL ANYBODY WHO YOU ARE.
IT'S MORE THAN JUST ME, ROSE.
THAT'S WHAT JUSTICE IS ABOUT--
--THE GREATER GOOD...
IF YOU SAY SO. TAKE IT OFF.
ROSE!
THE MASK, ALTAR BOY--

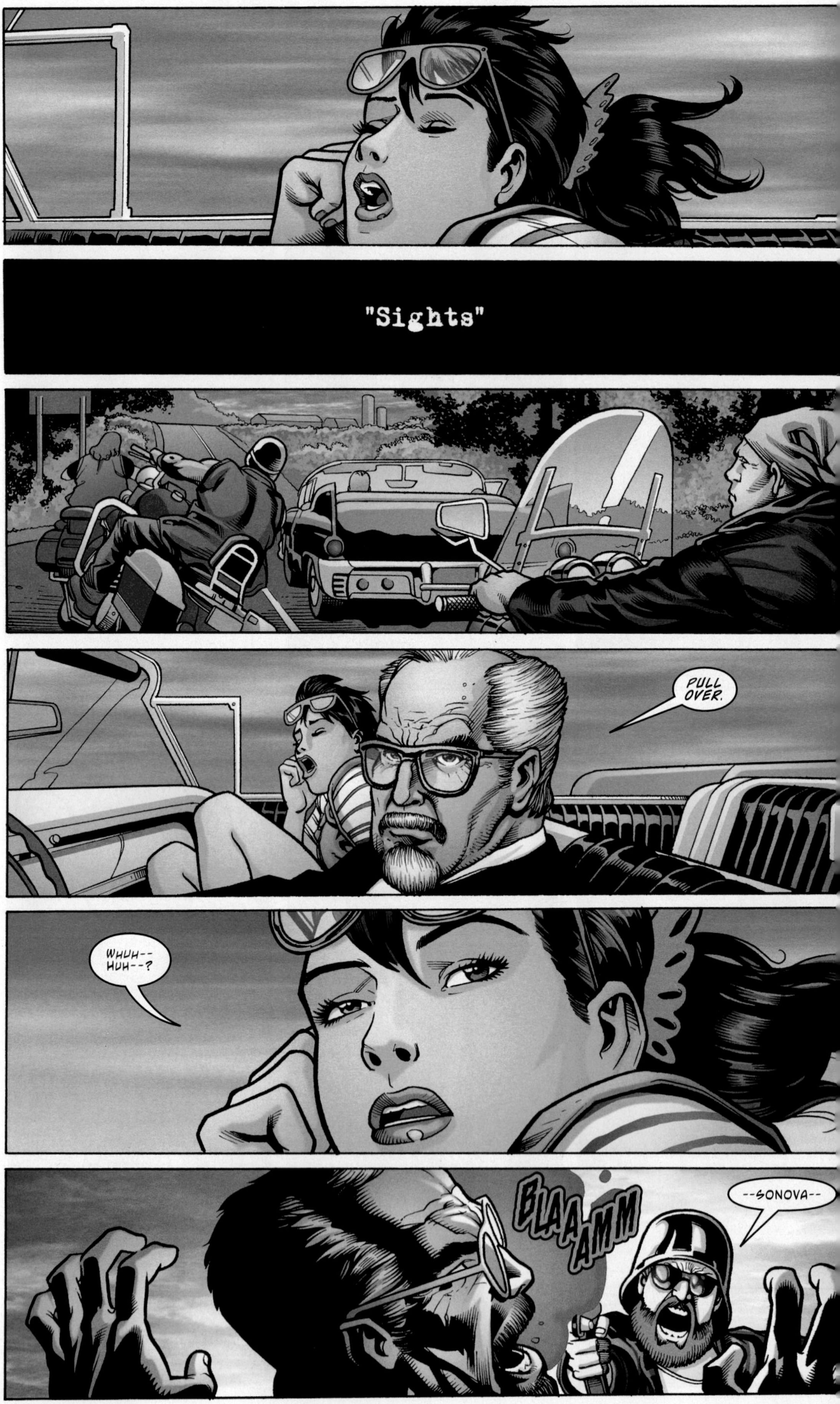
"Sights"
PULL OVER.
WHUH-- HUH--?
BLAAAMM
--SONOVA--

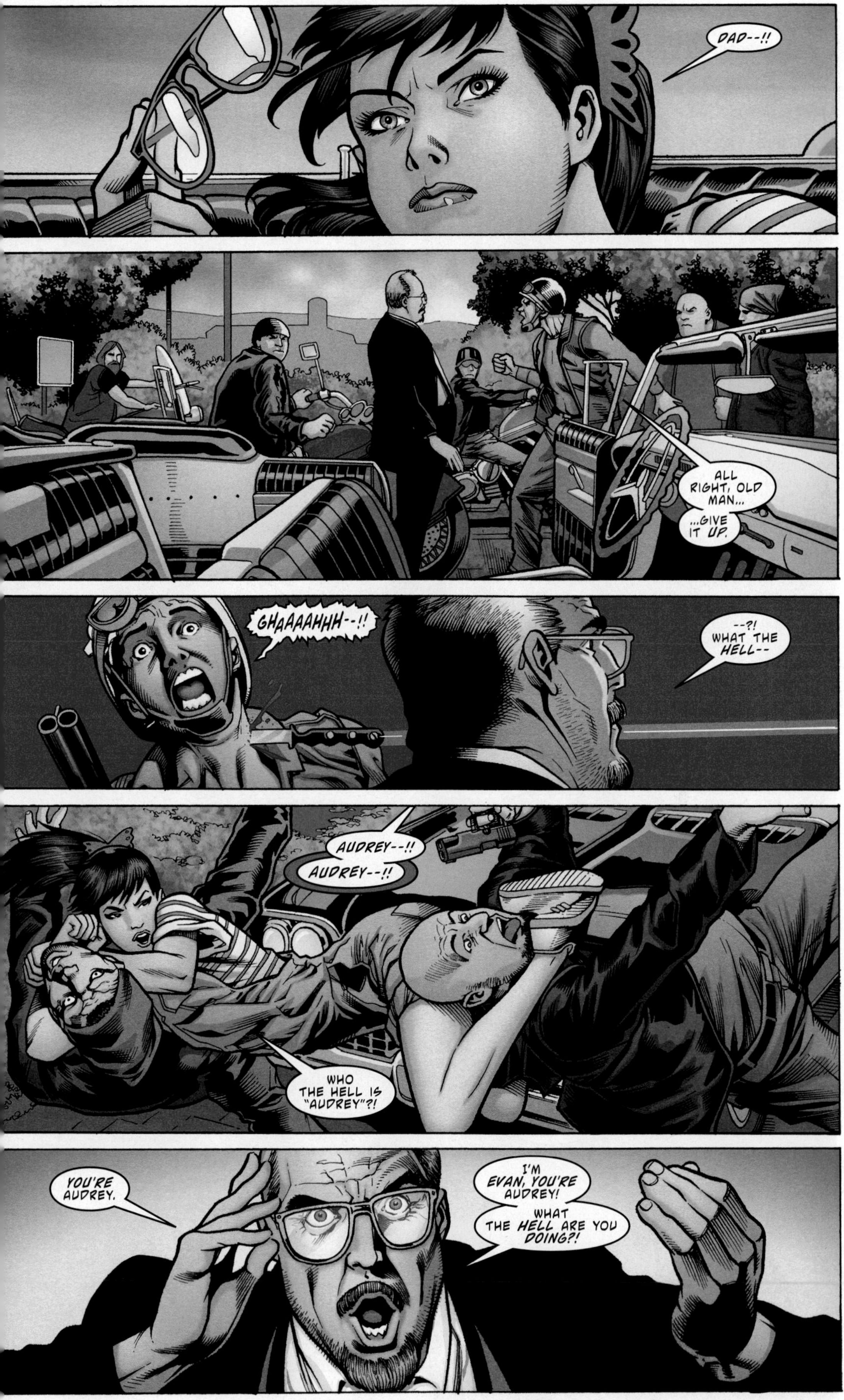
DAD--!!
ALL RIGHT, OLD MAN...
...GIVE IT UP.
GHAAAAHHH--!!
--?! WHAT THE HELL--
AUDREY--!!
AUDREY--!!
WHO THE HELL IS "AUDREY"?!
YOU'RE AUDREY.
I'M EVAN, YOU'RE AUDREY!
WHAT THE HELL ARE YOU DOING?!

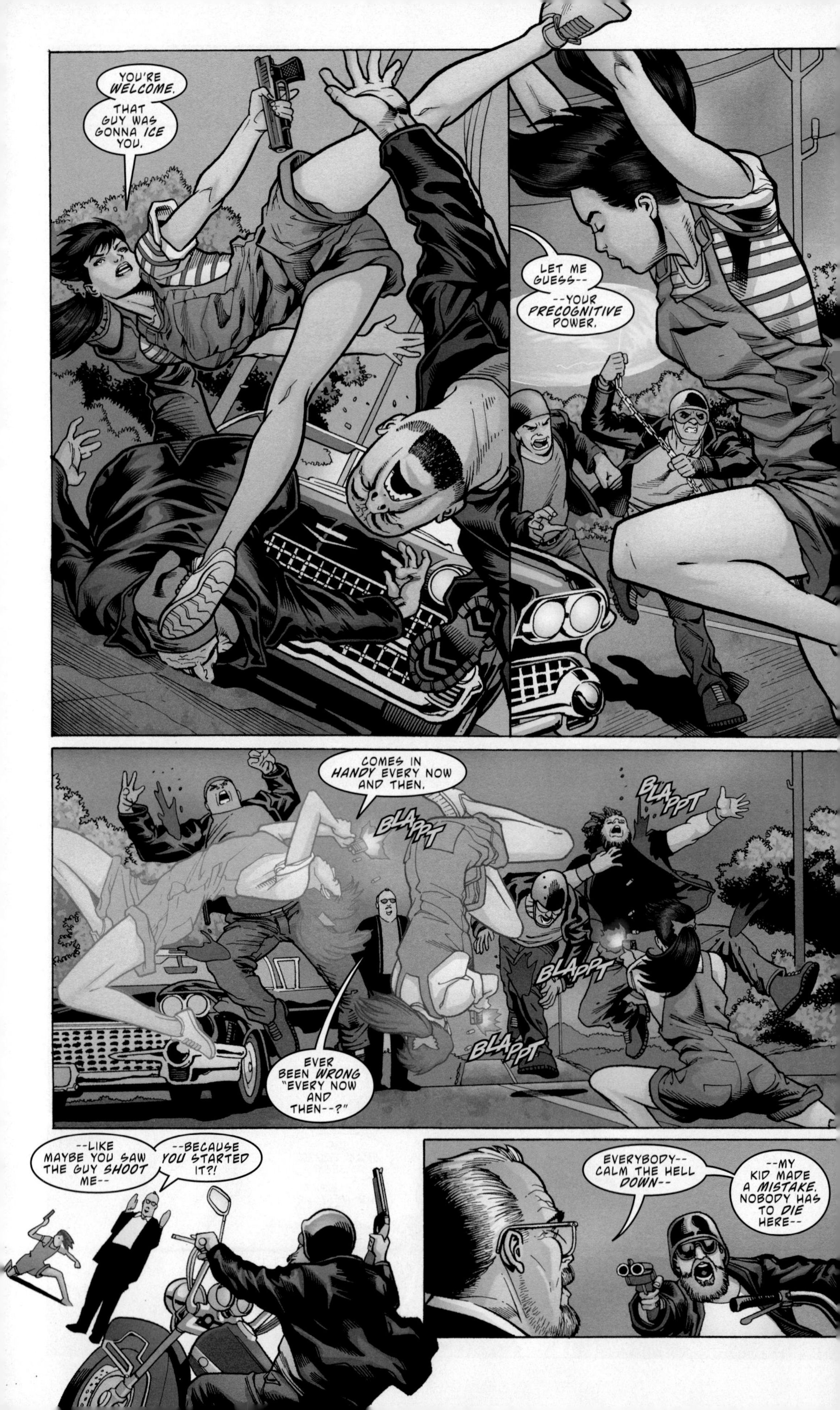

YOU'RE WELCOME. THAT GUY WAS GONNA ICE YOU.
LET ME GUESS--
--YOUR PRECOGNITIVE POWER.
COMES IN HANDY EVERY NOW AND THEN.
BLAPPT
BLAPPT
EVER BEEN WRONG "EVERY NOW AND THEN--?"
BLAPPT
BLAPPT
--LIKE MAYBE YOU SAW THE GUY SHOOT ME--
--BECAUSE YOU STARTED IT?!
EVERYBODY-- CALM THE HELL DOWN--
--MY KID MADE A MISTAKE. NOBODY HAS TO DIE HERE--

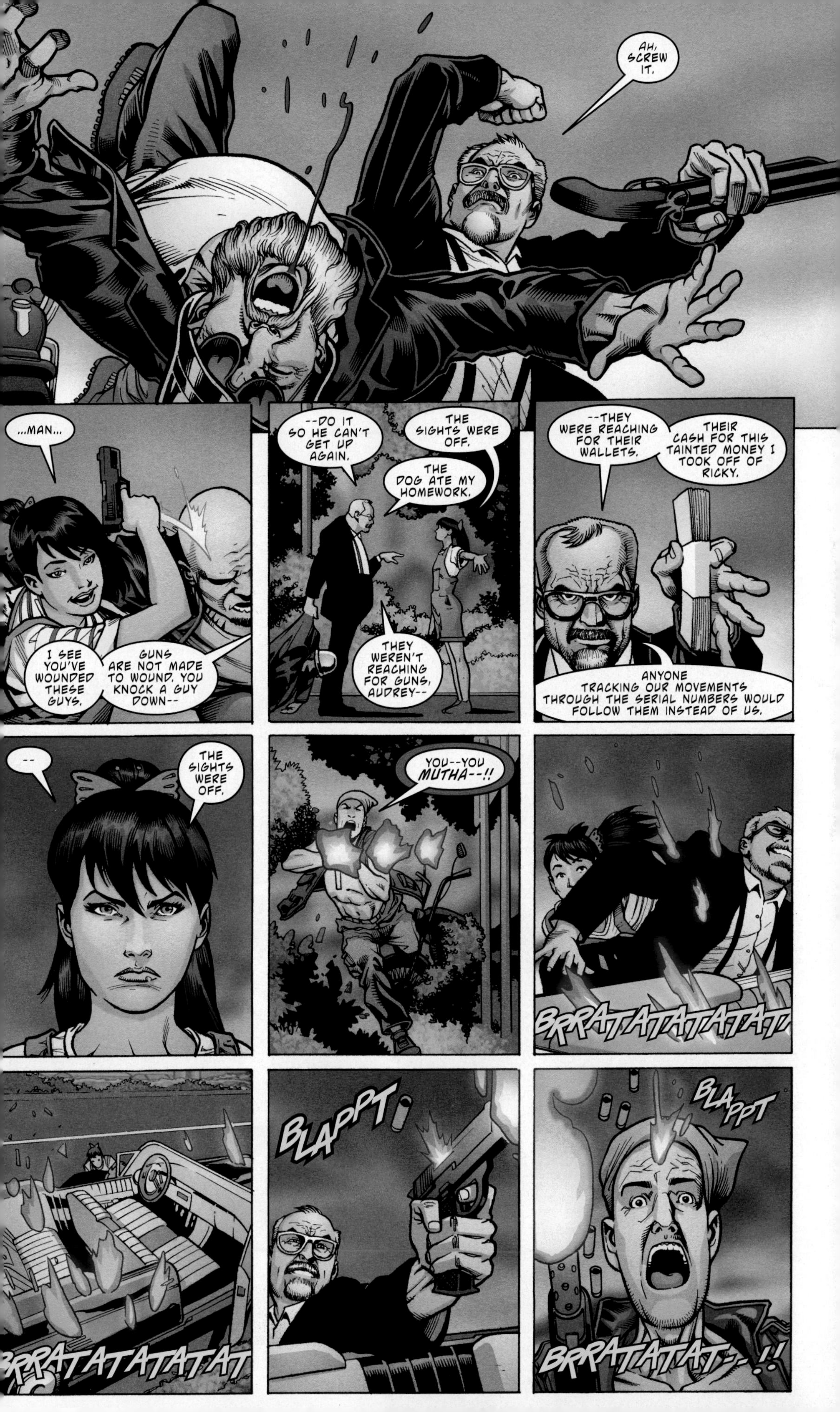
AH, SCREW IT.
...MAN...
I SEE YOU'VE WOUNDED THESE GUYS.
GUNS ARE NOT MADE TO WOUND. YOU KNOCK A GUY DOWN--
--DO IT SO HE CAN'T GET UP AGAIN.
THE SIGHTS WERE OFF.
THE DOG ATE MY HOMEWORK.
THEY WEREN'T REACHING FOR GUNS, AUDREY--
--THEY WERE REACHING FOR THEIR WALLETS.
THEIR CASH FOR THIS TAINTED MONEY I TOOK OFF OF RICKY.
ANYONE TRACKING OUR MOVEMENTS THROUGH THE SERIAL NUMBERS WOULD FOLLOW THEM INSTEAD OF US.
--
THE SIGHTS WERE OFF.
YOU--YOU MUTHA--!!
BRRATATATATATAT
BRRATATATATATAT
BLAPPT
BLAPPT
BRRATATAT--!!

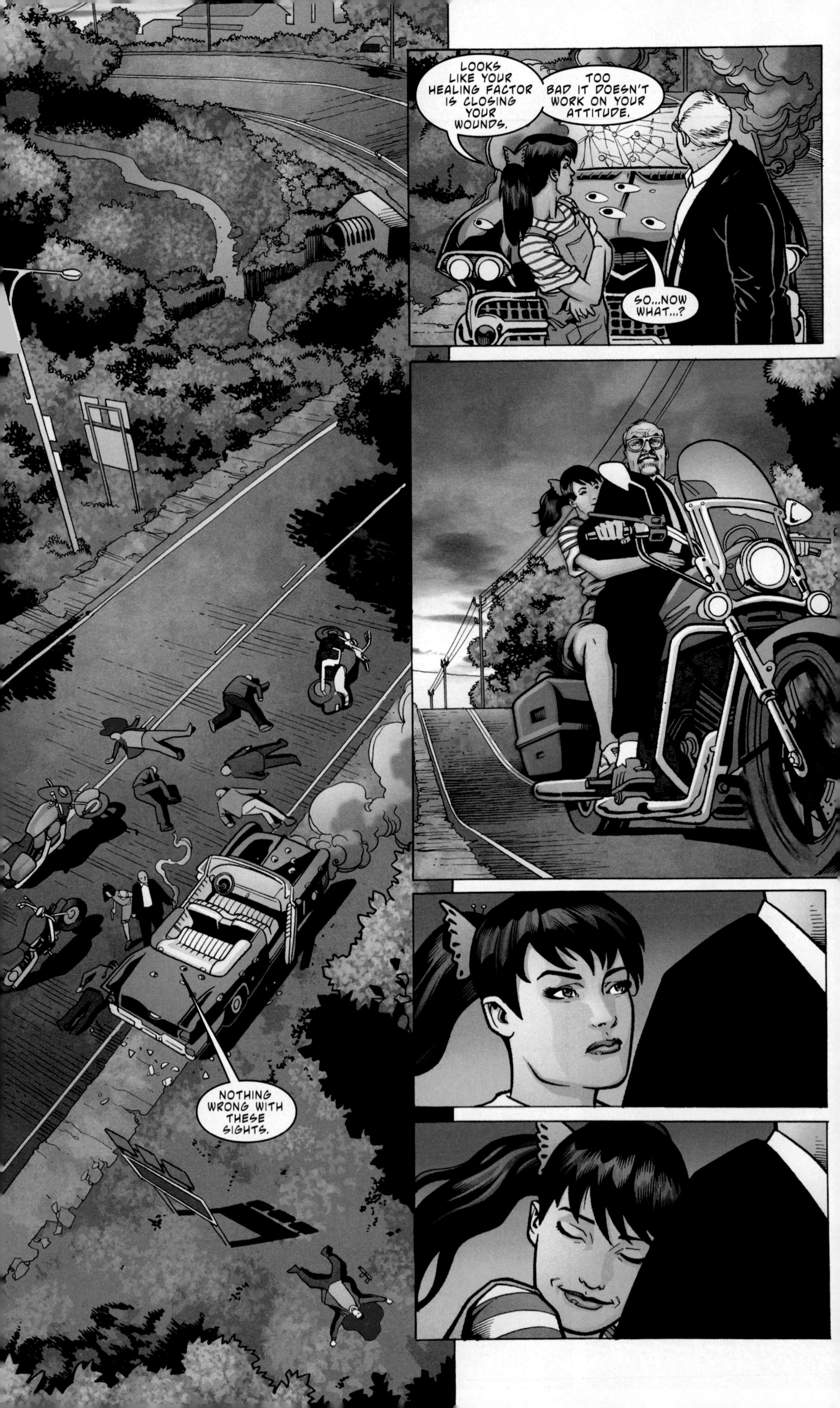

NOTHING WRONG WITH THESE SIGHTS.
LOOKS LIKE YOUR HEALING FACTOR IS CLOSING YOUR WOUNDS.
TOO BAD IT DOESN'T WORK ON YOUR ATTITUDE.
SO...NOW WHAT...?

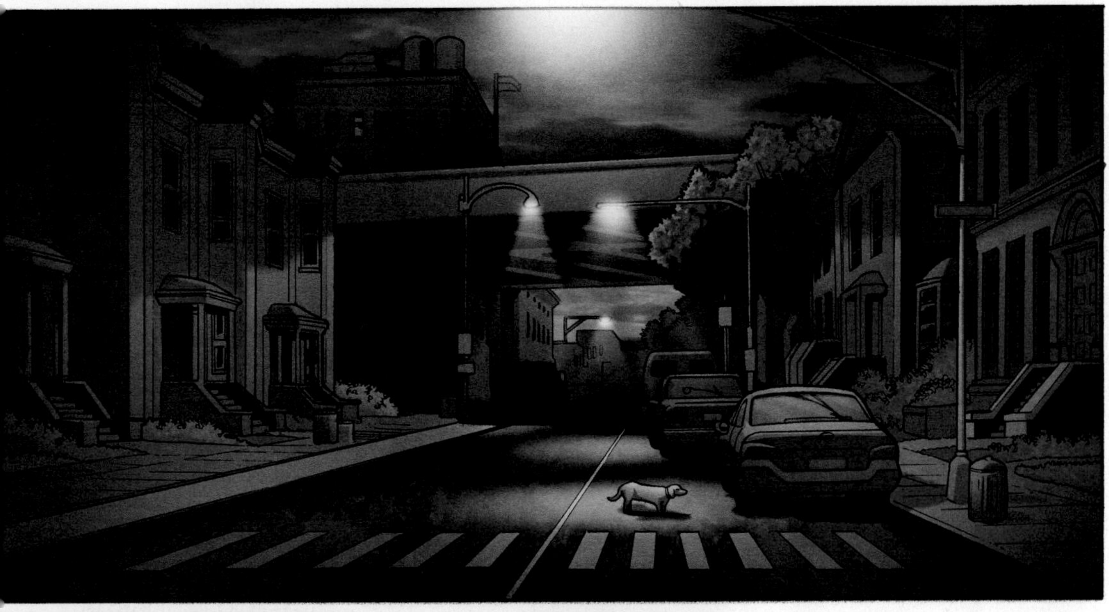

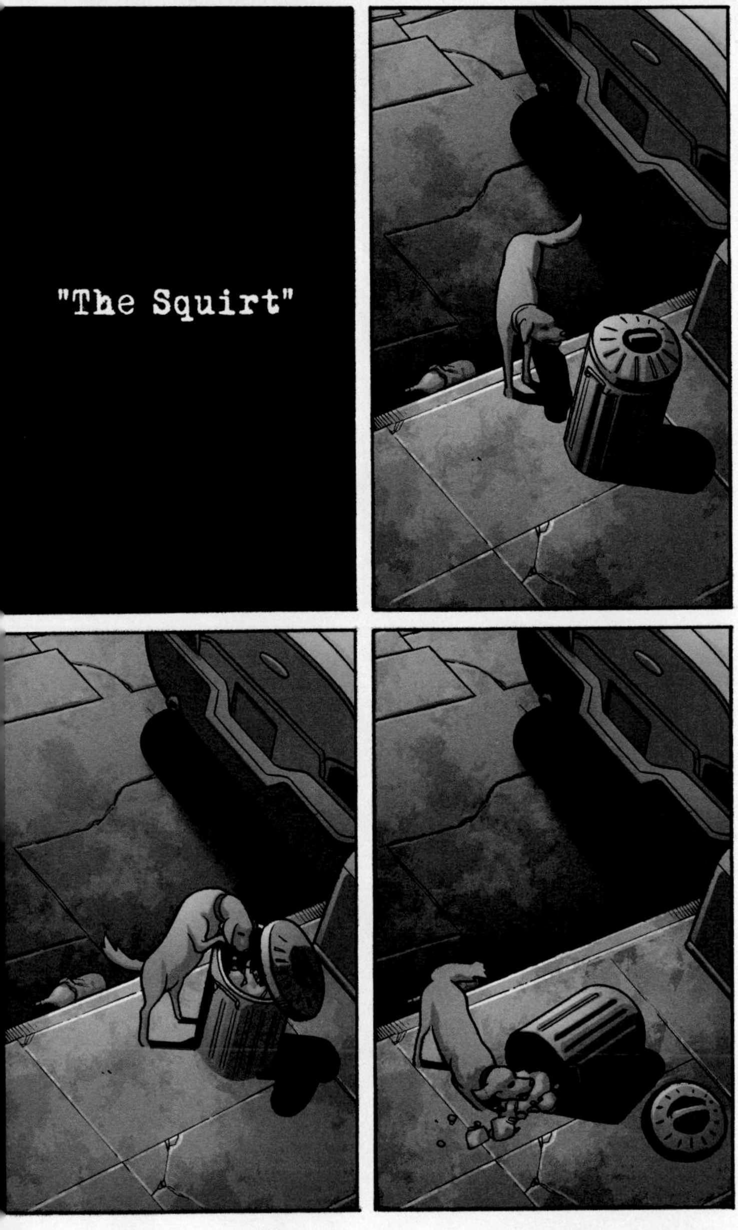
"The Squirt"

William Randolph Wintergreen

A-Squadron 22 HMS Special Air Service, Ret.

Slade couldn't be sure he would appear, but, suddenly, there he was: lost in the shadows of the Queensland Park El--the God Spot--surveying the area while remaining totally invisible. Slade scanned him several times and every scan came back with ever more useless data.

The man had almost no heat signature, which meant he was wearing body armor. Slade couldn't get his definitive height or weight because the man had a cloak he kept rearranging. He kept his mouth shut so no dental records were forthcoming. And he maintained complete radio silence.

The Batman.

The fact that Slade had spotted him at all meant Slade's cover was blown. Which, after all, was the plan.

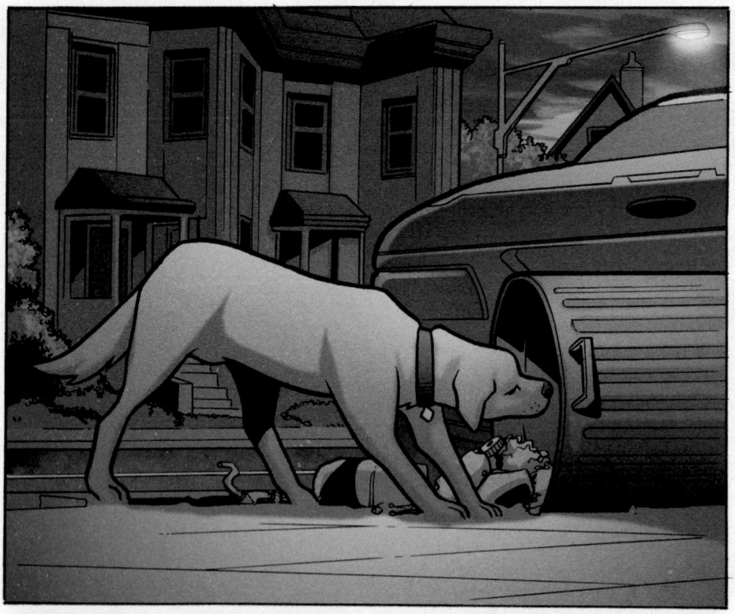

Slade couldn't help but admire Batman's tactics.

The infrared laser mic in the booze bottle. The ultrasonic whistle spiked into the lawn that summoned the stray dog with the heat sensor built into its flea collar. The impressive attempts to jam Slade's uplink to Hosun, Slade's hacker. Hosun had planted encrypted coordinates on the Gotham Police Commissioner's laptop.

Of course, the boy had no idea who he was actually working for.

Slade didn't doubt Batman would get his summons, but couldn't be sure he'd respond.

Slade often thought Batman would make a great assassin. He admired the work Batman did, and hoped he wouldn't have to kill him.

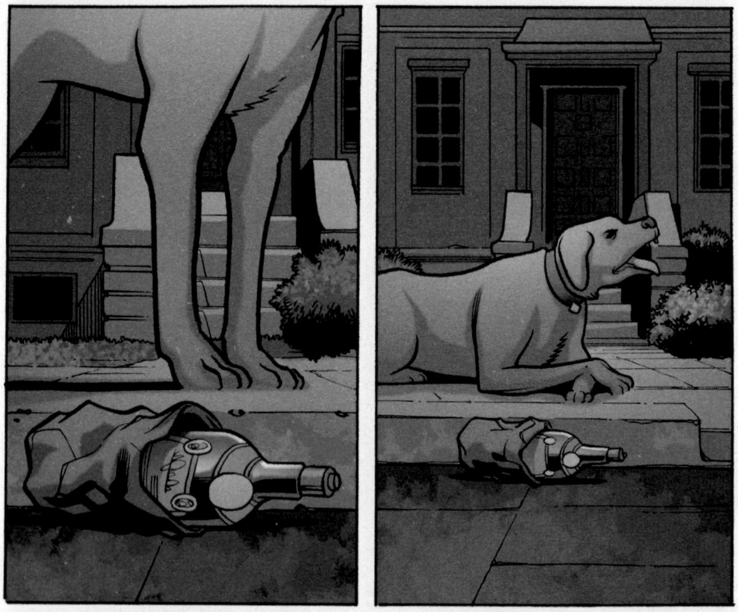

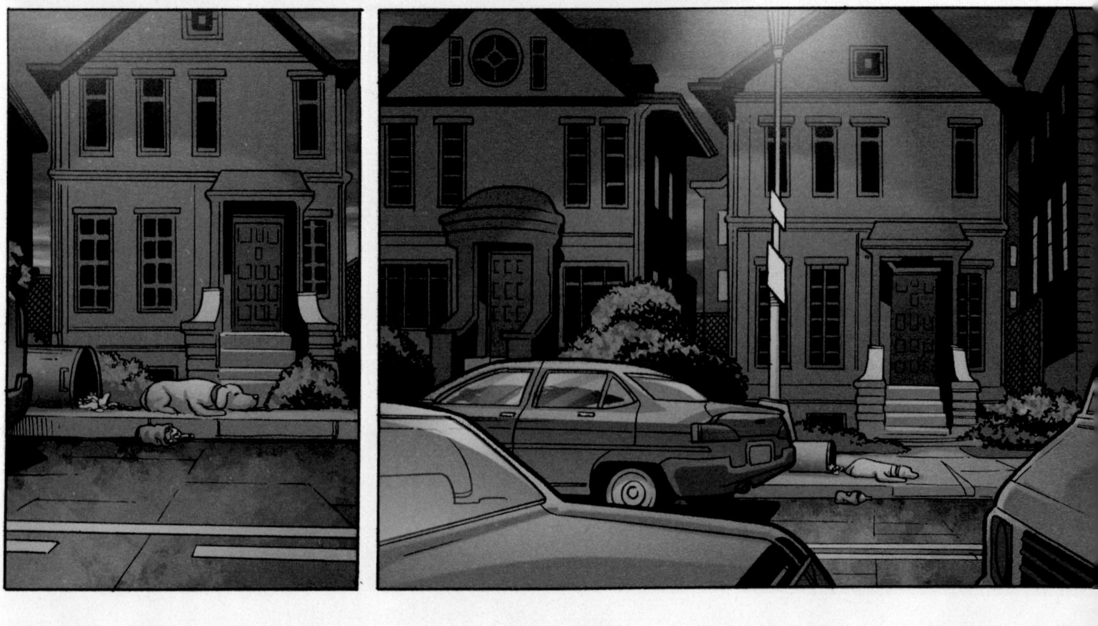

Right on cue.

Slade assumed if Batman didn't call in or make it home--

--someone would come looking for him. He assumed Batman was pretty useless in broad daylight.

Two things gave the boy away:

First, he had no heat signature. That meant some kind of armor.

Second, Hosun was very efficient. Slade knew who subscribed to the *Gotham Gazette*--and who didn't.

Slade knew the property tax status, current utility bills, and what time the sprinklers came on.

He knew when the mail arrived and what carrier was assigned the route. He knew the milk man's credit report.

He knew who was expecting parcel delivery, cable service, and whose car was about to be repossessed.

He knew the brakes on Mr. Freez-Cone's ice cream truck failed inspection three months ago.

The only thing Slade didn't know was what kind of sick bastard puts a child in the line of fire.

Batman had no reason to believe Slade wouldn't have killed his young accomplice on sight.

He admired Batman's apparently cold blood. And, in the eyeblink it took for Slade to experience that emotion--

--Batman vanished.

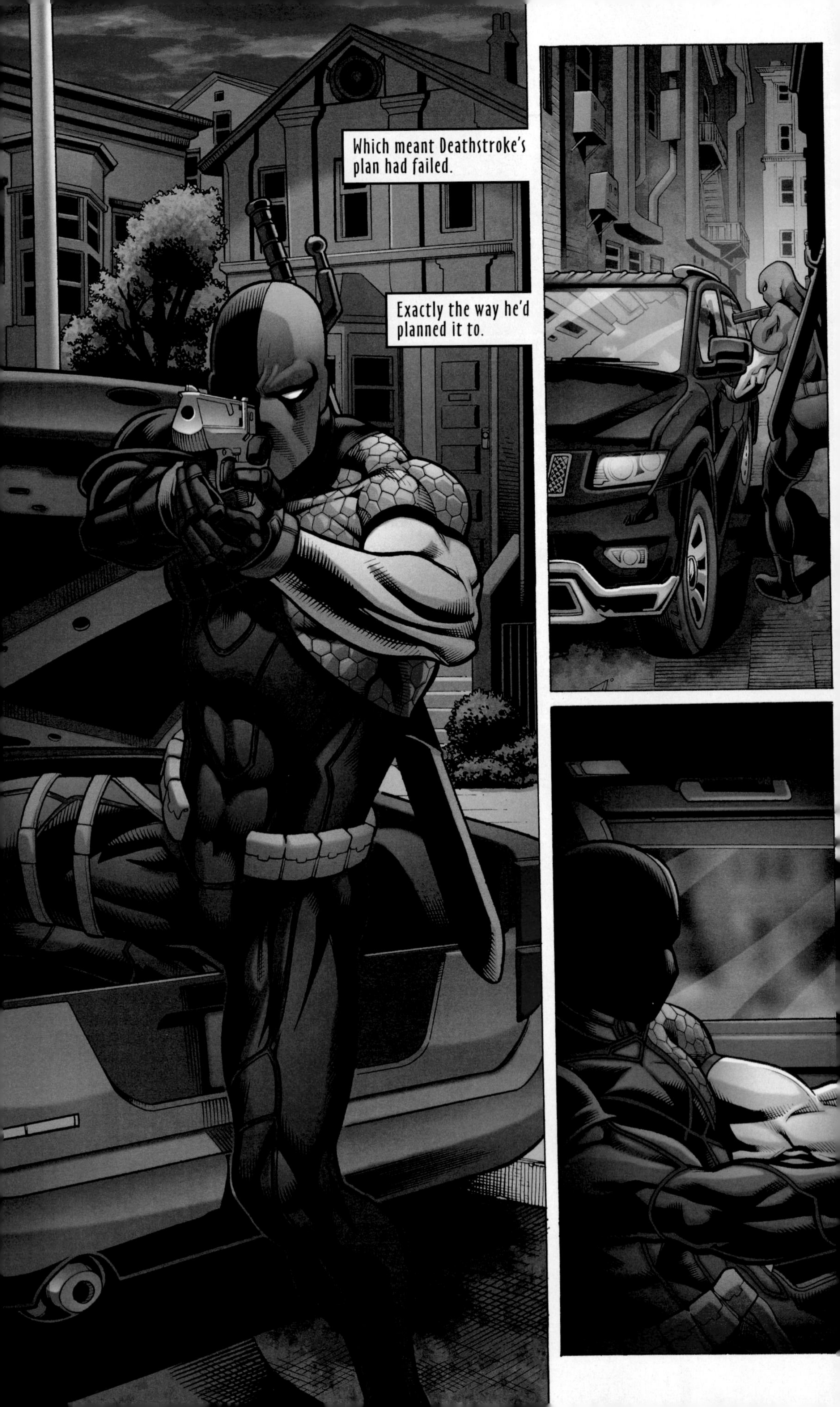
Which meant Deathstroke's plan had failed.
Exactly the way he'd planned it to.

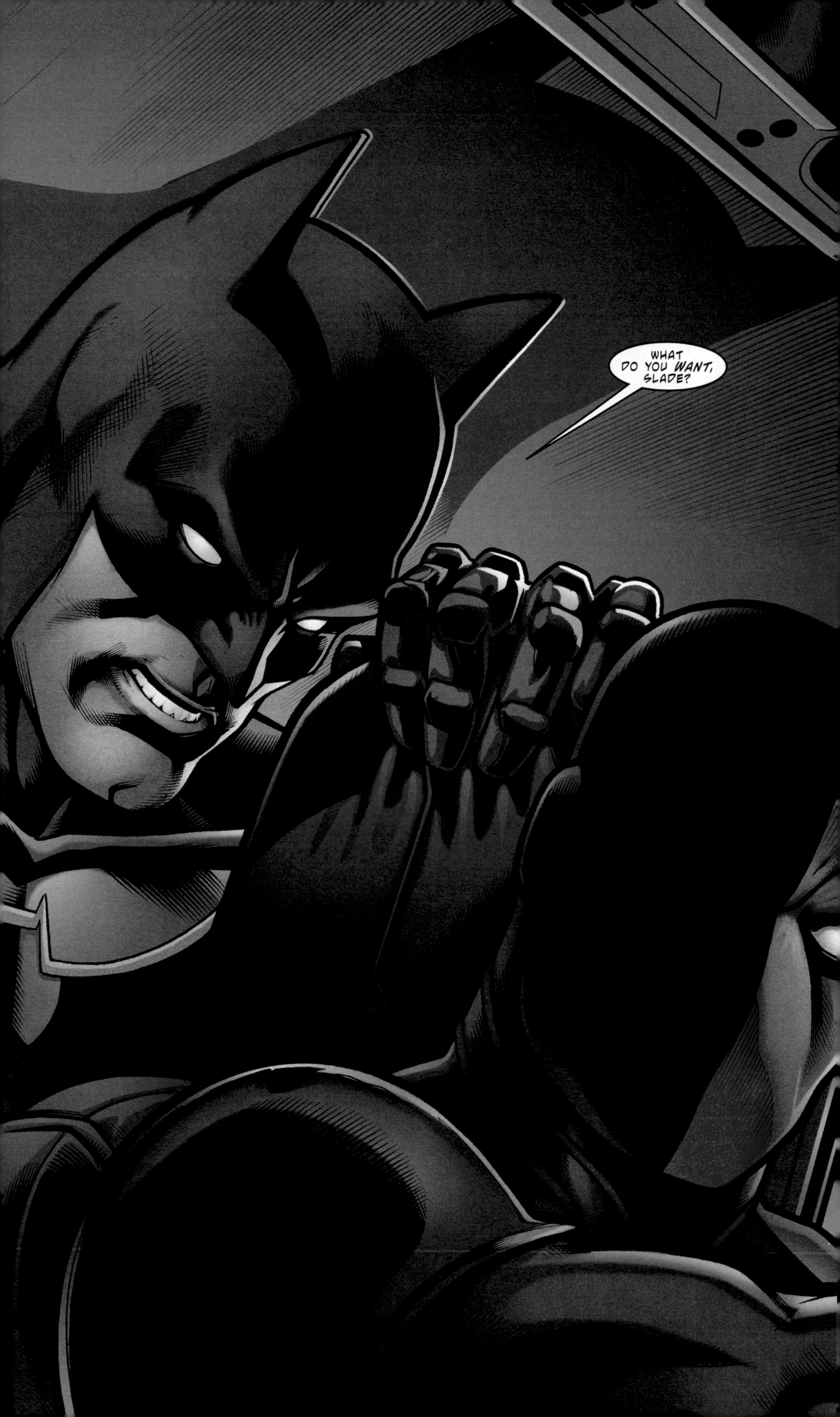
WHAT DO YOU WANT, SLADE?

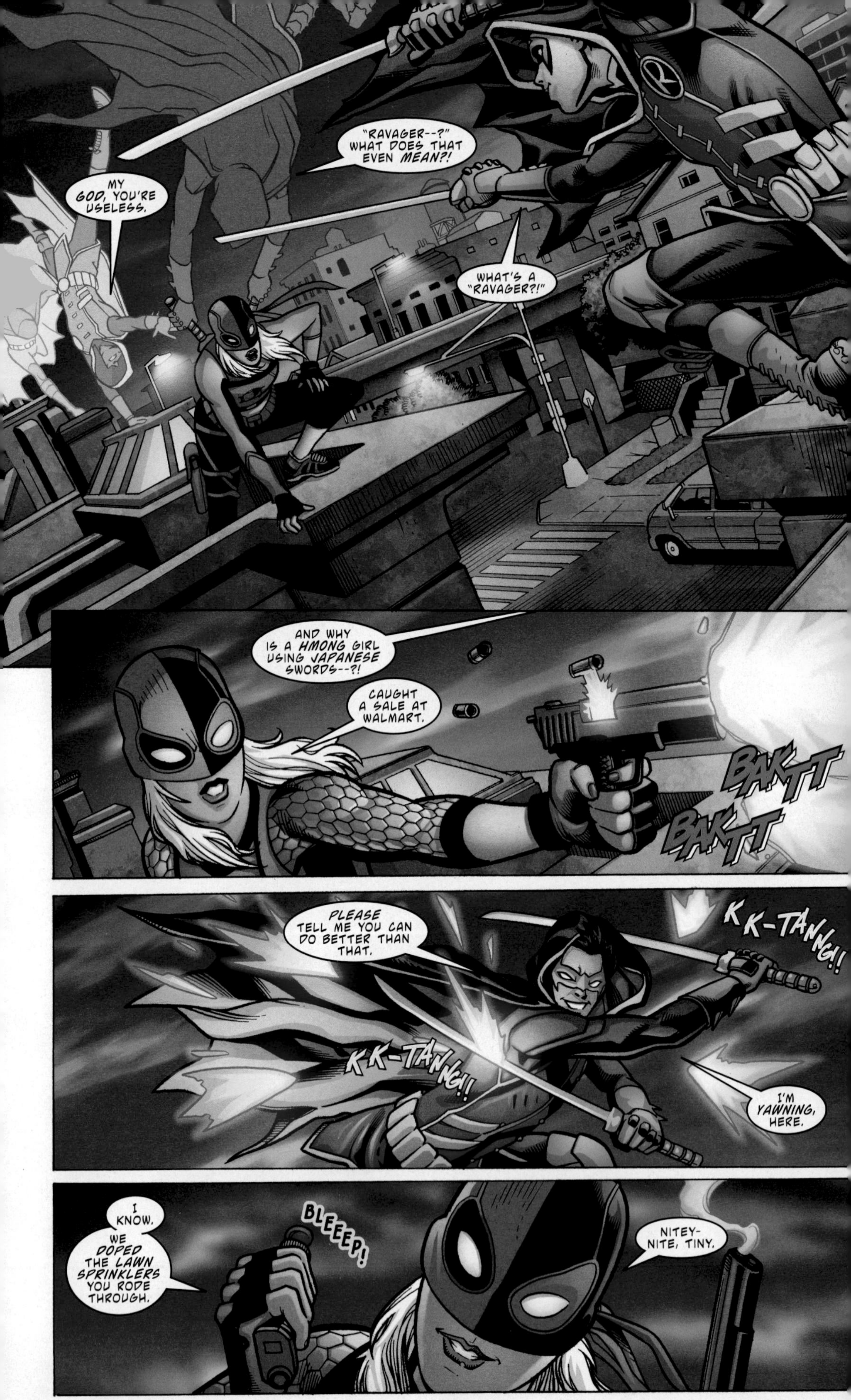

"RAVAGER--?" WHAT DOES THAT EVEN MEAN?!
MY GOD, YOU'RE USELESS.
WHAT'S A "RAVAGER?!"
AND WHY IS A HMONG GIRL USING JAPANESE SWORDS--?!
CAUGHT A SALE AT WALMART.
BAKTT
BAKTT
PLEASE TELL ME YOU CAN DO BETTER THAN THAT.
KK-TANNG!!
KK-TANNG!!
I'M YAWNING, HERE.
I KNOW.
WE DOPED THE LAWN SPRINKLERS YOU RODE THROUGH.
BLEEEP!
NITEY-NITE, TINY.

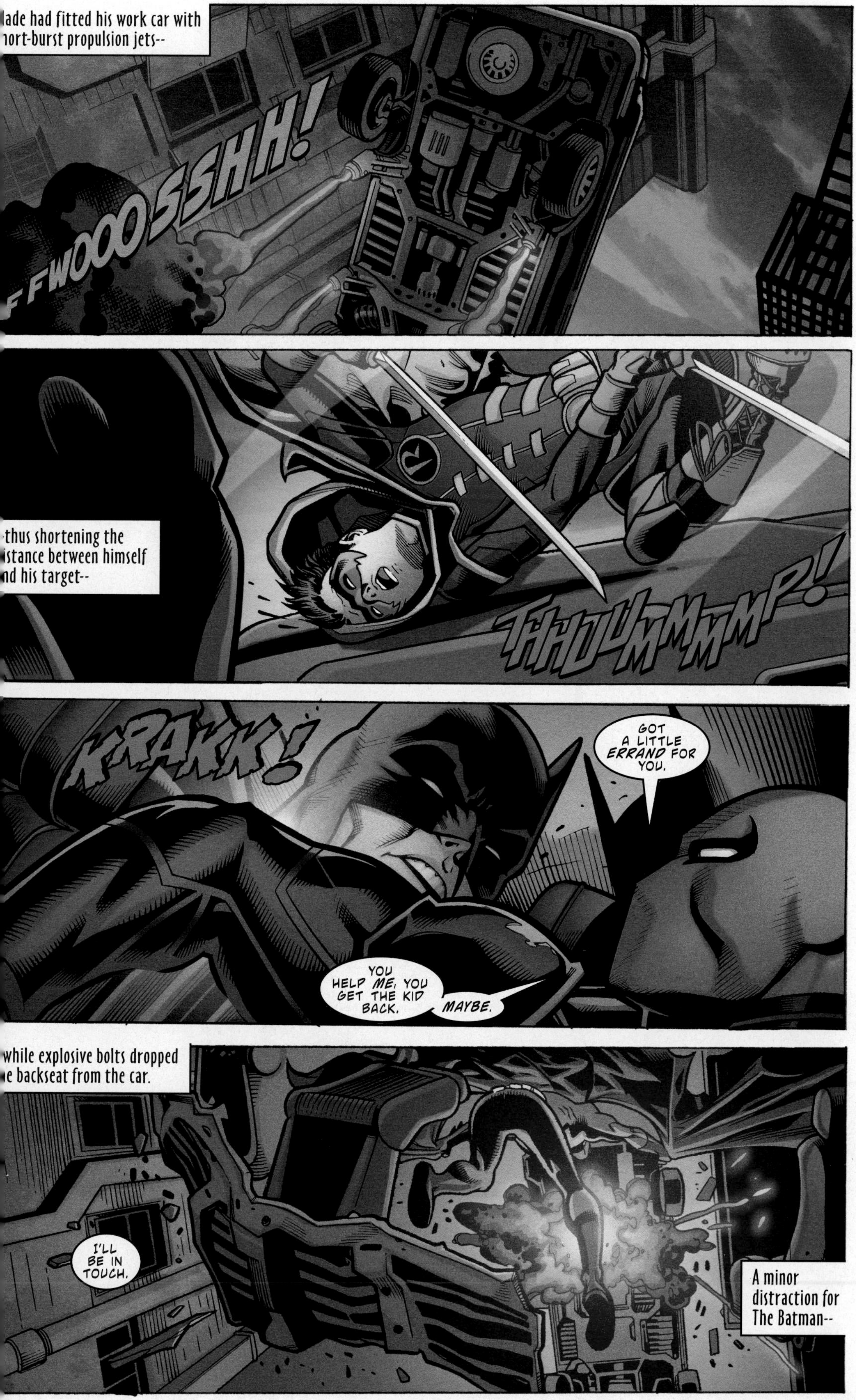

lade had fitted his work car with
hort-burst propulsion jets--
FFWOOOSSHH!
-thus shortening the
istance between himself
nd his target--
THHUMMMMP!
KRAKK!
GOT A LITTLE ERRAND FOR YOU.
YOU HELP ME, YOU GET THE KID BACK.
MAYBE.
while explosive bolts dropped
e backseat from the car.
I'LL BE IN TOUCH.
A minor
distraction for
The Batman--

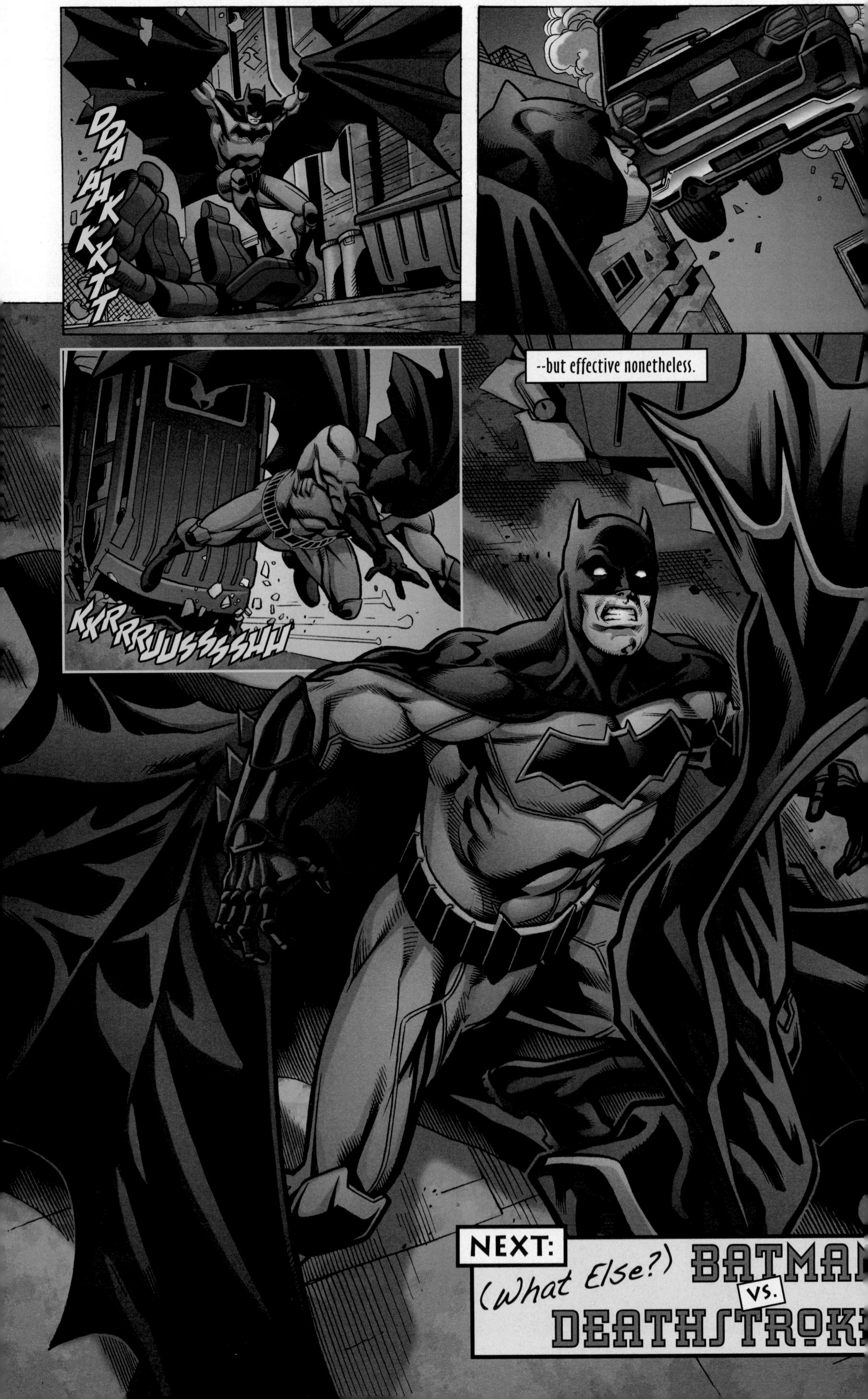
DDAAAKKKTT
KKRRRUUSSSSSHH
--but effective nonetheless.
NEXT:
(What Else?) BATMAN VS. DEATHSTROKE

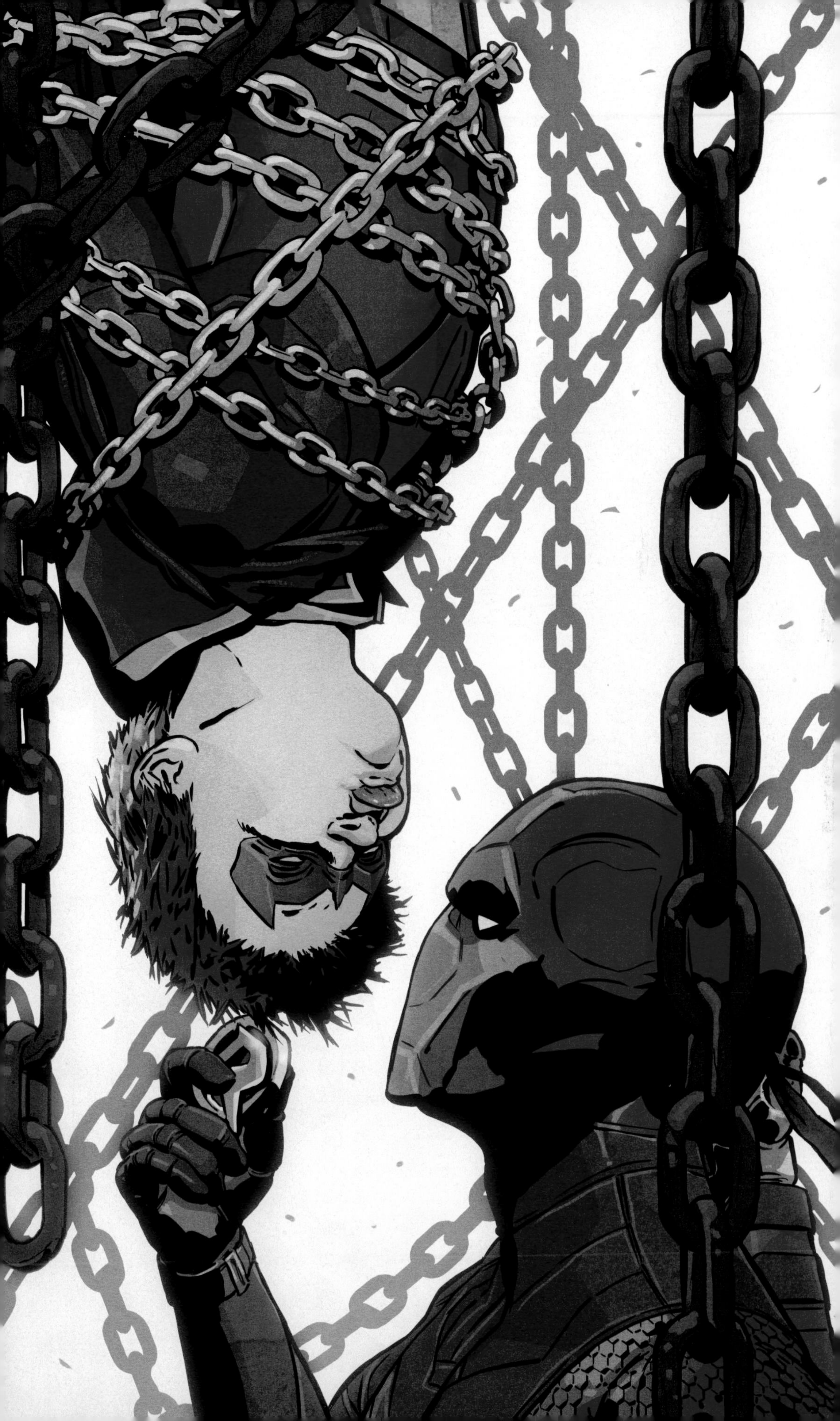

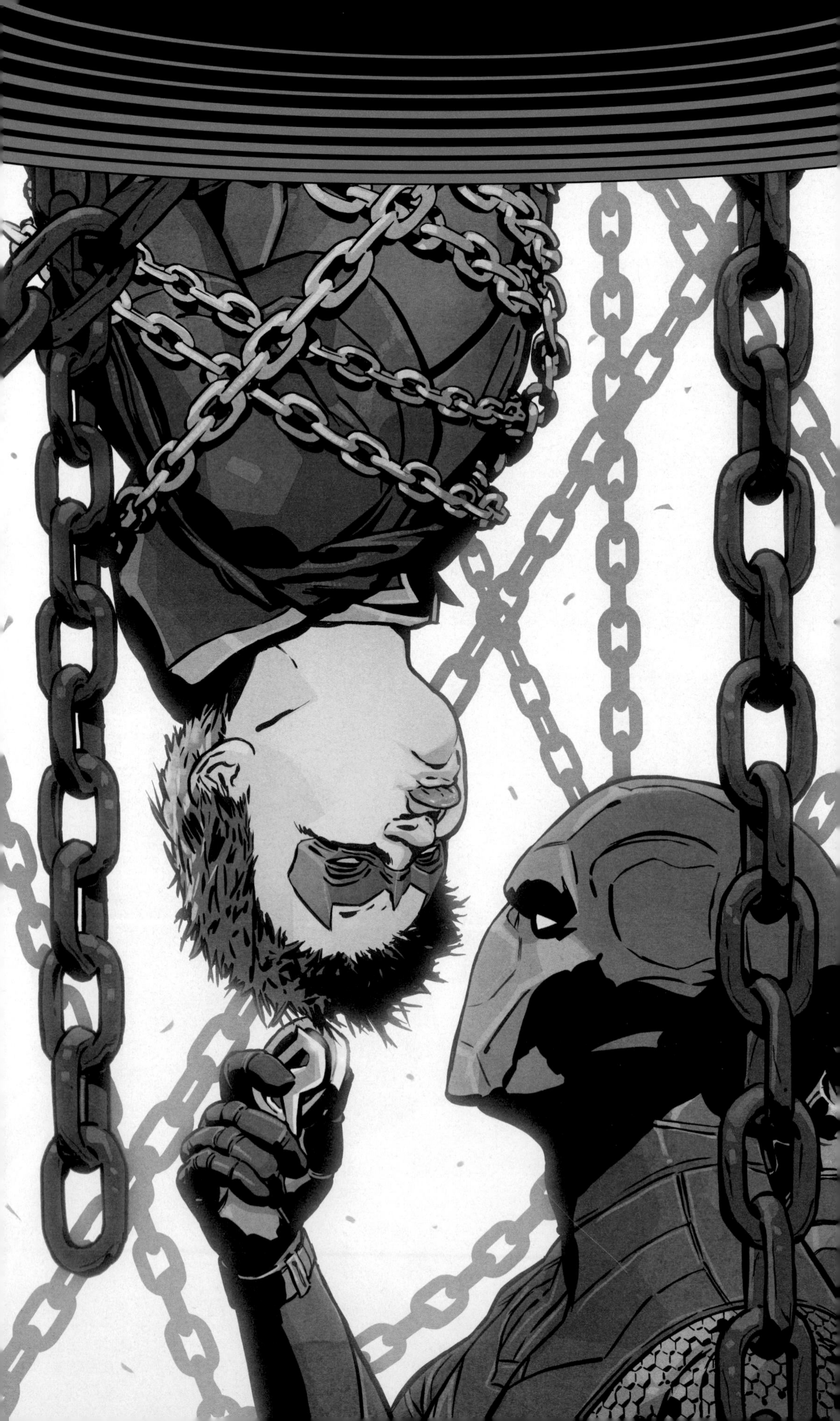

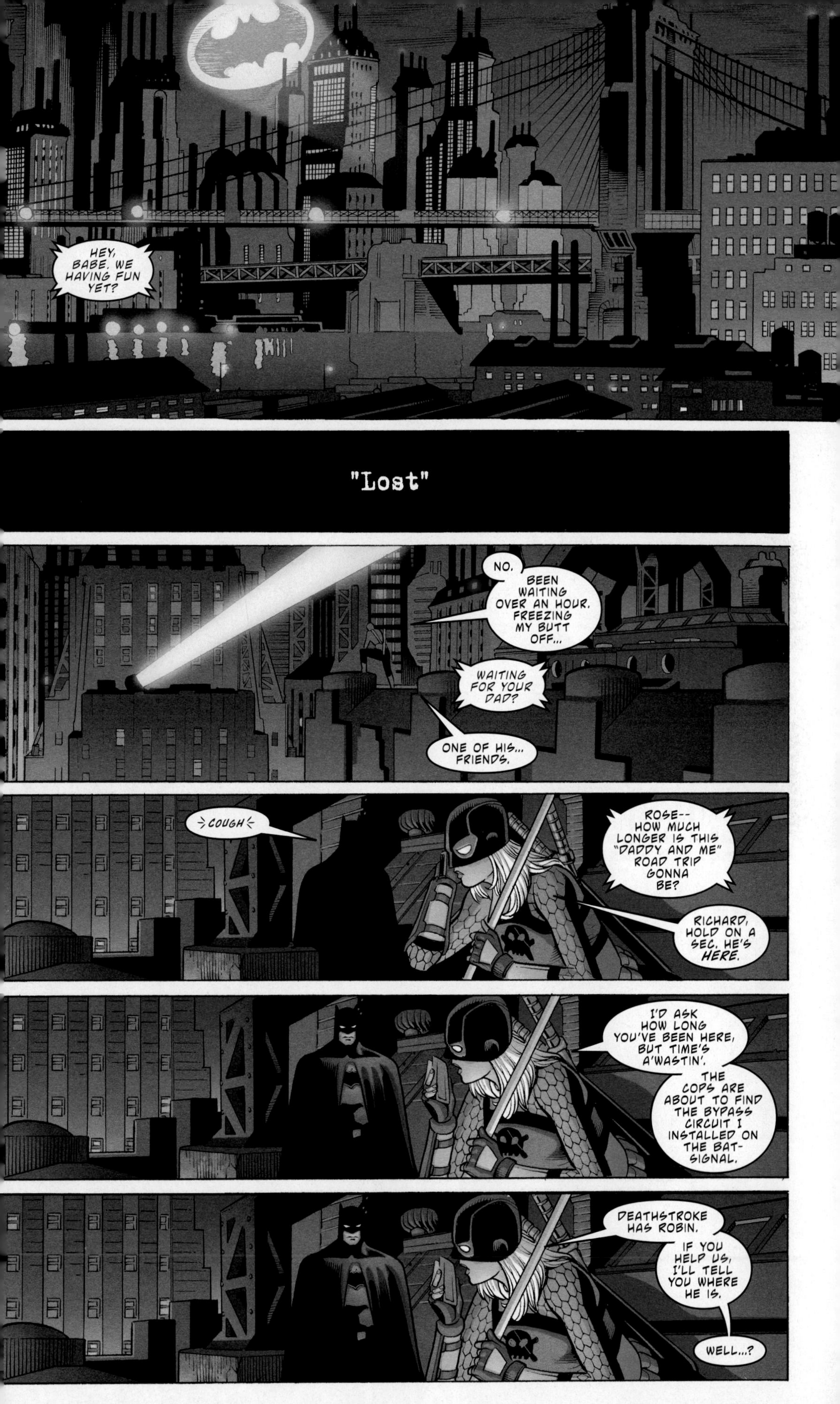
HEY, BABE. WE HAVING FUN YET?
"Lost"
NO.
BEEN WAITING OVER AN HOUR. FREEZING MY BUTT OFF...
WAITING FOR YOUR DAD?
ONE OF HIS... FRIENDS.
COUGH
ROSE-- HOW MUCH LONGER IS THIS "DADDY AND ME" ROAD TRIP GONNA BE?
RICHARD, HOLD ON A SEC. HE'S HERE.
I'D ASK HOW LONG YOU'VE BEEN HERE, BUT TIME'S A'WASTIN'.
THE COPS ARE ABOUT TO FIND THE BYPASS CIRCUIT I INSTALLED ON THE BAT-SIGNAL.
DEATHSTROKE HAS ROBIN.
IF YOU HELP US, I'LL TELL YOU WHERE HE IS.
WELL...?

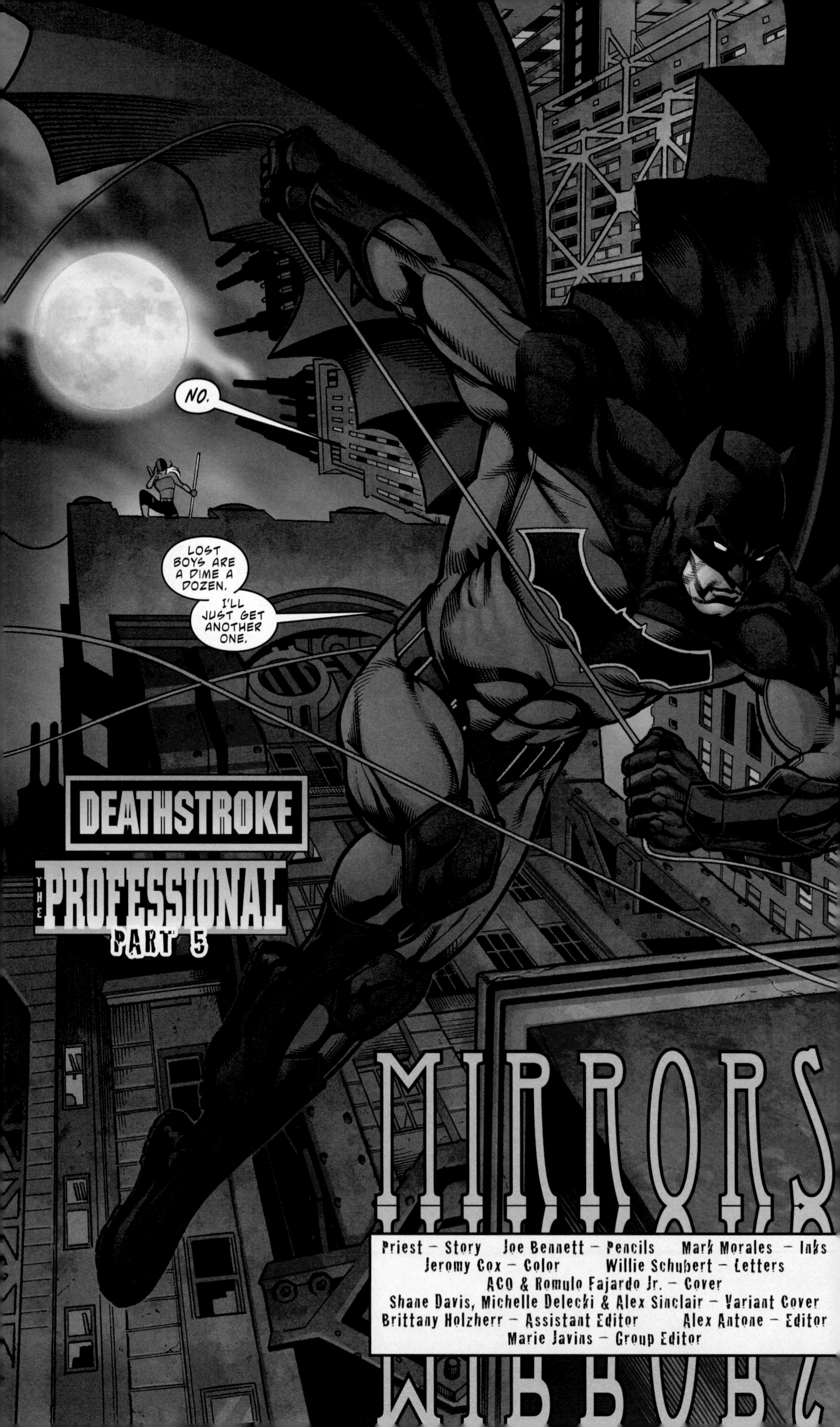

NO.
LOST BOYS ARE A DIME A DOZEN.
I'LL JUST GET ANOTHER ONE.
DEATHSTROKE
THE PROFESSIONAL
PART 5
MIRRORS
Priest – Story Joe Bennett – Pencils Mark Morales – Inks
Jeromy Cox – Color Willie Schubert – Letters
ACO & Romulo Fajardo Jr. – Cover
Shane Davis, Michelle Delecki & Alex Sinclair – Variant Cover
Brittany Holzherr – Assistant Editor Alex Antone – Editor
Marie Javins – Group Editor

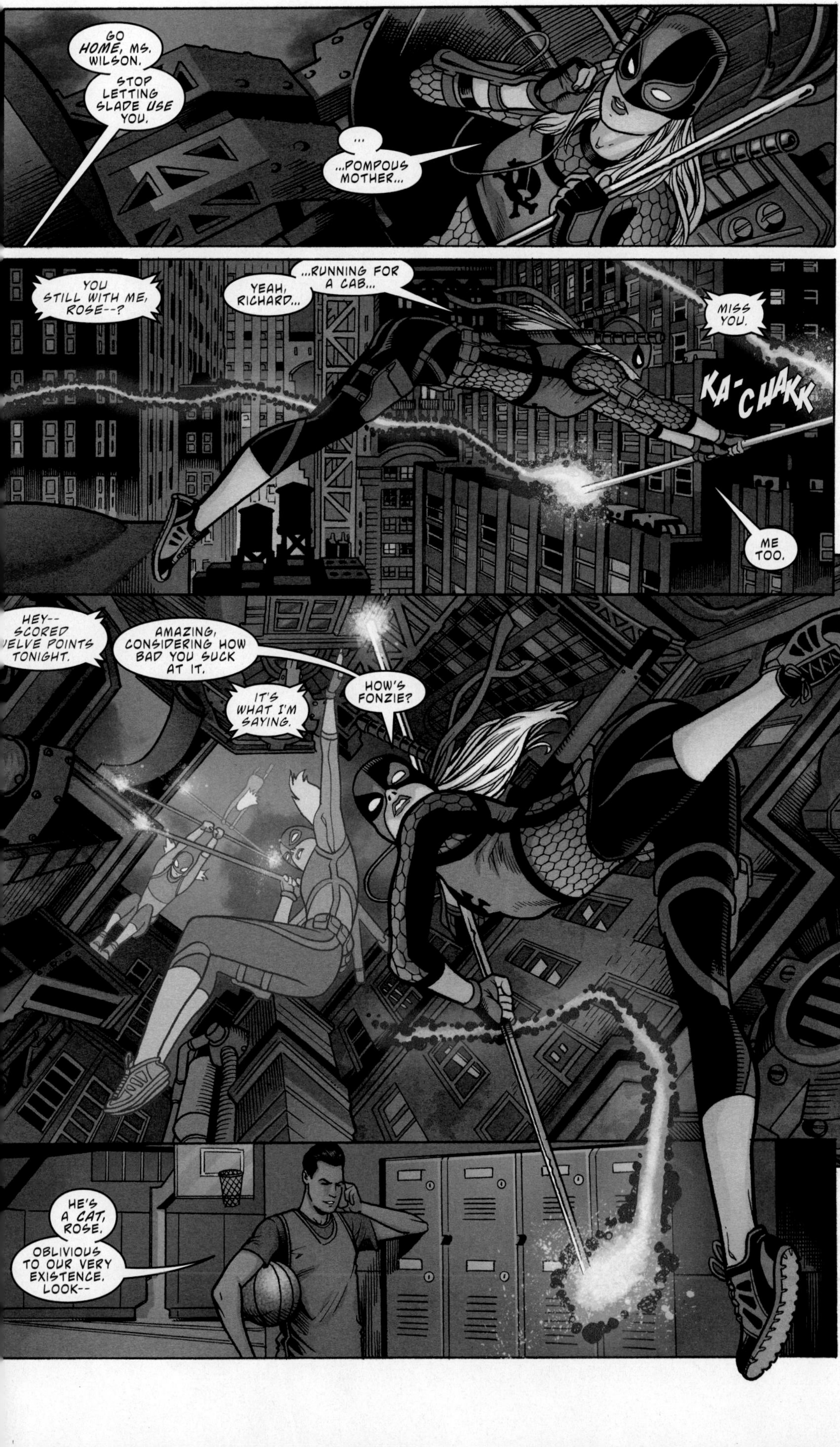
GO HOME, MS. WILSON.
STOP LETTING SLADE USE YOU.
...
...POMPOUS MOTHER...
YOU STILL WITH ME, ROSE--?
YEAH, RICHARD...
...RUNNING FOR A CAB...
MISS YOU.
KA-CHAKK
ME TOO.
HEY--SCORED TWELVE POINTS TONIGHT.
AMAZING, CONSIDERING HOW BAD YOU SUCK AT IT.
IT'S WHAT I'M SAYING.
HOW'S FONZIE?
HE'S A CAT, ROSE.
OBLIVIOUS TO OUR VERY EXISTENCE. LOOK--

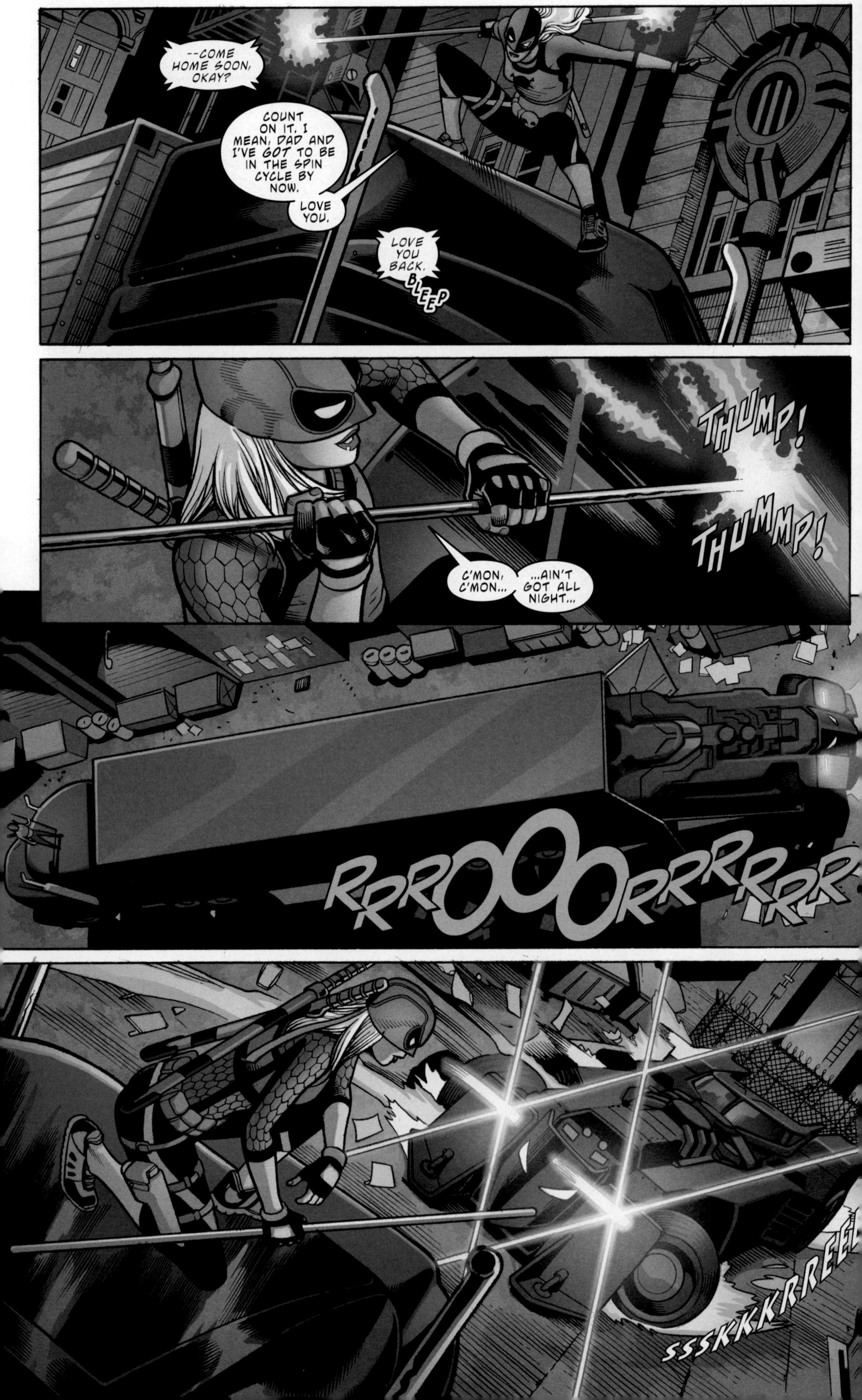
--COME HOME SOON, OKAY?
COUNT ON IT. I MEAN, DAD AND I'VE GOT TO BE IN THE SPIN CYCLE BY NOW.
LOVE YOU.
LOVE YOU BACK.
BLEEP
THUMP!
THUMMP!
C'MON, C'MON...
...AIN'T GOT ALL NIGHT...
RRROOORRRRRR
SSSKKKRREE!

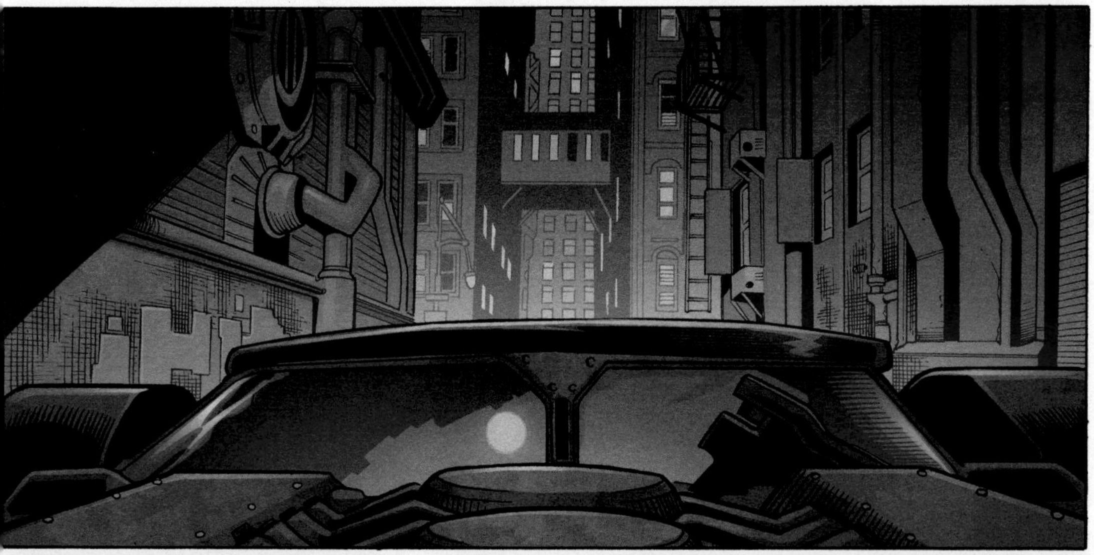

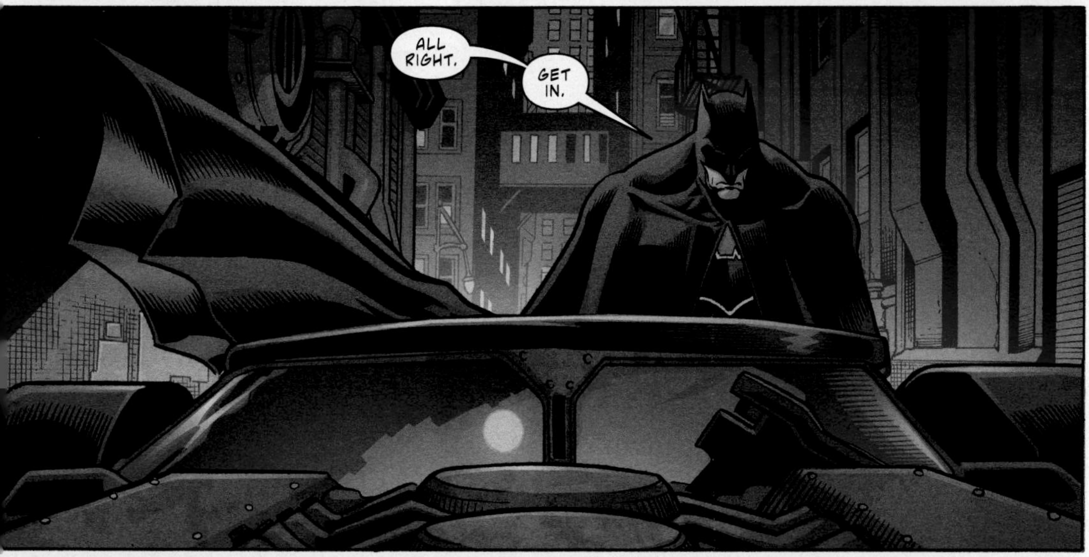

ALL RIGHT.
GET IN.

"In League"

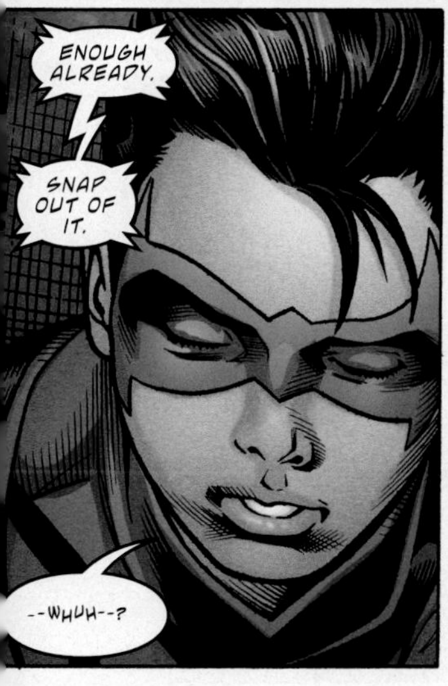

ENOUGH ALREADY.
SNAP OUT OF IT.
--WHUH--?

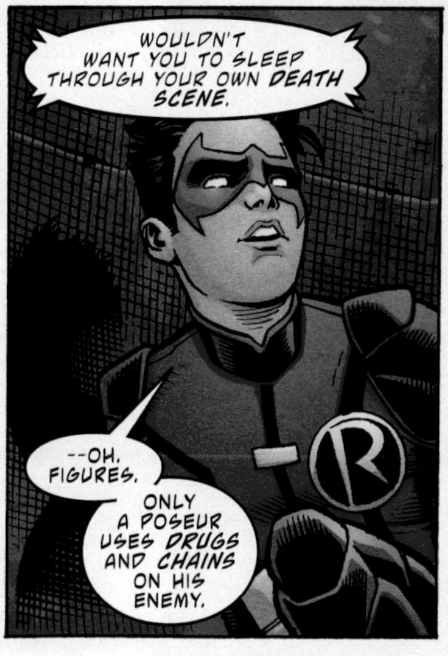

WOULDN'T WANT YOU TO SLEEP THROUGH YOUR OWN DEATH SCENE.
--OH. FIGURES.
ONLY A POSEUR USES DRUGS AND CHAINS ON HIS ENEMY.

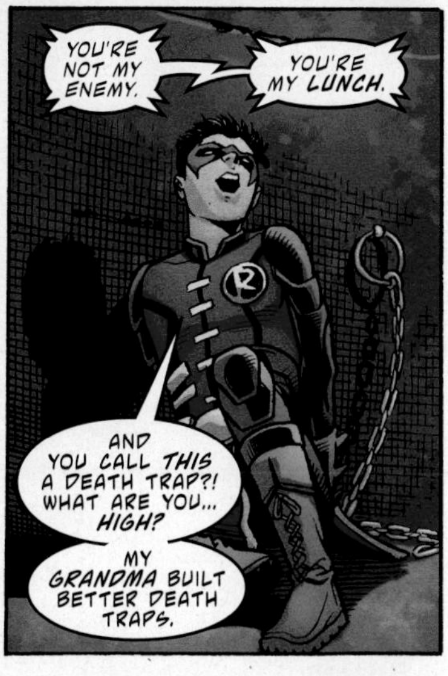

YOU'RE NOT MY ENEMY.
YOU'RE MY LUNCH.
AND YOU CALL THIS A DEATH TRAP?! WHAT ARE YOU... HIGH?
MY GRANDMA BUILT BETTER DEATH TRAPS.

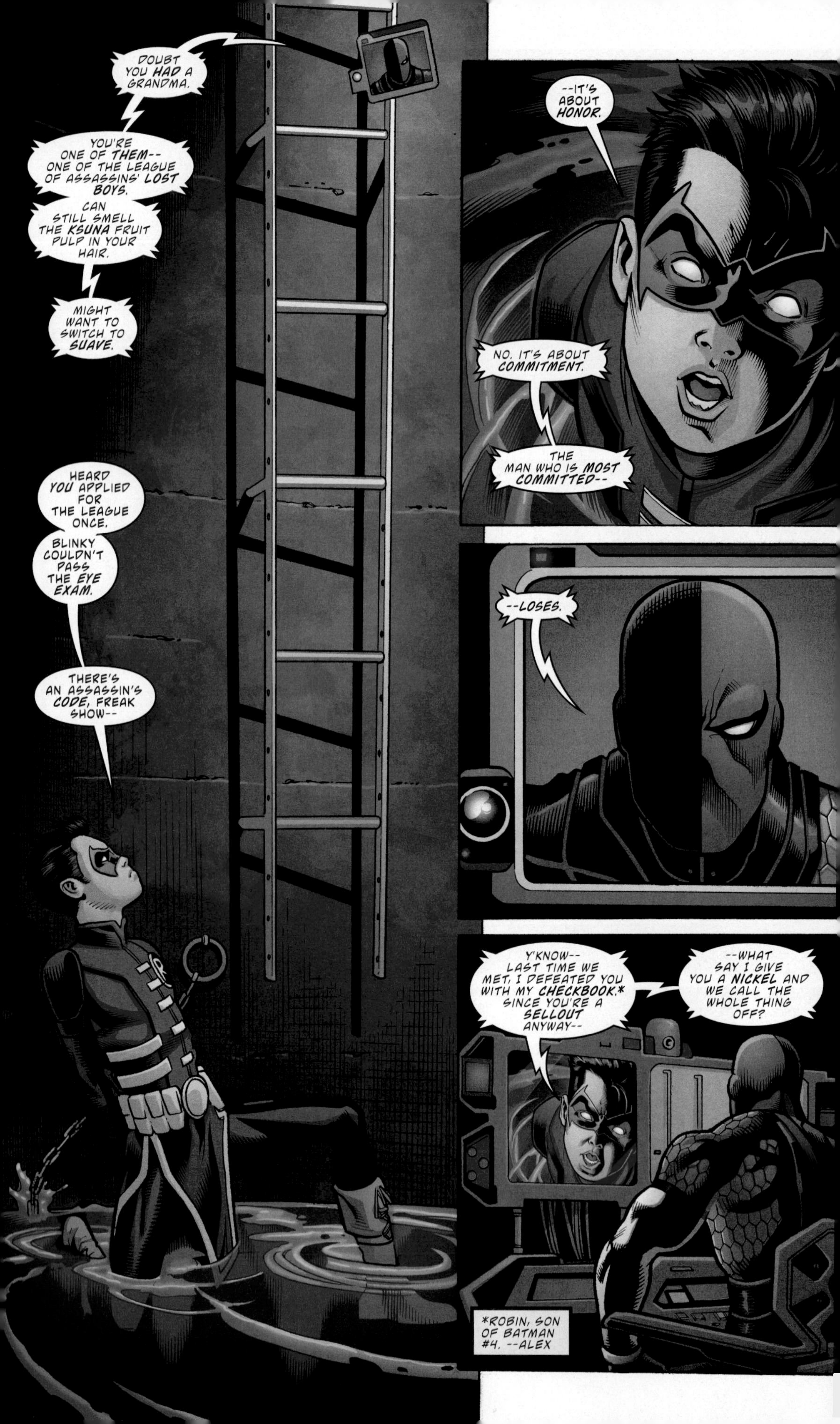
DOUBT YOU HAD A GRANDMA.
YOU'RE ONE OF THEM-- ONE OF THE LEAGUE OF ASSASSINS' LOST BOYS.
CAN STILL SMELL THE KSUNA FRUIT PULP IN YOUR HAIR.
MIGHT WANT TO SWITCH TO SUAVE.
HEARD YOU APPLIED FOR THE LEAGUE ONCE.
BLINKY COULDN'T PASS THE EYE EXAM.
THERE'S AN ASSASSIN'S CODE, FREAK SHOW--
--IT'S ABOUT HONOR.
NO. IT'S ABOUT COMMITMENT.
THE MAN WHO IS MOST COMMITTED--
--LOSES.
Y'KNOW-- LAST TIME WE MET, I DEFEATED YOU WITH MY CHECKBOOK.* SINCE YOU'RE A SELLOUT ANYWAY--
--WHAT SAY I GIVE YOU A NICKEL AND WE CALL THE WHOLE THING OFF?
*ROBIN, SON OF BATMAN #4. --ALEX

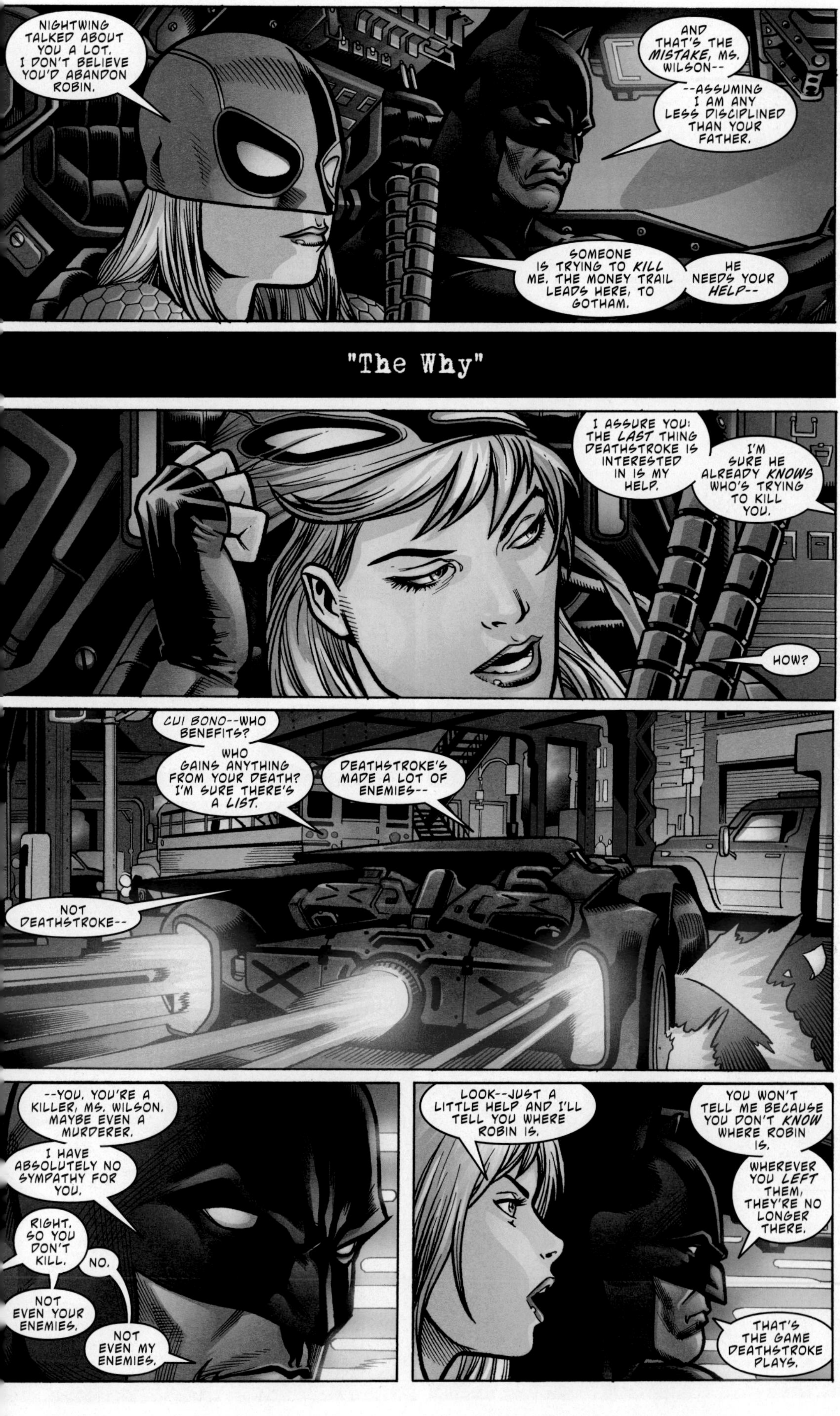
NIGHTWING TALKED ABOUT YOU A LOT. I DON'T BELIEVE YOU'D ABANDON ROBIN.
AND THAT'S THE MISTAKE, MS. WILSON--
--ASSUMING I AM ANY LESS DISCIPLINED THAN YOUR FATHER.
SOMEONE IS TRYING TO KILL ME. THE MONEY TRAIL LEADS HERE, TO GOTHAM.
HE NEEDS YOUR HELP--
"The Why"
I ASSURE YOU: THE LAST THING DEATHSTROKE IS INTERESTED IN IS MY HELP.
I'M SURE HE ALREADY KNOWS WHO'S TRYING TO KILL YOU.
HOW?
CUI BONO--WHO BENEFITS?
WHO GAINS ANYTHING FROM YOUR DEATH? I'M SURE THERE'S A LIST.
DEATHSTROKE'S MADE A LOT OF ENEMIES--
NOT DEATHSTROKE--
--YOU. YOU'RE A KILLER, MS. WILSON. MAYBE EVEN A MURDERER.
I HAVE ABSOLUTELY NO SYMPATHY FOR YOU.
RIGHT. SO YOU DON'T KILL.
NO.
NOT EVEN YOUR ENEMIES.
NOT EVEN MY ENEMIES.
LOOK--JUST A LITTLE HELP AND I'LL TELL YOU WHERE ROBIN IS.
YOU WON'T TELL ME BECAUSE YOU DON'T KNOW WHERE ROBIN IS.
WHEREVER YOU LEFT THEM, THEY'RE NO LONGER THERE.
THAT'S THE GAME DEATHSTROKE PLAYS.

"Father's Day"

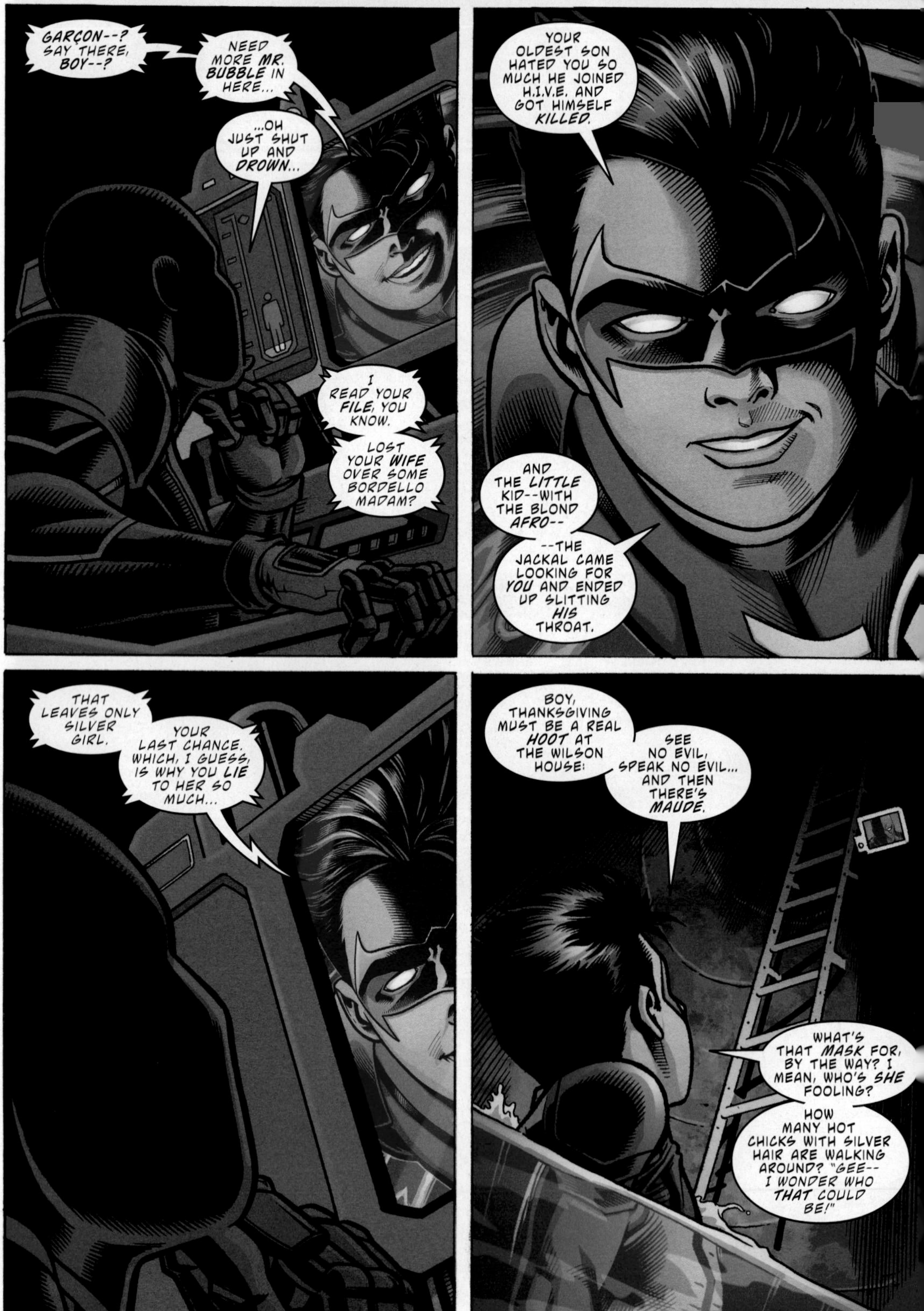
GARÇON--? SAY THERE, BOY--?
NEED MORE MR. BUBBLE IN HERE...
...OH JUST SHUT UP AND DROWN...
I READ YOUR FILE, YOU KNOW.
LOST YOUR WIFE OVER SOME BORDELLO MADAM?
YOUR OLDEST SON HATED YOU SO MUCH HE JOINED H.I.V.E. AND GOT HIMSELF KILLED.
AND THE LITTLE KID--WITH THE BLOND AFRO--
--THE JACKAL CAME LOOKING FOR YOU AND ENDED UP SLITTING HIS THROAT.
THAT LEAVES ONLY SILVER GIRL.
YOUR LAST CHANCE. WHICH, I GUESS, IS WHY YOU LIE TO HER SO MUCH...
BOY, THANKSGIVING MUST BE A REAL HOOT AT THE WILSON HOUSE:
SEE NO EVIL, SPEAK NO EVIL... AND THEN THERE'S MAUDE.
WHAT'S THAT MASK FOR, BY THE WAY? I MEAN, WHO'S SHE FOOLING?
HOW MANY HOT CHICKS WITH SILVER HAIR ARE WALKING AROUND? "GEE--I WONDER WHO THAT COULD BE!"

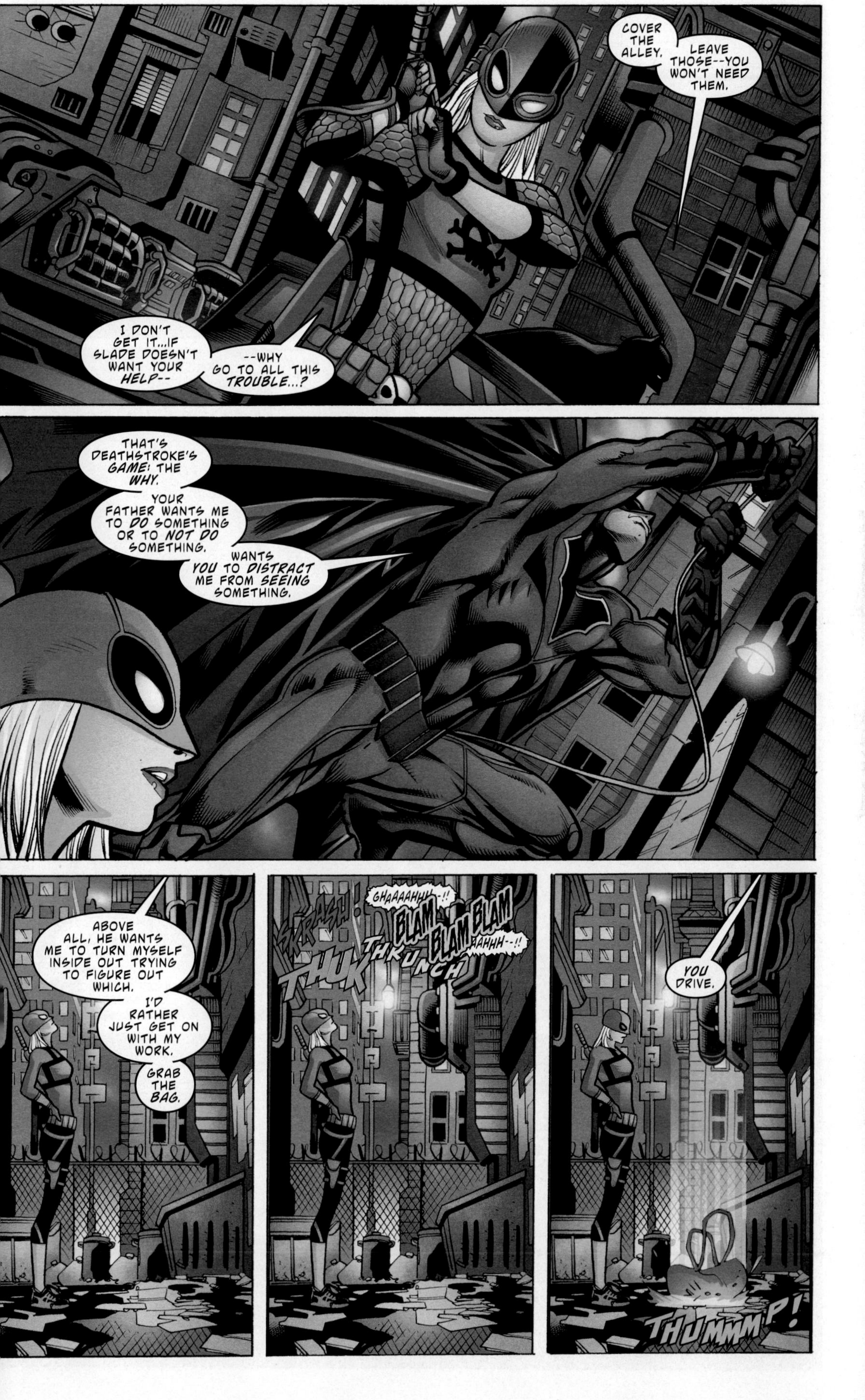
COVER THE ALLEY.
LEAVE THOSE--YOU WON'T NEED THEM.
I DON'T GET IT...IF SLADE DOESN'T WANT YOUR *HELP*--
--WHY GO TO ALL THIS *TROUBLE*...?
THAT'S DEATHSTROKE'S *GAME*: THE *WHY*.
YOUR FATHER WANTS ME TO *DO* SOMETHING OR TO *NOT DO* SOMETHING.
WANTS *YOU* TO *DISTRACT* ME FROM *SEEING* SOMETHING.
ABOVE ALL, HE WANTS ME TO TURN MYSELF INSIDE OUT TRYING TO FIGURE OUT WHICH.
I'D RATHER JUST GET ON WITH MY WORK.
GRAB THE *BAG*.
SKRASH!
GHAAAAHH--!!
BLAM
BLAM BLAM
AHHHH--!!
THUK
THKUNCH
YOU DRIVE.
THUMMMP!

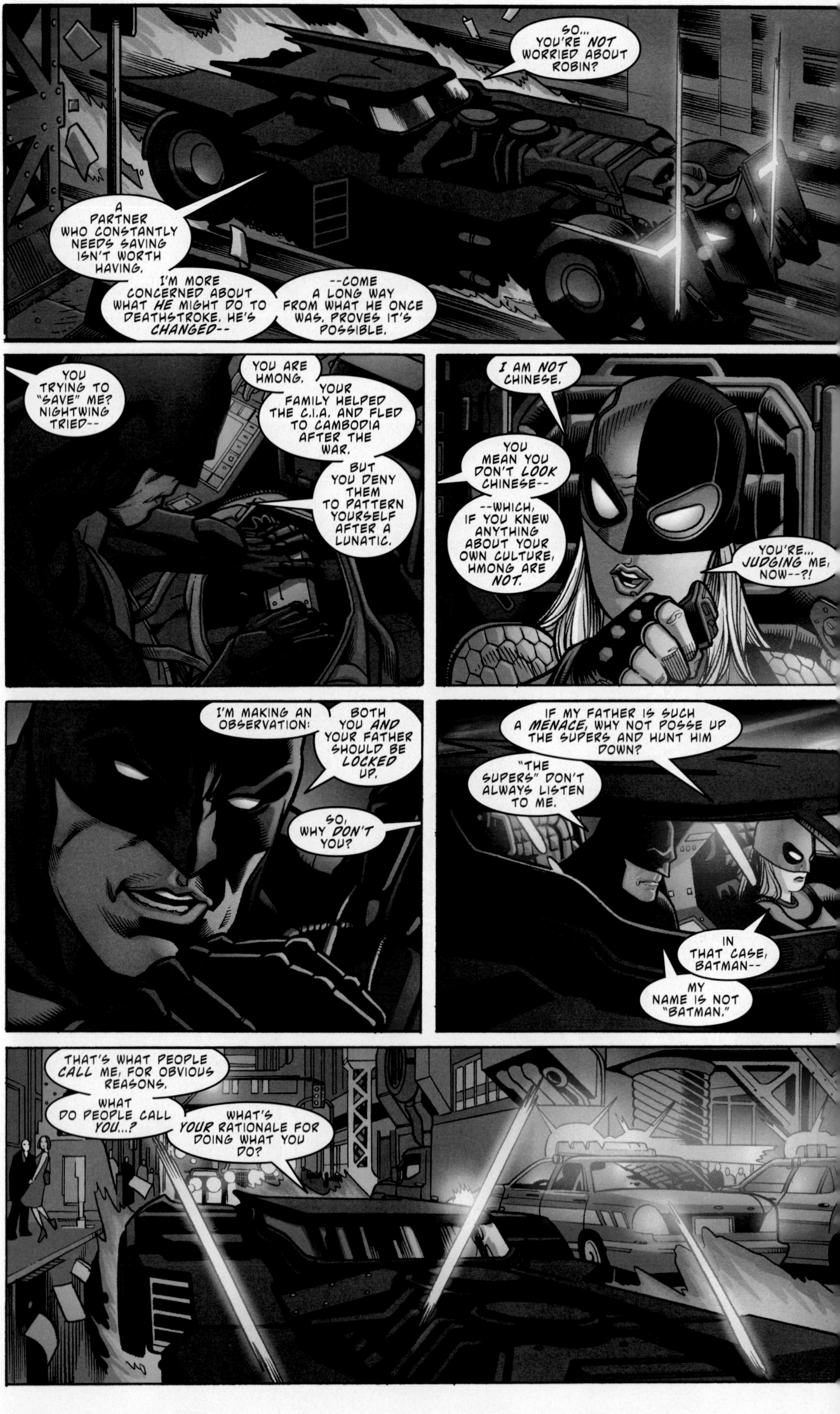
SO... YOU'RE NOT WORRIED ABOUT ROBIN?
A PARTNER WHO CONSTANTLY NEEDS SAVING ISN'T WORTH HAVING.
I'M MORE CONCERNED ABOUT WHAT HE MIGHT DO TO DEATHSTROKE. HE'S CHANGED--
--COME A LONG WAY FROM WHAT HE ONCE WAS. PROVES IT'S POSSIBLE.
YOU TRYING TO "SAVE" ME? NIGHTWING TRIED--
YOU ARE HMONG.
YOUR FAMILY HELPED THE C.I.A. AND FLED TO CAMBODIA AFTER THE WAR.
BUT YOU DENY THEM TO PATTERN YOURSELF AFTER A LUNATIC.
I AM NOT CHINESE.
YOU MEAN YOU DON'T LOOK CHINESE--
--WHICH, IF YOU KNEW ANYTHING ABOUT YOUR OWN CULTURE, HMONG ARE NOT.
YOU'RE... JUDGING ME, NOW--?!
I'M MAKING AN OBSERVATION:
BOTH YOU AND YOUR FATHER SHOULD BE LOCKED UP.
SO, WHY DON'T YOU?
IF MY FATHER IS SUCH A MENACE, WHY NOT POSSE UP THE SUPERS AND HUNT HIM DOWN?
"THE SUPERS" DON'T ALWAYS LISTEN TO ME.
IN THAT CASE, BATMAN--
MY NAME IS NOT "BATMAN."
THAT'S WHAT PEOPLE CALL ME, FOR OBVIOUS REASONS.
WHAT DO PEOPLE CALL YOU...?
WHAT'S YOUR RATIONALE FOR DOING WHAT YOU DO?

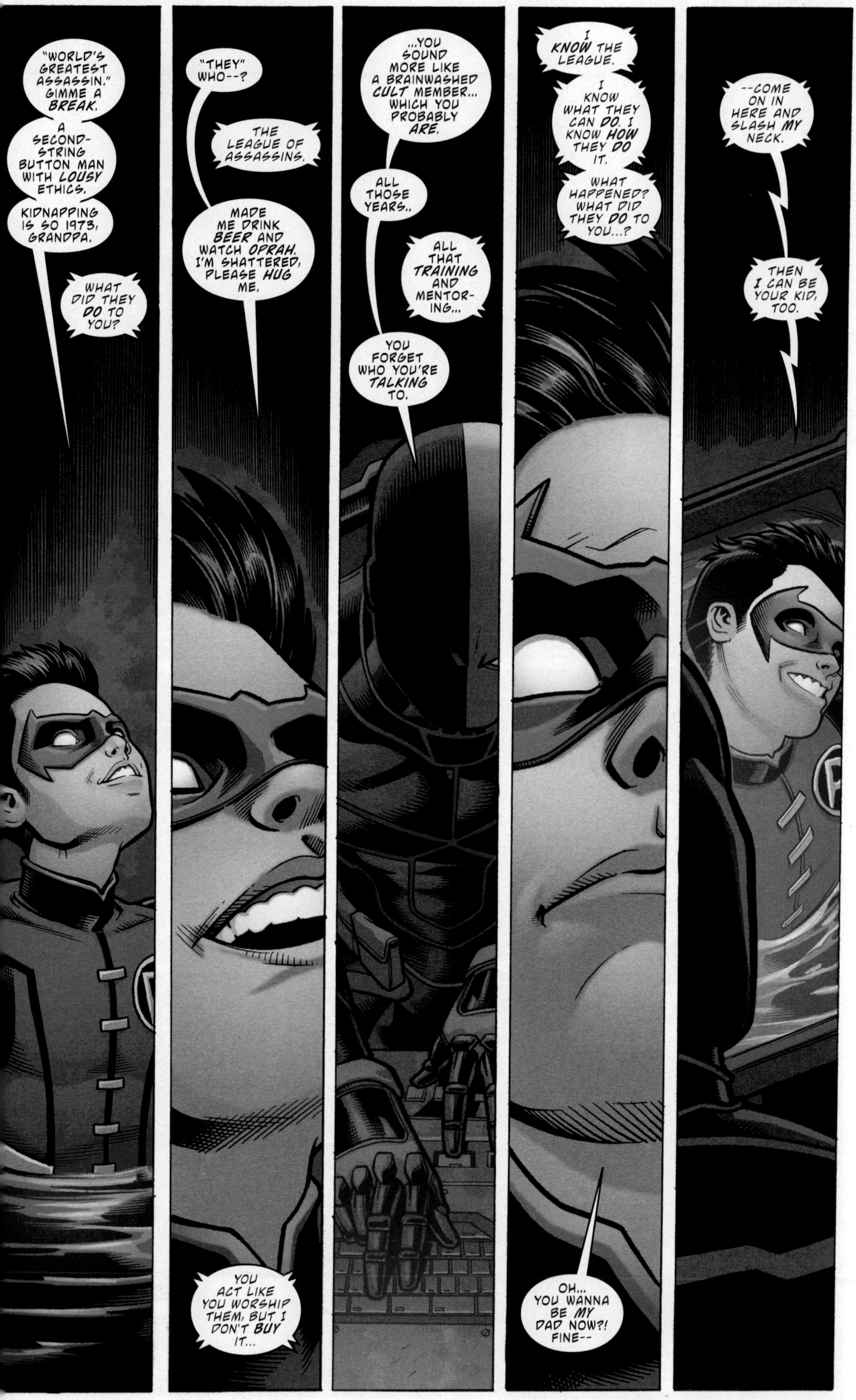
"WORLD'S GREATEST ASSASSIN." GIMME A BREAK.
A SECOND-STRING BUTTON MAN WITH LOUSY ETHICS.
KIDNAPPING IS SO 1973, GRANDPA.
WHAT DID THEY DO TO YOU?
"THEY" WHO--?
THE LEAGUE OF ASSASSINS.
MADE ME DRINK BEER AND WATCH OPRAH. I'M SHATTERED, PLEASE HUG ME.
YOU ACT LIKE YOU WORSHIP THEM, BUT I DON'T BUY IT...
...YOU SOUND MORE LIKE A BRAINWASHED CULT MEMBER... WHICH YOU PROBABLY ARE.
ALL THOSE YEARS..
ALL THAT TRAINING AND MENTOR-ING...
YOU FORGET WHO YOU'RE TALKING TO.
I KNOW THE LEAGUE.
I KNOW WHAT THEY CAN DO. I KNOW HOW THEY DO IT.
WHAT HAPPENED? WHAT DID THEY DO TO YOU...?
OH... YOU WANNA BE MY DAD NOW?! FINE--
--COME ON IN HERE AND SLASH MY NECK.
THEN I CAN BE YOUR KID, TOO.

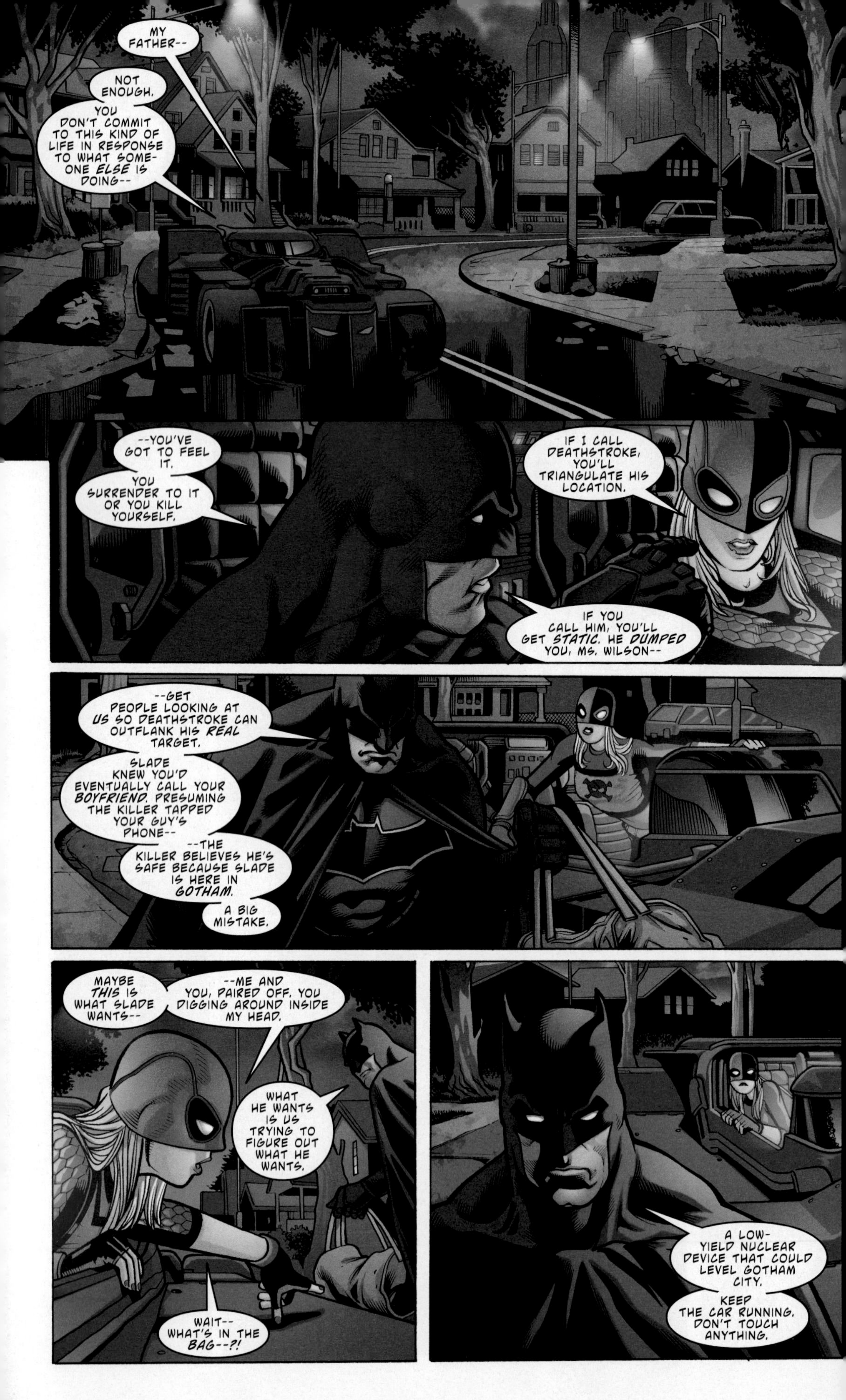
MY FATHER--
NOT ENOUGH.
YOU DON'T COMMIT TO THIS KIND OF LIFE IN RESPONSE TO WHAT SOME-ONE *ELSE* IS DOING--
--YOU'VE GOT TO FEEL IT.
YOU SURRENDER TO IT OR YOU KILL YOURSELF.
IF I CALL DEATHSTROKE, YOU'LL TRIANGULATE HIS LOCATION.
IF YOU CALL HIM, YOU'LL GET *STATIC*. HE *DUMPED* YOU, MS. WILSON--
--GET PEOPLE LOOKING AT *US* SO DEATHSTROKE CAN OUTFLANK HIS *REAL* TARGET.
SLADE KNEW YOU'D EVENTUALLY CALL YOUR *BOYFRIEND*. PRESUMING THE KILLER TAPPED YOUR GUY'S PHONE--
--THE KILLER BELIEVES HE'S SAFE BECAUSE SLADE IS HERE IN *GOTHAM*.
A BIG MISTAKE.
MAYBE *THIS* IS WHAT SLADE WANTS--
--ME AND YOU, PAIRED OFF. YOU DIGGING AROUND INSIDE MY HEAD.
WHAT HE WANTS IS US TRYING TO FIGURE OUT WHAT HE WANTS.
WAIT-- WHAT'S IN THE *BAG*--?!
A LOW-YIELD NUCLEAR DEVICE THAT COULD LEVEL GOTHAM CITY.
KEEP THE CAR RUNNING. DON'T TOUCH ANYTHING.

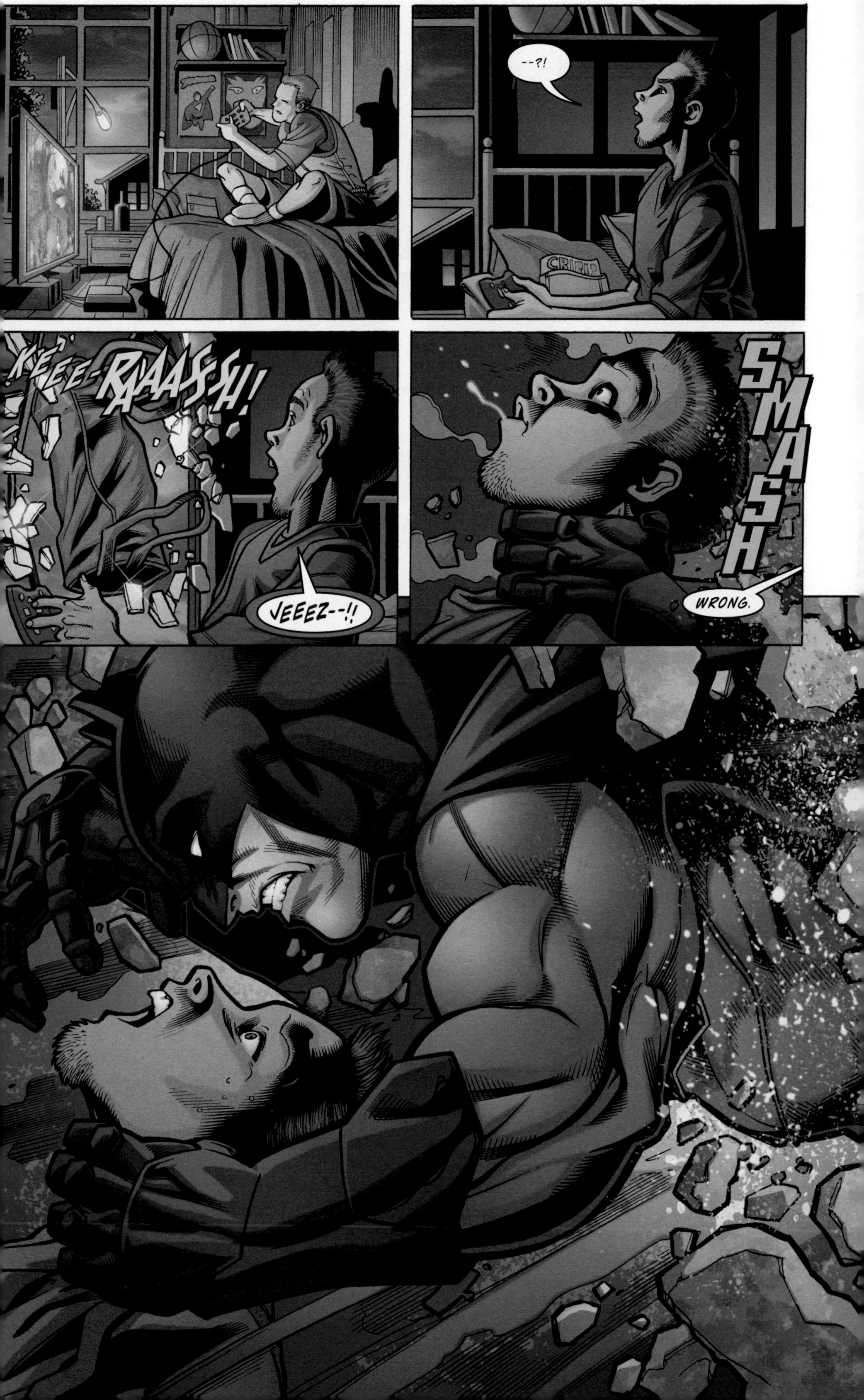
--?!
KEEE-RAAASSH!
JEEEZ--!!
SMASH
WRONG.

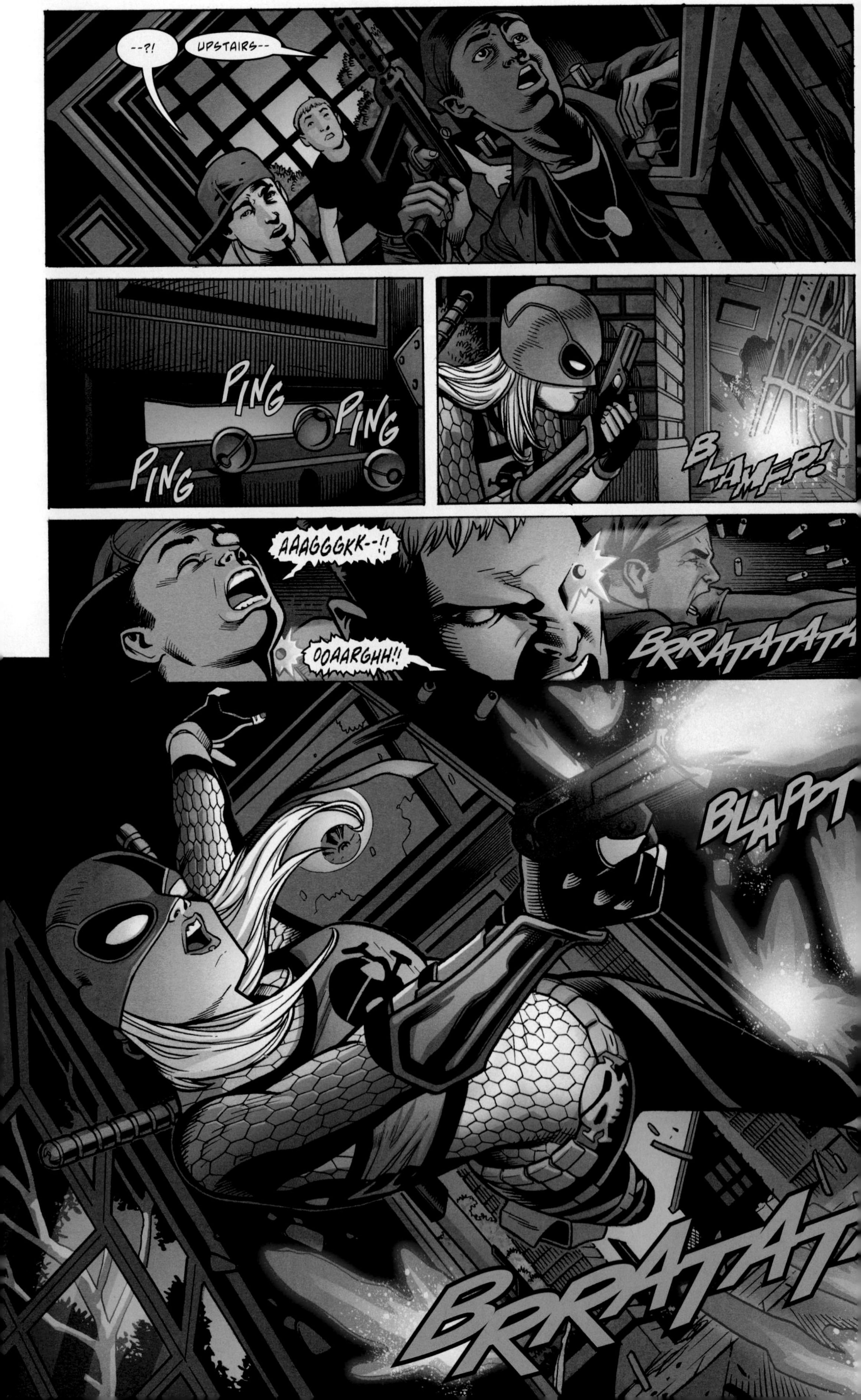
--?!
UPSTAIRS--
PING
PING
PING
BLAM-P!
AAAGGGKK--!!
OOAARGHH!!
BRRATATATA
BLAPPT
BRRATATAT

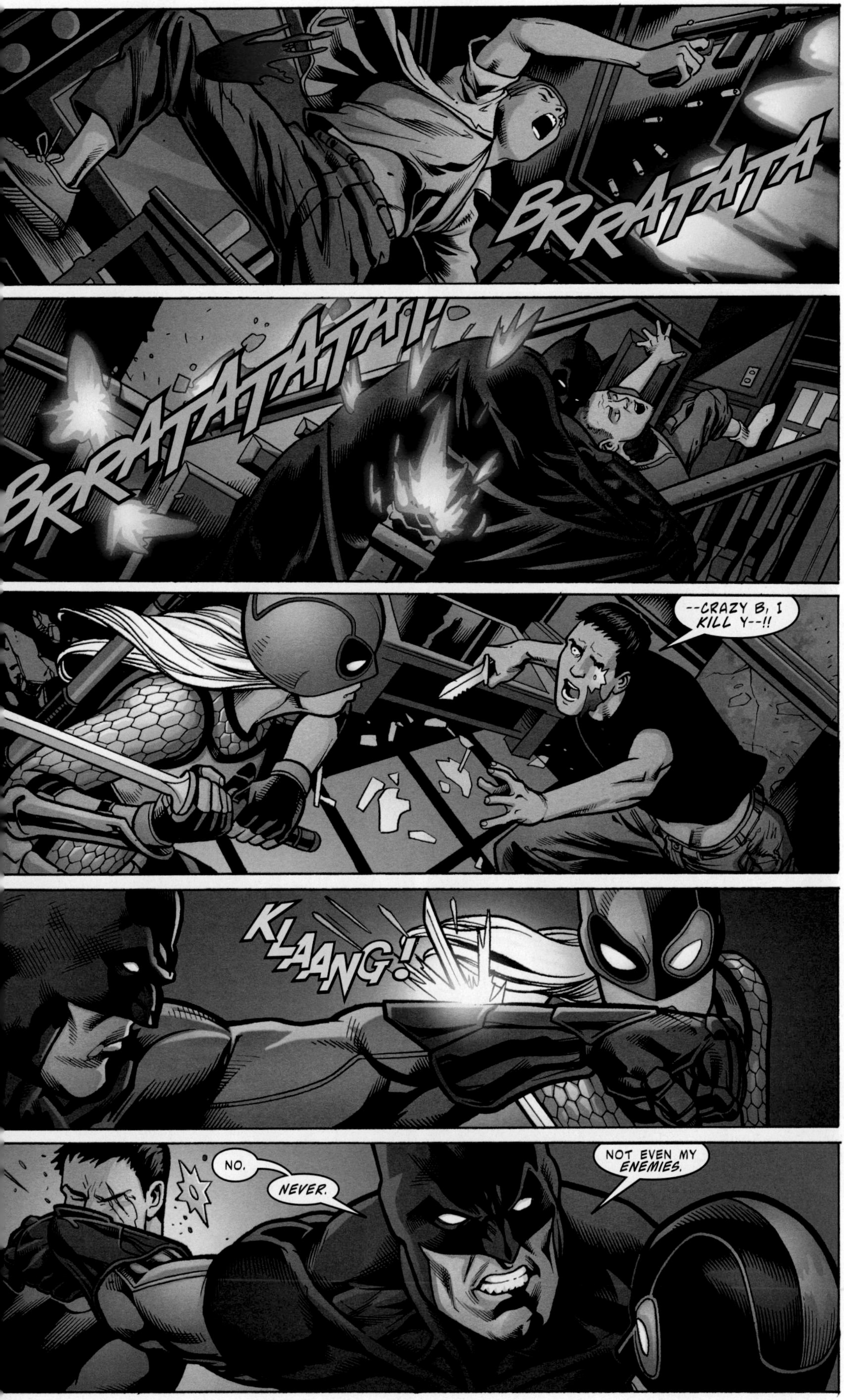

BRRATATA
BRRATATATA!!
--CRAZY B, I KILL Y--!!
KLAANG!!
NO.
NEVER.
NOT EVEN MY ENEMIES.

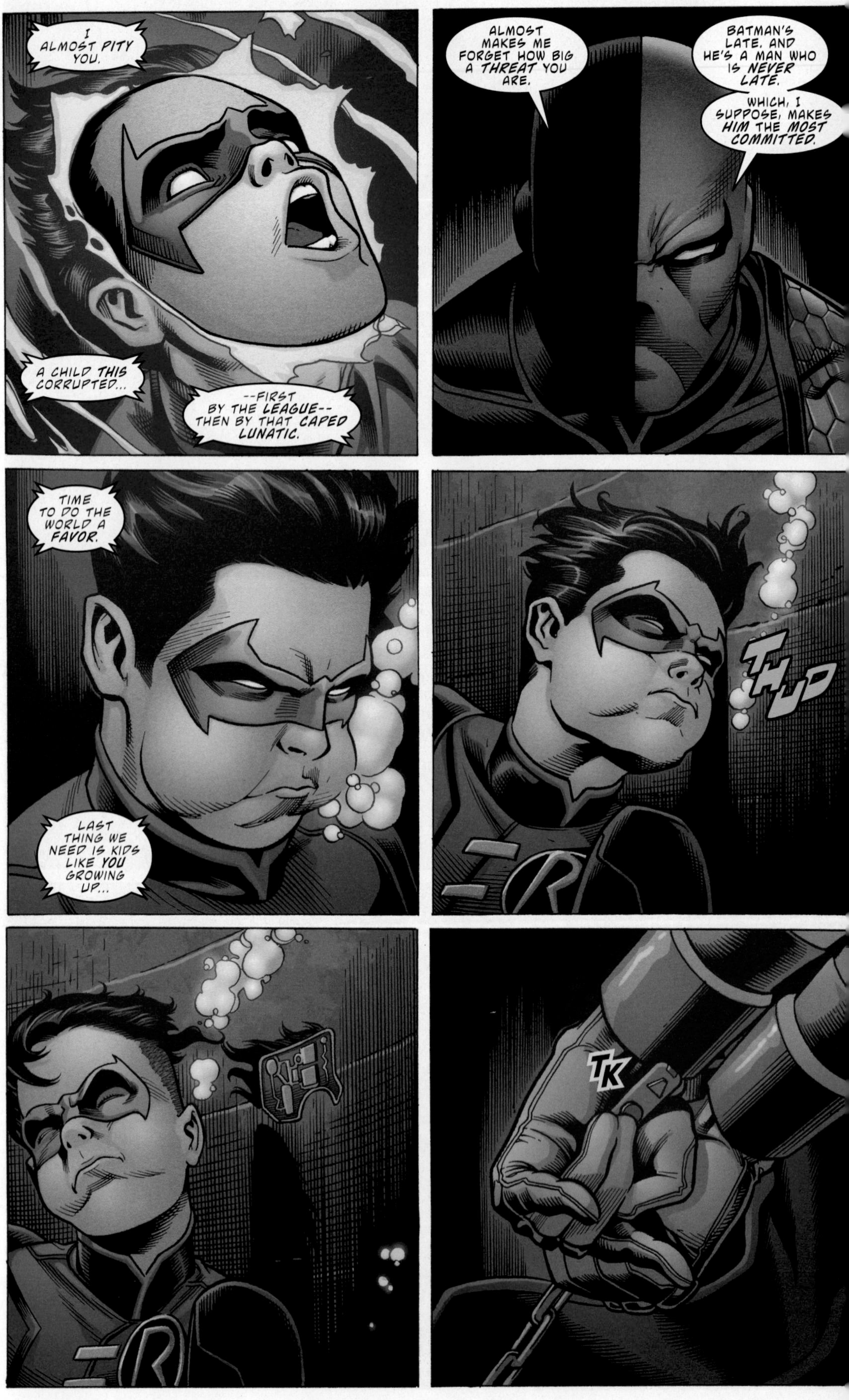
I ALMOST PITY YOU.
A CHILD THIS CORRUPTED...
--FIRST BY THE LEAGUE-- THEN BY THAT CAPED LUNATIC.
ALMOST MAKES ME FORGET HOW BIG A THREAT YOU ARE.
BATMAN'S LATE. AND HE'S A MAN WHO IS NEVER LATE.
WHICH, I SUPPOSE, MAKES HIM THE MOST COMMITTED.
TIME TO DO THE WORLD A FAVOR.
LAST THING WE NEED IS KIDS LIKE YOU GROWING UP...
THUD
TK

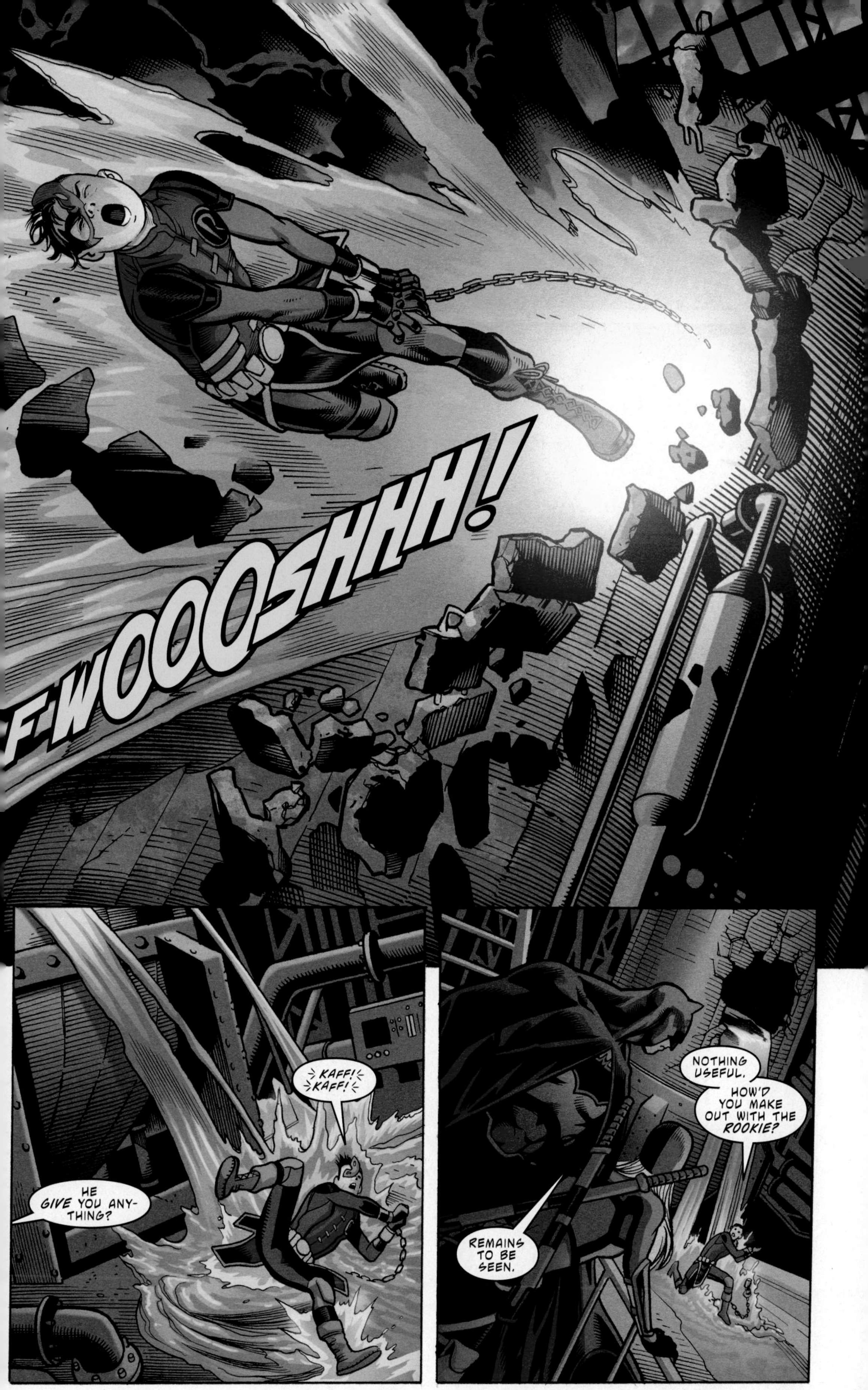
F-WOOOSHHH!
KAFF! KAFF!
HE GIVE YOU ANY-THING?
NOTHING USEFUL.
HOW'D YOU MAKE OUT WITH THE ROOKIE?
REMAINS TO BE SEEN.

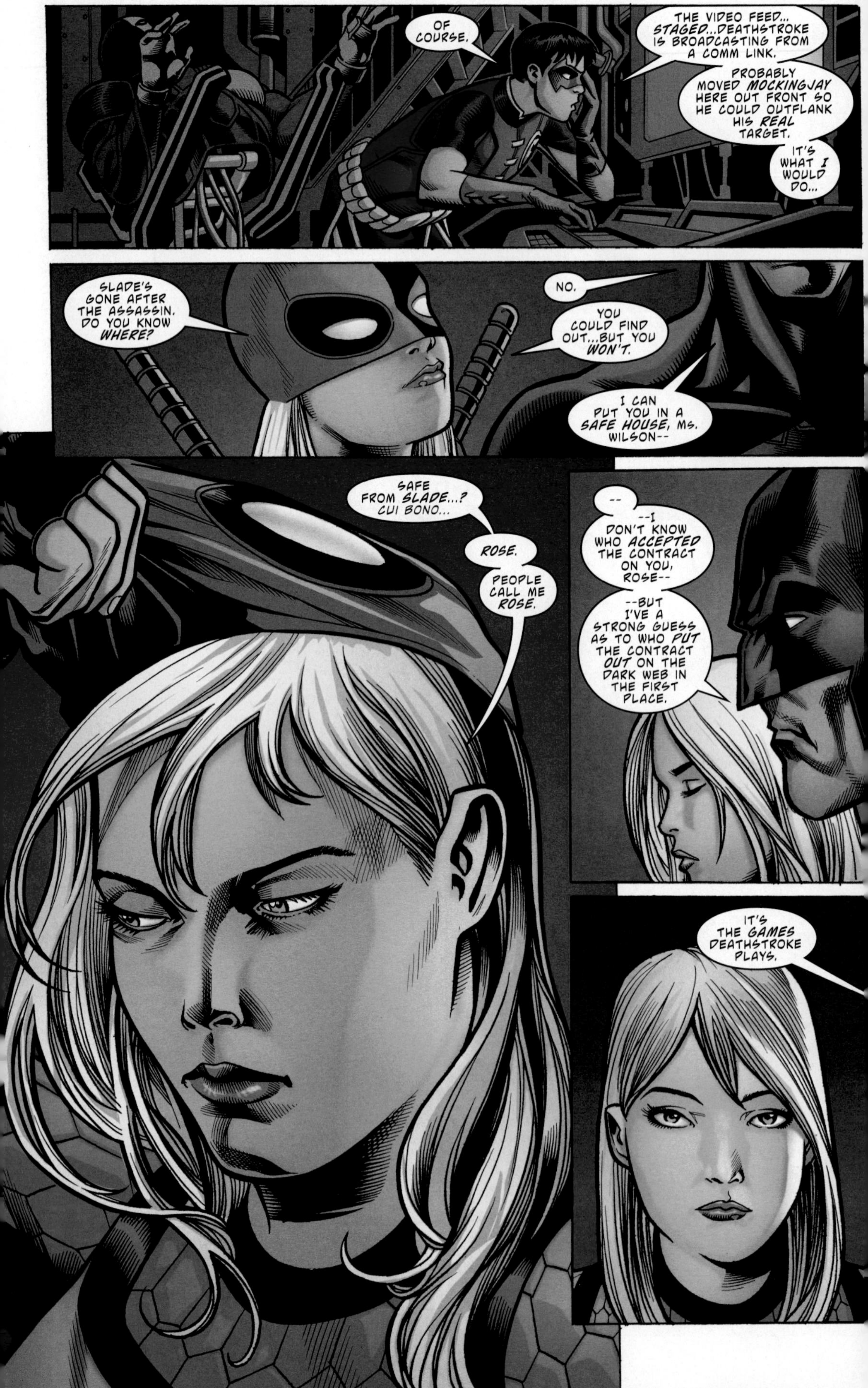
OF COURSE.
THE VIDEO FEED... STAGED...DEATHSTROKE IS BROADCASTING FROM A COMM LINK.
PROBABLY MOVED MOCKINGJAY HERE OUT FRONT SO HE COULD OUTFLANK HIS REAL TARGET.
IT'S WHAT I WOULD DO...
SLADE'S GONE AFTER THE ASSASSIN. DO YOU KNOW WHERE?
NO.
YOU COULD FIND OUT...BUT YOU WON'T.
I CAN PUT YOU IN A SAFE HOUSE, MS. WILSON--
SAFE FROM SLADE...? CUI BONO...
ROSE.
PEOPLE CALL ME ROSE.
--
--I DON'T KNOW WHO ACCEPTED THE CONTRACT ON YOU, ROSE--
--BUT I'VE A STRONG GUESS AS TO WHO PUT THE CONTRACT OUT ON THE DARK WEB IN THE FIRST PLACE.
IT'S THE GAMES DEATHSTROKE PLAYS.

"Home"

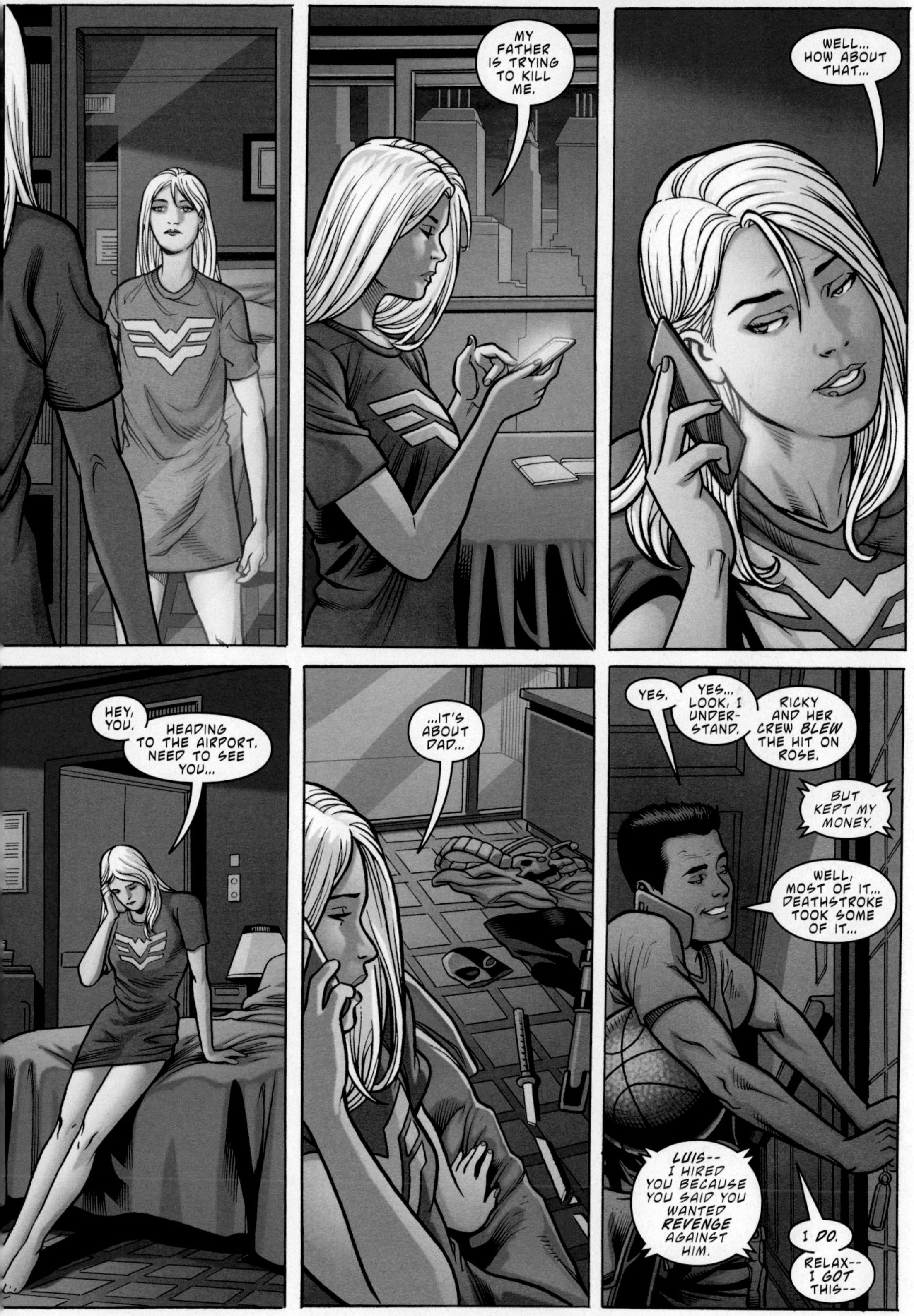

MY FATHER IS TRYING TO KILL ME.
WELL... HOW ABOUT THAT...
HEY, YOU.
HEADING TO THE AIRPORT. NEED TO SEE YOU...
...IT'S ABOUT DAD...
YES.
YES... LOOK, I UNDER-STAND.
RICKY AND HER CREW BLEW THE HIT ON ROSE.
BUT KEPT MY MONEY.
WELL, MOST OF IT... DEATHSTROKE TOOK SOME OF IT...
LUIS-- I HIRED YOU BECAUSE YOU SAID YOU WANTED REVENGE AGAINST HIM.
I DO.
RELAX-- I GOT THIS--

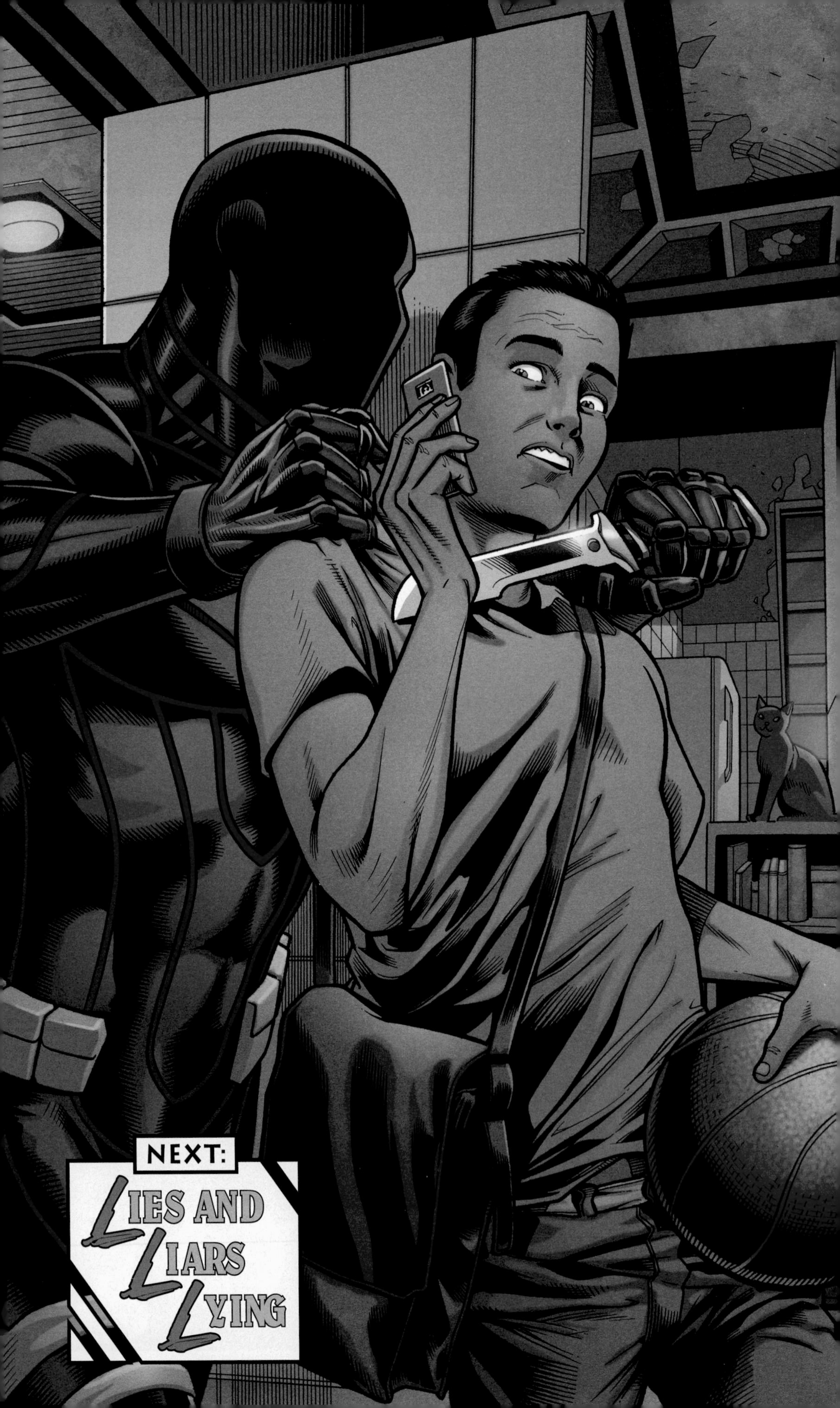
NEXT:
LIES AND LIARS LYING

VARIANT COVER GALLERY

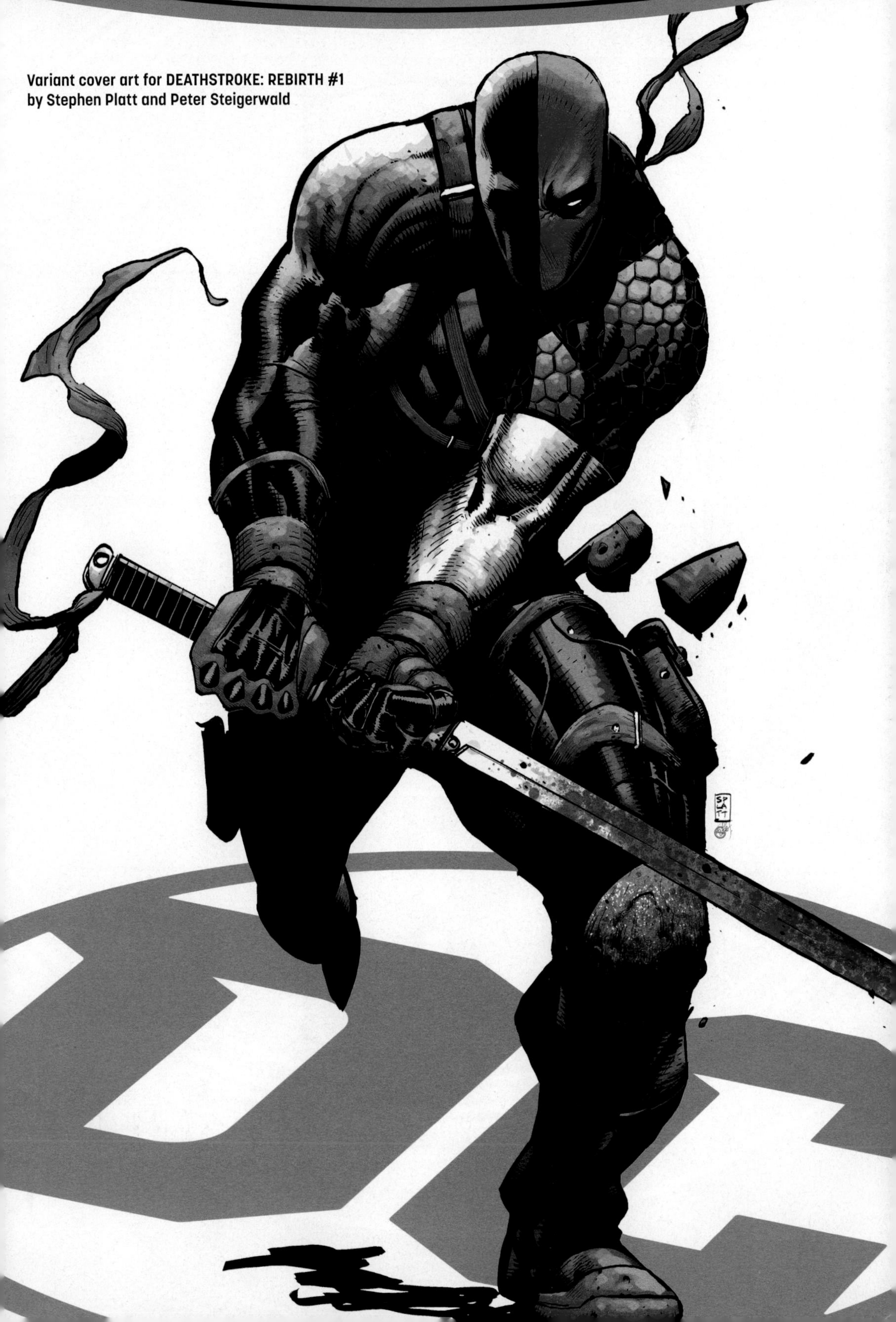

Variant cover art for DEATHSTROKE: REBIRTH #1
by Stephen Platt and Peter Steigerwald

Variant cover art for DEATHSTROKE #1
by Shane Davis, Michelle Delecki and Alex Sinclair

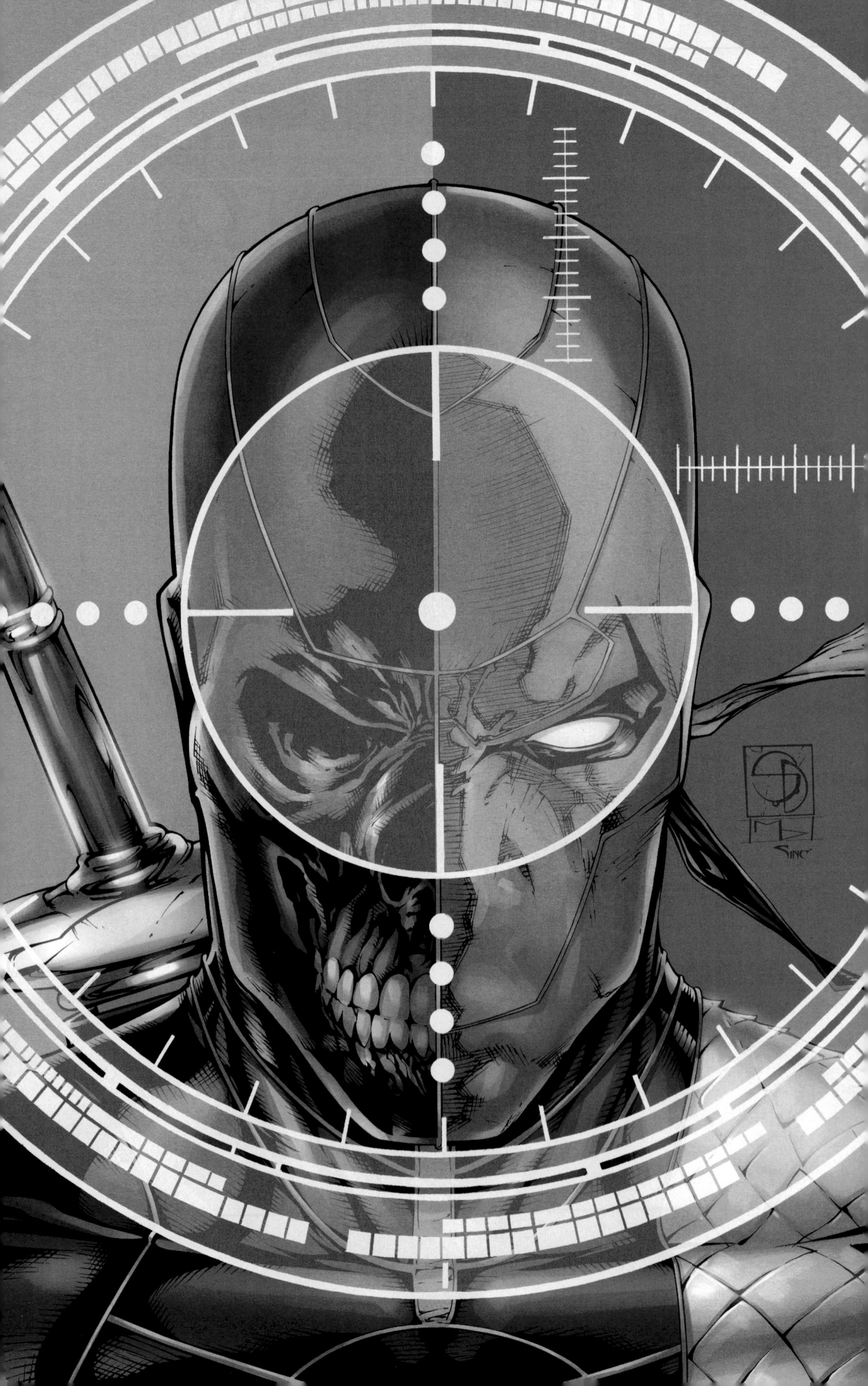

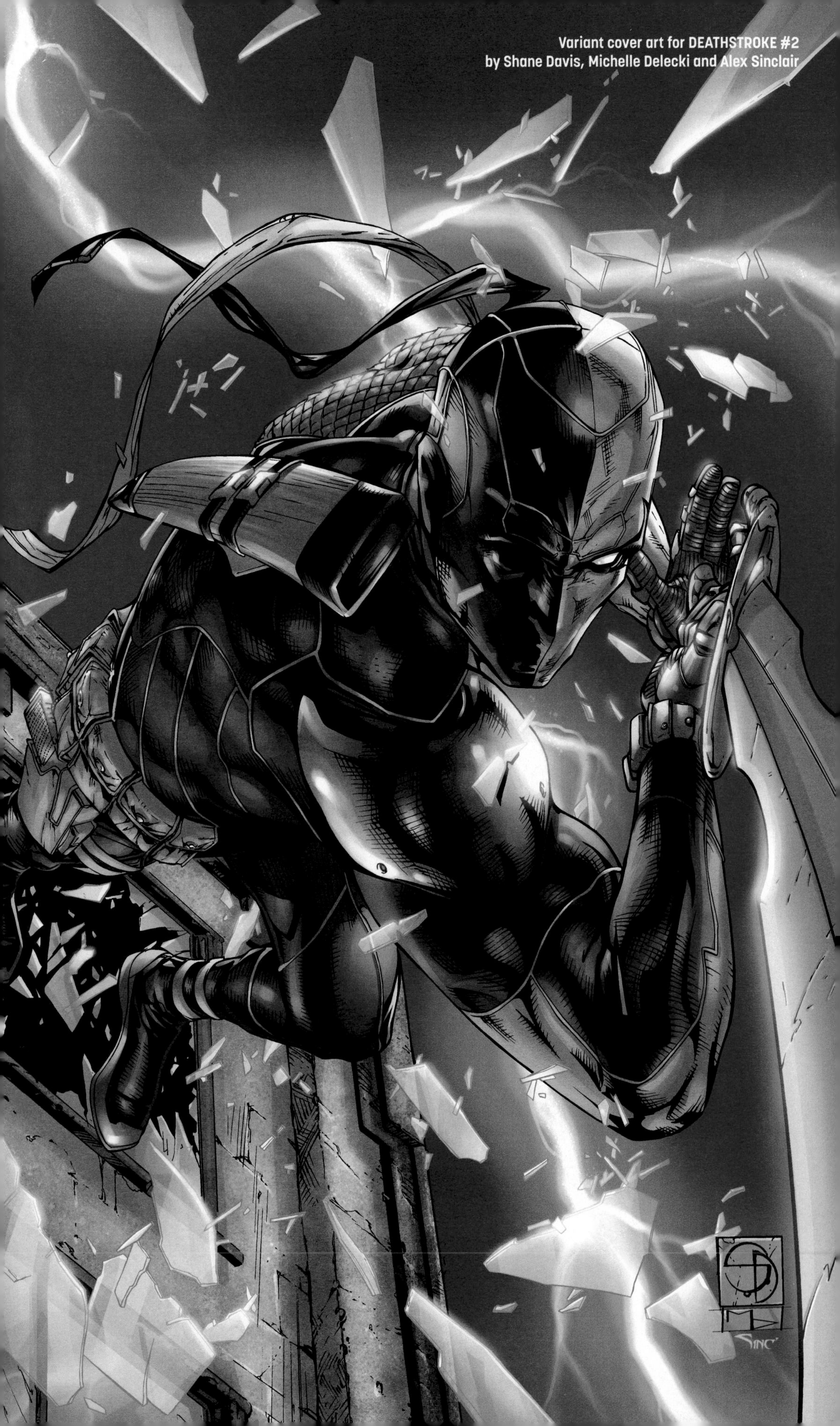

Variant cover art for DEATHSTROKE #2
by Shane Davis, Michelle Delecki and Alex Sinclair

Variant cover art for DEATHSTROKE #3
by Shane Davis, Michelle Delecki and Alex Sinclair

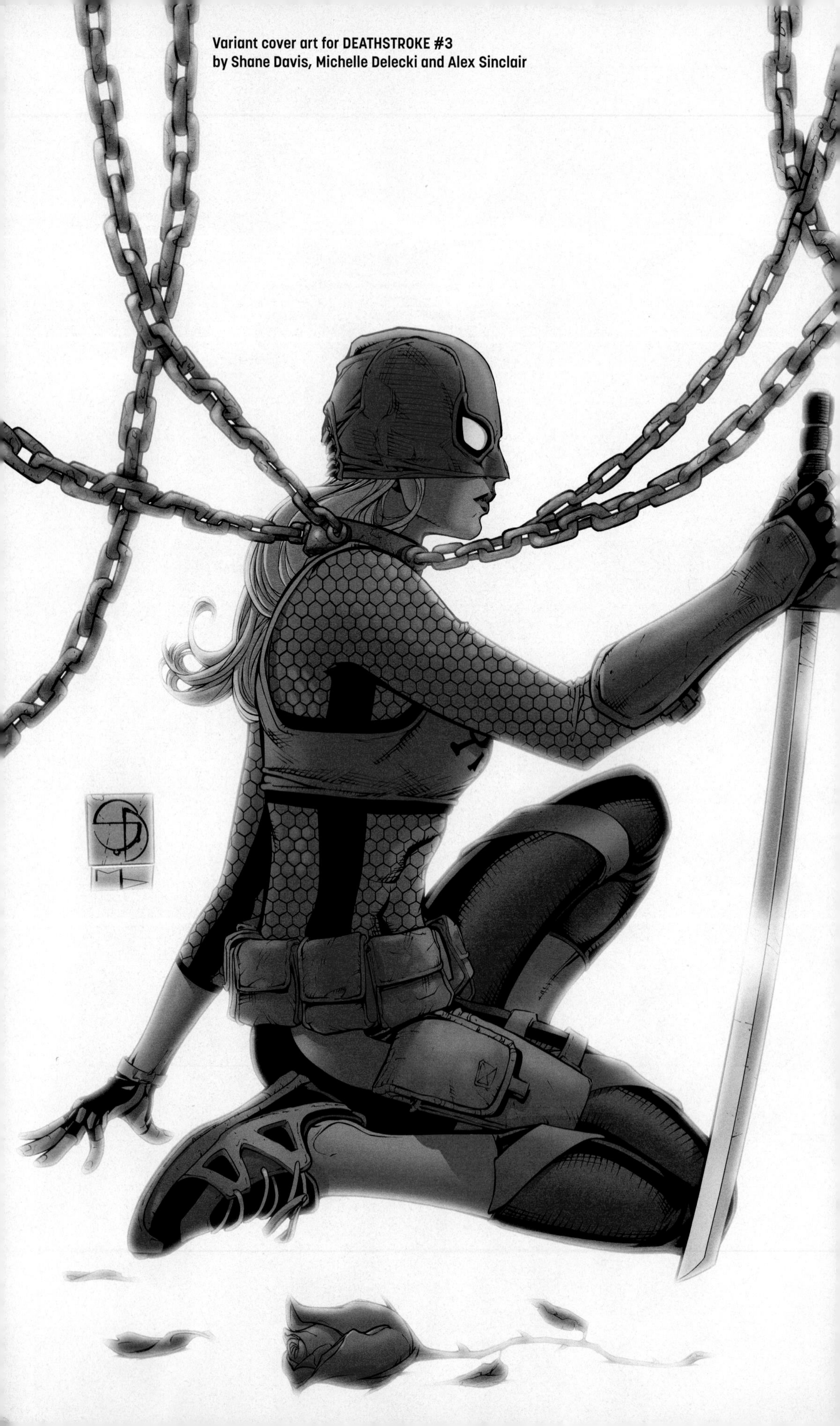

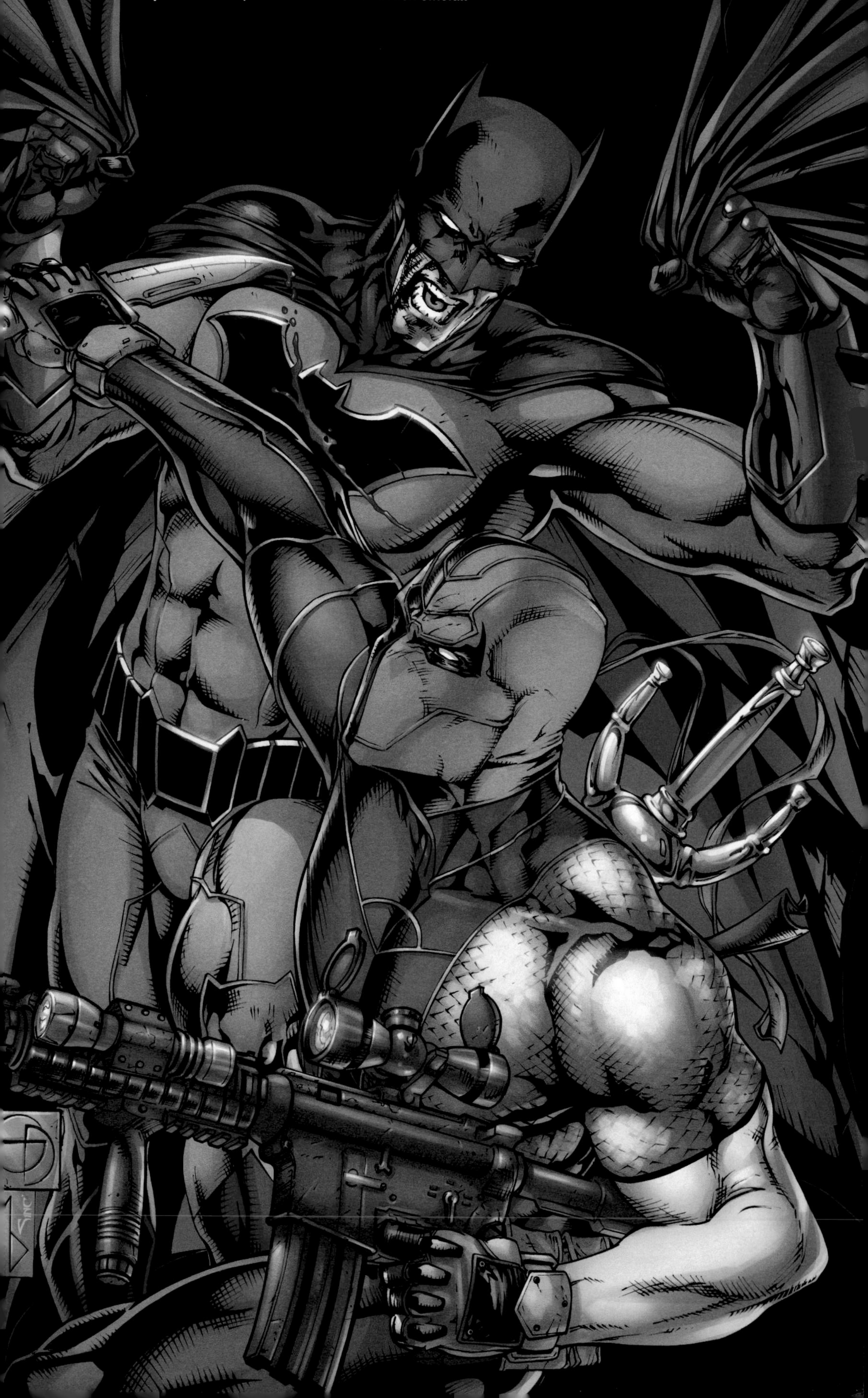

Variant cover art for DEATHSTROKE #4
by Shane Davis, Michelle Delecki and Alex Sinclair

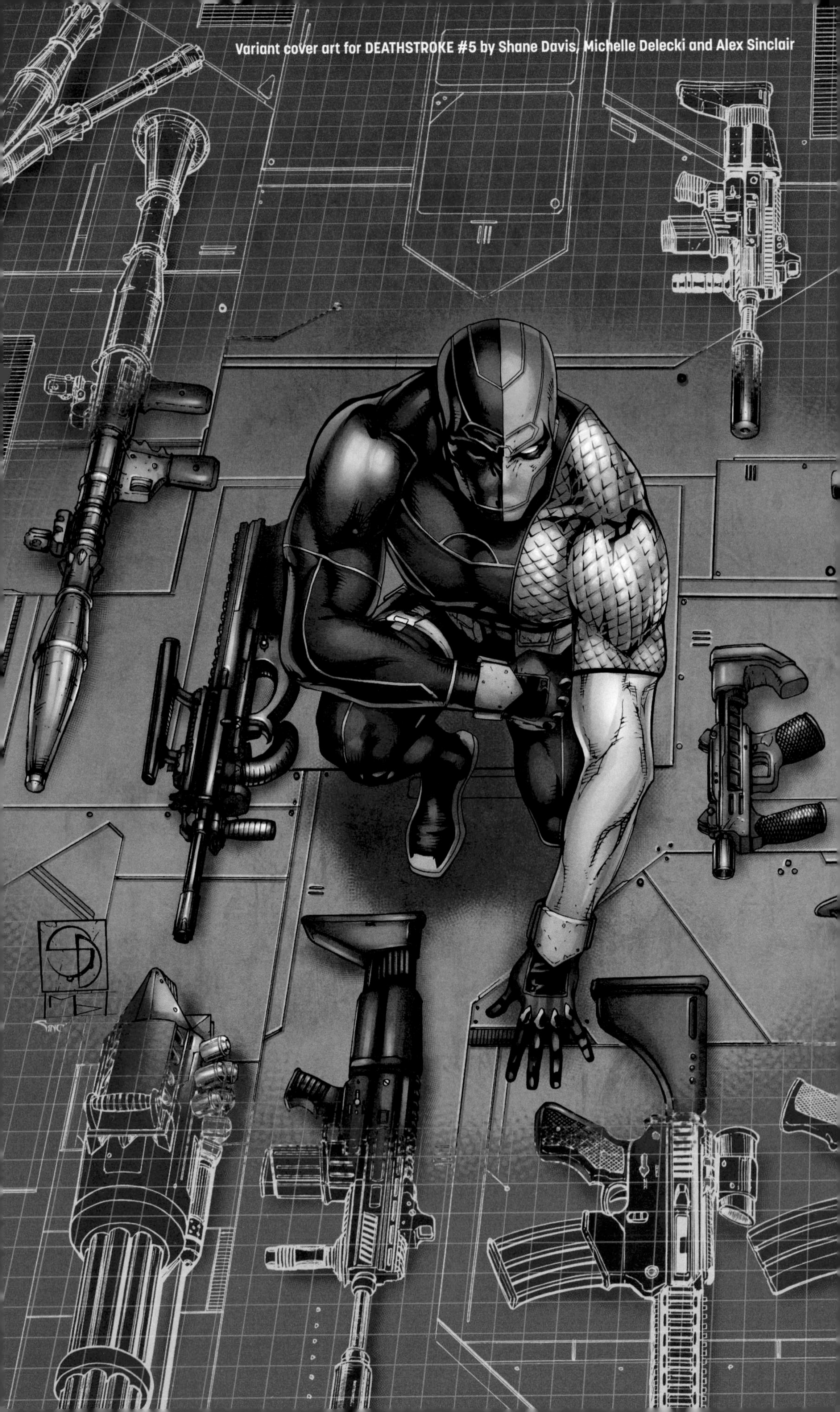

Variant cover art for DEATHSTROKE #5 by Shane Davis, Michelle Delecki and Alex Sinclair

's nice to see one of the best comics of the
e '80s return so strongly."
Comic Book Resources

's high energy from page one through to the
t page." – **BATMAN NEWS**

C UNIVERSE REBIRTH

SUICIDE
SQUAD

L. 1: THE BLACK VAULT

OB WILLIAMS
ith JIM LEE and others

VOL.1 THE BLACK VAULT

ROB WILLIAMS • JIM LEE • PHILIP TAN • JASON FABOK • IVAN REIS • GARY FRANK

VOL.1 THE POISON TRUTH
SIMON OLIVER • MORITAT • ANDRE SZYMANOWICZ

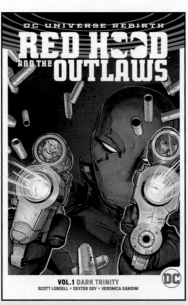

VOL.1 DARK TRINITY
SCOTT LOBDELL • DEXTER SOY • VERONICA GANDINI

VOL.1 DIE LAUGHING
AMANDA CONNER • JIMMY PALMIOTTI • CHAD HARDIN • JOHN TIMMS

THE HELLBLAZER VOL. 1:
THE POISON TRUTH

RED HOOD AND THE OUTLAWS VOL. 1:
DARK TRINITY

HARLEY QUINN VOL. 1:
DIE LAUGHING

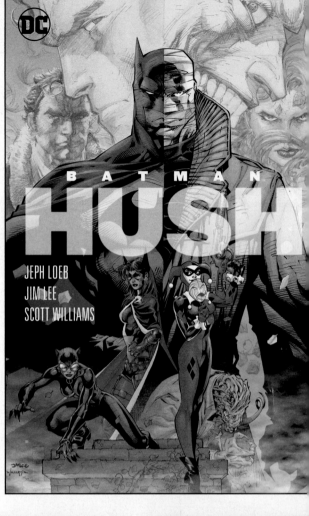
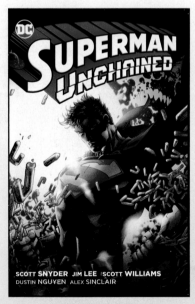